William Marx

A Scholar's Life

Translated by Nicholas Elliott

Hermits United
London · Paris

Published in Great Britain by Hermits United Ltd. 2026

Translated from William Marx, *Vie du lettré*
(Les Éditions de Minuit, Paris, France, 2009)

Copyright © Les Éditions de Minuit, 2009
English translation © Hermits United, 2026
This edition © Hermits United, 2026

All rights reserved
Printed in France

A catalogue record for this book is available from the British Library
ISBN 978-1-916658-20-2

www.hermits-united.com

A Scholar's Life

To my teachers,

and to my teachers' teachers.

I come back to that simple and uncompromising idea that 'literature' (because, when it comes down to it, my project is 'literary') is always made out of 'life'.

Roland Barthes,
The Preparation of the Novel,
16 DECEMBER 1978[1]

For me, culture as 'training' (≠ method) evokes the image of a kind of dispatching along an eccentric path: stumbling among snatches, between the bounds of different fields of knowledge, flavours.

Roland Barthes,
How to Live Together,
12 JANUARY 1977[2]

Contents

Preamble		13
I	Birth	19
II	The Body	24
III	Gender	31
IV	Schedule	37
V	Education	42
VI	The Examination	52
VII	The Study	57
VIII	Economy	68
IX	The Home	76
X	The Garden	81
XI	The Animal	89
XII	Sexuality	97
XIII	Food	104
XIV	Melancholy	111
XV	The Soul	120
XVI	Religion	130
XVII	Quarrel	143
XVIII	The Academy	153

XIX	Politics	161
XX	War	171
XXI	The Coronation	178
XXII	The Island	185
XXIII	The Night	190
XXIV	Death	194
Notes		201
Bibliography		231
Index		251

Preamble

What is a scholar? Someone whose physical and intellectual existence is organised around texts and books. The scholar lives among and from books, uses his own life to keep them alive, and, in particular, to read them.

This definition entails a series of consequences.

The scholar's existence is not in the natural order of things. Leopardi is right to remind us of this: literature is made first for non-scholars.[1] To set literature as the principal aim of a life is in many respects an extraordinary, if not pathological, pursuit.

This is why a scholar, however learned and erudite, is not necessarily a wise man or a saint: some scholars are mad, vicious, and best avoided.

The scholar is not always a philosopher or even a writer: though there are obviously scholars who are writers, this is not true of all of them, just as not all writers are scholars. On balance, a scholar is more like a reader than a writer: he has sacrificed his life to ensure others' voices are heard.

*

A scholar does not live in his own time. Or at the very least, he knows that this time period is only one among others; that it isn't the most important; that it may not even be central to history. The scholar's melancholy probably stems from this feeling that he belongs to the margins of the centuries, that he only occupies a jump seat in the crowd of living beings who have passed over this earth. He knows that the memory of his place, however minimal, will only endure if other scholars come after him to continue his work, to use it and quote it, citing his name in a footnote. A fragile hope. The scholar's existence hangs on a thread – or a quill.

The real scholar is at great risk of remaining unknown. Hence the paradox of his biography: it claims to show what is actually hidden.

*

Scholars form both the base of a civilisation (they guarantee its continuity) and a destructive body, a support and a threat: they allow for an order to be created, but participate in contesting it. For the power of texts of the past is precisely that they have been, in other words that they are not (or no longer); if the revolution consists in replacing what exists with what does not exist, nothing is more revolutionary than the past. What arises from the present reinforces it: it is simply its development. But the unnatural permanence of what belongs to the past and should no longer be alters the normal course of history: by returning, the past destroys the present, despite the fact that it produced the present – and because it produced it.

Today the real role of the practice and teaching of letters is to keep active literature's double postulation, considered simultaneously as the expression of reality and a power that wrenches one away from that same reality, and to let itself be wiped out by those texts that built our world, that are us and at the same time not us – or else to wipe them out, which amounts to the same thing. A door must be left open to negation in this world. This is precisely where the difference between culture and entertainment plays out.

*

The scholar makes truth prevail over every form of power. He is the only one to guarantee the accuracy of the sources, the authenticity of the text, and the pertinence of the original context, so as to remain as close as possible to the original intention. Other interpretations and commentaries are also needed, but they will come later, and if the scholar has not first done his work, however brilliant these interpretations, they will be vain.

In the expanding universe, the galaxies all seem to be moving away from each other. Similarly, the past is always moving away from us. Through his philological work, the scholar attempts to tame the past, to make it comprehensible, to reduce the distance. Or simply to make it exist again, though in a new form. A Sisyphean task, always demanding to be started again as time slips away.

But let us be clear: scholarly reading is also an interpretation, since everything is interpretation, but it is an interpretation in which the interpreter disappears behind the text as much as he can. In other words, scholarly reading stands out from other readings through a particular ethical dimension: the interpreter's ego is detestable there. It is understood that a text has no ultimate truth, but it's important to suppose a criterion of truth, which makes certain interpretations more probable or acceptable than others. At least that's what the scholar believes.

This ethical dimension is what justifies this book. Any approach to a text is inseparable from a position in life. Reading demands all of the reader's being: it reveals him, and he reveals himself in it. The scholar defines himself by a particular relationship to time, texts, and himself.

*

Hence the possibility of gathering under the name of the scholar individuals who are the product of cultures and eras utterly heterogeneous with one exception: the role they assign the scholar. The approach adopted here will be transhistorical.

Of course, some eras are favourable to scholars. Scholars ideally emerge in troubled times, at a turning point between ages when one world is about to vanish and another to appear: the Hellenistic period, the end of the Roman republic, the crisis of the papacy in the fourteenth century, the religious crisis in the sixteenth, the crisis of modernity in the nineteenth, etc. But scholars have also cropped up very nicely outside of these particular contexts.

So it goes with the advent of the internet, which will not lead to the disappearance of scholars: they survived the invention of the printing press, after all. But they will be transformed.

These pages therefore presuppose a shared existential position, beyond the differences of culture, religion, and civilisation. It is good to anchor literary study in the most concrete existence. Literature is also a question of being.

*

This is the existential commitment I will try to bring to light over the course of twenty-four chapters tracing the life – or a day in the life – of an imaginary scholar composed of all the scholars who have succeeded one another. A course that is also a founding myth of written civilisations, from the Egyptian and Babylonian scribe to today's academics.

The documents drawn on will be multiple and diverse: letters, biographies, first-hand accounts, objects, images. It takes all sorts to create a myth.

Literary fiction will be examined with caution, as it often presents scholars in a ridiculous light. Think of Anatole France's Sylvestre Bonnard and Marcel Proust's Professor Brichot. Literature most often delights in ridiculing the scholar and erudite knowledge. Perhaps to eliminate a competitor while concurrently promoting the figure of the artist? Yet there is something solemn and profound about the scholar's relationship to the world and other people. Something far more serious than the simple quirk of absent-mindedness he is sometimes saddled with.

The mirror held up here aims to be as faithful as possible. Reader, expect to find a wide variety of scholars from across the ages, continents, and cultures. You might even recognise yourself there.

I
Birth

The scholar was born in 551 BC, in the state of Lu, in the present-day province of Shandong. His mother conceived him after praying on a hill, which may explain why the edges of the newborn's skull were strangely raised, as if it were a hillock.[1]

A second scholar was born on 3 January in the year 106 BC, in Italy. According to Plutarch, the delivery took place 'without travail or pain'.[2] A ghost appeared to the wet nurse to announce that the Romans would be forever grateful to this child.

What do these two bizarre birth tales have in common other than their bizarreness? The two events are accompanied by omens that indicate the newborn's exceptional nature: a congenital malformation in Confucius's case, and a supernatural apparition in Cicero's. Everything suggests that both were born scholars from head to toe, issuing from their mothers' womb swathed in with knowledge and diplomas, or at least that they were summoned by fate to become scholars without fail.

Yet nothing is less plausible. One can be many things at birth: brown- or blond-haired, tall or short, girl or boy. One can have two heads or three legs. At a push, one might be born gifted or even a prodigy, equipped with all the talents necessary to accumulate knowledge over the course of a life. But, strictly speaking, one cannot be born a scholar. One cannot even be born fated to become a scholar, for to say so would be to deny the freedom of a series of choices made at every instant of an entire life.

Nine months is not enough to make a scholar. His gestation continues throughout his existence: '[Confucius] said, "At fifteen, I set my mind on learning; by thirty, I had found my footing; at forty, I was free from perplexity; by fifty, I understood the will of Heaven; by sixty, I learned to give ear to others; by seventy, I could follow my heart's desires without overstepping the line."'[3] It takes an entire life for culture to be embodied in a man and become his second nature. You can die a scholar, but you cannot be born a scholar.

When it comes down to it, these two birth stories say exactly that: their clearly fabulous nature, at the outset of biographies basically intended to be realistic, invites one to consider them *cum grano salis*. Above all, they affirm the impossibility of describing a scholar's birth or, more precisely, of making it coincide with the raw data in the civil records.

But while these stories have every trait of pious legends, the richness of their substance prevents us from considering them sterile. They indicate that the scholar, no less than gods or heroes, can be the object of myth. Like them, he is entitled to a miraculous birth. His life sufficiently elevated him above ordinary mortals for his nativity to be retrospectively illuminated.

This retrospective aspect reveals a typical process of scholarly activity. The time it deals with is time reversed: the scholar builds bridges between eras; he makes the past accessible, reconfiguring it in light of the demands of the present and passing down the memory of this past to future generations. Since he breathes new life into the collective past through the dynamic of culture itself, the least he can do is also to transform his own life. The past must always be reinvented. It is the scholar's task to make that happen.

This was true of Ezra, the first and greatest of the Hebrew scribes, who was charged by King Artaxerxes with re-establishing the religion of the Temple in Jerusalem. After leaving Babylon, Ezra succeeded Moses as the second founder of Judaism by gathering and publishing the texts of the Torah. Over the course of seven days, he read and commented on the Law of God before the assembled people.[4]

The scholar's missions are to preserve the texts, to understand them, and to interpret them. His birth is always accompanied by a rebirth, a renaissance. This explains why the chronicler did not find it necessary to describe the circumstances of Ezra's birth: the scholar is born an adult.

But he does not appear in every time period. Certain eras are favoured: the moments of crisis. The decline of the Zhou dynasty and the beginning of the epoch referred to by Confucius himself as 'Spring and Autumn'; the exile's return to Jerusalem in ruins; the troubled end of the Roman republic: Confucius, Ezra, and Cicero each faced the challenge of a world undergoing radical change or on the verge of collapsing. Confucius responded by collecting writings and poems from ancient times and making culture a requirement for human dignity. Ezra established the text of Divine Law and shared it with his people. Cicero brought the forms and concepts of Greek thought to Rome and offered his fellow citizens an ideal of life that turned all the accepted values upside down: *cum dignitate otium*,[5] in other words the possibility of leading a perfectly honourable life despite staying far from the business and political struggles that were supposed to take up every Roman citizen's time.

Like Ezra returning from Babylon, the scholar in some way always wants to return from exile. Confucius criticised the reality of his time in the name of a mythical era he constantly refers to as if he still lived in it: that of the early days of the Zhou dynasty, or even of the previous dynasties, the Xia and the Shang.[6] In Cicero, one recognises the mind of a man who has returned from Greece: while others banally arrive back from the colonies or a safari, his crocodiles and panthers are philosophers, whom he tries as best he can to acclimate to Rome. But his exile was also temporal: he would have liked to bring back to life the Republic's great historic figures, Cato the Elder and the Scipios.

Much later, Renaissance humanists would also try to rekindle ties with a classical antiquity which they believed with a sudden conviction had been cut off by their immediate predecessors. Thus the scholar becomes aware, sometimes tragically, that no tradition is established once and for all, to last for all eternity: it is always to be recreated, and reinvented. The past does not pass itself down. It needs our help.

Confucius's biographer has reason to point out that 'soon after his birth [his father] Shu-liang-hch died and was buried at Mount Fang in the east of Lu.' He continues to say that, 'Later Confucius suspected that his father's grave was there, but his mother hid the truth from him.'[7] It is a remarkable symbol that the father of all scholars did not know his own father, that he did not even know where he was buried: a symbol of a grief that never ends, a constituent incompleteness or an original fault that makes the scholar sensitive to every flaw of knowledge and memory, and renders the work of erudition and archival research all the more necessary. But it's also the sign of a filiation with gaps: the scholar always thinks of himself as more intensely connected to his most distant ancestors than to his closest kin. He sees himself less as a son than as a grandson or a great-grandson. This is also where the feeling of exile arises.

The scholar was not born with history, but with the awareness of history and the passing of time, which seem to have dawned on humanity all at once: at opposite ends of Asia, Confucius and Ezra are near contemporaries. One could add Herodotus, whom Cicero called 'the father of history' (*patrem historiae*),[8] and who appeared in an era when Greece seemed on the verge of collapsing under the blows of the Persian empire. All these names are remembered as those of the world's first scholars.

Or at least the first to be known and celebrated by name, and of whom we have some memory. For in and through these scholars, other even more ancient scholarly traditions are imperceptibly carried on and transformed: through Herodotus's journeys to Egypt and Ezra's royal mission to Jerusalem, the great line of Egyptian and Babylonian scribes is reinvented and spread to other cultures, raised to a greater power.

The transition from the scribe's work to the scholar's is an epistemological leap in human history. By losing his anonymity, the scribe acquires another dimension: reflexivity. Driven by the urgency of the times and the need to set a precedent, he becomes aware of himself and the importance of his function and he tells both his own story and that of his people. His name is passed down with the chronicle. The myth of the scholar can finally be born, the cult of the scholar takes shape and his life can begin.

II
The Body

Many will recall Ernst Kantorowicz's analyses of the king's double body: the 'body natural', subject to all the vicissitudes of life, and the 'body politic', which is immortal and incorruptible.[1] Like the king, the scholar has a double body: it is limited and extensive.

The former belongs to the physical order: it is open to the five senses, participates in life's ordinary pleasures and pains, and is subject to the passions, illness, and death. It is no different from any other human being's body – at least, at first glance. We will soon take note of a few differences.

For its part, the extensive body has nothing in common with the previous one: it belongs to the immaterial order, is composed of all the works and texts produced by the scholar, and has a tendency to grow with time as his writings multiply. Its life span, though incommensurable with the limited body's, is not infinite: worms, water, fire, and censorship can affect and destroy it.

Sometimes the scholar's extensive body can perish before his limited body. This happens more often than one thinks. Think of students who abandon their thesis along the way and let their early drafts rot in a basement: while their limited body is still in the bloom of health, their extensive body turns to dust. There are multitudes of these stillborn scholars, but one cannot point to any famous examples, for the very reason that the life of their extensive body has been cut short.

Indeed, the extensive body grows not only through all the texts written by the scholar himself, but also through all those texts the scholar's own texts have more or less directly produced (editions, commentaries), all the citations from his own texts, all the citations of these citations, and so on. The extensive body's development is virtually unlimited, until it reaches the end of the world – or of libraries and human knowledge. Consider the presocratic philosophers: only a few fragments of their work have survived – bits of sentences, sometimes only isolated words – but their extensive body still regularly expands, thanks to successive editions of the fragments and the reflections they provoke.

A few principles can be determined. The scholar's extensive body has a tendency to grow indefinitely, though the pace of this expansion varies. Growth can stop for a more or less long period, measurable in decades, centuries, even millennia. When the extensive body is not growing, it tends to be rendered nearly invisible by the other extensive bodies rapidly expanding. These periods of stagnation correspond with what is known as oblivion. In general, oblivion is provisional, in which case it is known as purgatory.

Any extensive body, if in the least bit extensive, is destined to eventually grow (as in the example of the pre-Socratics). Yet when under certain circumstances an extensive body vanishes entirely, nothing can bring it back to life. The range of accidents conceivable is quite varied: library fire, war, change of civilisation, disappearance of a language or writing system (if no one thought to pass down a grammar, dictionary, or deciphering tool like the Rosetta stone), or the extinction of humankind and any form of extraterrestrial intelligence. Happily, these accidents are rare – at least the latter ones. But in this regard, insignificant actions can have consequences nearly as disastrous as a nuclear war: in a library, an inaccurately written file card or an incorrectly shelved book can interrupt an extensive body's growth for centuries – until the next inventory check.

The scholar's limited body has nothing in common with his extensive body, though some portraits seem to indicate the contrary. From this perspective, the Chinese tradition about the father of all scholars is particularly deceptive. According to the historian Sima Qian, 'Confucius was nine feet six inches tall.' He adds: 'Everybody marveled at his height.'[2] Which is understandable, given that being over nine feet tall remains remarkable to our day. It is likely that the biographer's report on Confucius's height is significantly exaggerated. To be more precise, the biographer symbolically ascribed the extensive body's height to the limited body's. For a scholar's second body does indeed make him a giant. Rabelais was on to this when he created Pantagruel and Gargantua, two paragons of Renaissance humanism whose appetite for knowledge was equaled only by their appetite plain and simple.

If the scholar's limited body reflected his extensive body's reality, libraries would be frequented by armies of basketball pros and high jumpers. That's far from the case: as is widely known, the typical book lover is more like a worm. Which has not prevented certain visionary architects from building libraries on the scale of the scholar's extensive body. Witness the Bibliothèque Nationale de France, which stands on the banks of the Seine like a megalithic monument erected by giants, with four massive towers, heavy metal doors, endless ambulatories, and 90-foot ceilings.[3]

Any reader who has paced up and down the Bibliothèque Nationale's halls and pushed open its weighty doors knows from experience that the scholar's extensive body and limited body are bound by contrast: one is frail, the other vigorous. The mythology of the scholar frequently emphasises this contrast. As early as the first century AD, the doctor Celsus noted that 'almost all those fond of letters' (*omnes paene cupidi litterarum*) were among 'the weak' (*imbecili*).[4] The limited body also earned its name by comparison with non-scholars.

Picking up where Celsus left off, Giacomo Leopardi was exceptionally persistent in developing the theory of the opposition between the scholar's two bodies. His theory was based on personal experience: this puny hunchbacked poet with poor eyesight and a susceptibility to multiple illnesses was convinced that all his problems were due to the frenzied studying he had engaged in from a very young age. 'I have ruined myself with seven years of mad and most desperate study during that age when my constitution was growing and should have grown strong', he admitted in 1818, when he was not even twenty. 'And I have ruined myself unhappily and beyond remedy for my whole life, and rendered my aspect miserable, contemptible all that great portion of man which is alone regarded by the many.'[5]

But if Leopardi had not devoted himself to scholarly research and learned Latin, Greek, Hebrew, and the modern languages, would he really have become an athlete or, at the very least, a man in good health? That's far from certain. What's important is that this is what Leopardi believed, and so believing, he constructed from this palpable individual reality an entire doctrine of scholarly life liable to give meaning to his own existence. A soul of Leopardi's caliber preferred to think of himself as subject to the general law of scholars, however unjust, rather than a victim of random fate: the order of knowledge weighed less heavily on him than the unpredictable blows of destiny.

It follows that the poet's journals are full of remarks that ultimately create a system: 'It has already been observed that physical vigour damages the intellectual faculties and favours the imagination, whereas a poor physique greatly favours reflection.'[6] Elsewhere he writes:

> Bodily weakness benefits the exercise and development of the mental faculties, especially those pertaining to reason, and physical vigour harms them. And conversely, the exercise and development of these faculties greatly harms the vigour and well-being of the body. Thus Celsus holds that the enfeeblement of men, and illnesses, derive from study, and each thinker or scholar (*studioso*) experiences it for himself as regards the individual deterioration of his body.[7]

And also: 'Study is an extremely tiring thing.'[8] Or: 'Hunchbacks have a lot of wit.'[9]

There is a moving quality to this litany of general statements, candidly intended to hide the horror of an individual fate behind a universal human tragedy. The scholar will be less unhappy if he knows he is a member of a community suffering from the same ills and can explicitly identify the guilty party. The guilty party, here, is no other than Lady Nature, accused of having invested all her plans in the body, without leaving any room for the development of the intelligence.

Nothing is less natural, indeed, than works of the mind. There was probably once a time, Leopardi recognises, when physical vigour wasn't incompatible with intellectual exercises, in the blessed era of Plato and Cicero. The reason is simple: in classical antiquity, knowledge wasn't as developed as it is now; mastering it did not require as much study. Today this is no longer the case:[10] the poet had no choice but to acknowledge that the culture he belonged to had deliberately constructed itself against the natural order and the basic necessities of the body.

But unlike Rousseau, Leopardi doesn't see this as a reason to condemn civilisation. Instead, he chooses to incriminate nature, a nature to which he refuses to submit his own existence or humankind's. The scholar's calling is to belong to the camp of *antiphysis*: he is decidedly not of this world. Leopardi would pay a heavy price for the freedom he claimed: he was carried off by disease before his fortieth birthday. Nature had taken its revenge for all his accusations.

Alas, Leopardi was neither the first nor the last of nature's scholarly victims, though times have certainly changed. Today many scholars go to the gym and take their weekly jog, as if to celebrate the new alliance of body and mind. Revenge is therefore more subtle, or ironic: Jorge Luis Borges became blind upon being appointed director of Argentina's national library in 1955; eight hundred thousand books were simultaneously given to him and taken away. Other holders of this prestigious position had met the same fate: José Marmol and Paul Groussac.[11] But Borges responded to nature's cruel and repetitive irony with his own greater and prouder irony by making his blindness part of his own legend and using it as a source of poetic inspiration:

> From hunger and from thirst (in the Greek story)
> a king lies dying among gardens and fountains.
> Aimlessly, endlessly, I trace the confines,
> high and profound, of this blind library.[12]

It is tempting to apply what Borges describes here to the condition of every scholar, in every era. There's no need to be blind to endure the torment of Tantalus: faced with the enormity of the knowledge that awaits him, the student bitterly experiences his physical incapacity to take it all in. The body refuses to stay awake, the eyes close, the mind becomes muddled, the stomach tightens, the limbs stiffen: his entire being calls out to him, 'You won't be finishing this page today.' But he will finish it eventually, and other pages too, deep into the night. The scholar's courage is to sacrifice the limited body to the benefit of the extensive body.

III

Gender

For centuries, the idea of a woman scholar evoked at best a chimera, at worse, a character in a farce, or, as was often the case, both at once: in Molière, learned ladies were undoubtedly comical, but were neither truly learned nor actually women.

There is no biological or genetic reason for this imbalance between the sexes: it remains to be proven that the scholar gene is specifically linked to the Y chromosome, and it is unlikely that it ever will be, if it's true that the scholarly life can only be conceived in opposition to any kind of determinism. The scholar is fundamentally a free being, unencumbered by the immediate constraints of his existence. Texts have delivered him from his own context.

But if the scholar is a miracle, the woman scholar is doubly so. For the means of this freedom must also be granted and the choice permitted. Rare are the societies that offer all individuals the chance to commit themselves to the direction that best suits their talents and the values they wish to champion.

Virginia Woolf imagined the childhood of a little sister to William Shakespeare, Judith.[1] She watches her brother leave for school while she remains at home; she steals some rare moments from her domestic duties to secretly read some of the books he brings home. When he leaves for London to embark on a career in the theatre, her father forces her to take a husband. If she resists and runs away, she is fated to sooner or later get caught in the snare of a man who will impregnate her. Domestic life will inevitably prevail. Woolf cannot imagine any way out for her other than suicide.

When girls aren't allowed the liberal education to which boys are entitled, when universities are closed to them (Woolf emphasises that in her era, the 1920s, women were still barred from entering certain Oxford and Cambridge libraries alone),[2] when half of humankind is congenitally fated to ignorance or a mere sheen of knowledge suited to social occasions, how can the word *scholar* be applied to a woman? The potential in some words takes many centuries to be realised.

Sadly, the acknowledgement of this exclusion, repeated many times over the last centuries, remains topical in certain countries. But we owe one of its most penetrating and eloquent formulations to perhaps the most learned woman of the eighteenth century, a member of the aristocratic elite whose story arouses both admiration and compassion. Émilie du Châtelet had two major passions in life: one was for the sciences, the other for Voltaire. Her love of science led her to translate Newton and Leibniz and correspond as an equal with the most eminent scholars in Europe. Her second passion was fulfilled in a few happy years shared with her great man. But her life ended in a manner characteristic of the fate of women over many long centuries: she died at forty-two, after giving birth to a daughter by her lover, the poet Saint-Lambert.

In the preceding months, to avoid 'losing the fruit of [her] labour, in case [she] should die in childbirth', she threw herself into a desperate race against time: 'I get up at 9,' she wrote, 'sometimes at 8, I work until 3, take my coffee at 3, I return to work at 4, I leave it at 10 to have a bite to eat alone, I chat until midnight with monsieur de Voltaire, who is present at my supper, and I return to work at midnight, until 5 a.m.'[3] An admirable display of courage and lucidity in the face of biological fate.

It's probably no coincidence that a woman is the one to have given us the most acute account of the truly existential nature of the scholar's work. Indeed, in her *Discours sur le bonheur* [Discourse on Happiness], Madame du Châtelet offers one of the most beautiful and pertinent panegyrics to the quest for knowledge, whose role she analyses in life in general and in the lives of women in particular.

Her argument consists of two points. First, 'the love of studying is of all the passions that which contributes most to our happiness.' This is because 'it contains a passion from which an elevated soul is never free, that of glory', a glory not necessarily provided by one's contemporaries. On the contrary, the glory specific to the scholar primarily comes with posterity: that is what they base their existence on.

No doubt that the hope for this future glory is most often vain – and glory may by definition be an illusion. But the pleasure this vanity provides 'is not an illusion: for it proves to us the actual good in enjoying our future reputation.' Even in the most immediate present, we need to enjoy the future. If it were otherwise, 'who would work for his children, for the grandeur of his house?' The desire for future glory produces a powerful reason to live, in which study has a place of the highest importance.

Granted, Madame du Châtelet's argument is not entirely original. It bears the influence of Cicero and the moralist discourse on self-esteem.[4] Additionally, her remarks apply only to those scholars who have produced writing, effectively excluding mere readers. But one has to admit that few writers have set out in so few words and with such clarity the truly existential necessity of the scholar's work.

So what part do women play in this business? This is where Madame du Châtelet's reasoning takes an unprecedented turn. Once the love of glory has been established as a life principle, it must be admitted that men have far more chances to satisfy this principle than women do. Public careers are open to men – in war, politics, diplomacy – while, as the marquise observes, 'women are excluded, due to their state, from any kind of glory and when, by chance, one happens to be born with an elevated soul, all that remains for her is to study so she may be consoled for all the exclusions and dependencies to which she is condemned by her state.' The following conclusion becomes unavoidable: 'the love of studying is far less necessary to the happiness of men than of women.' For 'half the world', studying is in fact the only way to achieve glory, and yet 'it is precisely for that half that education removes the means and makes the taste for it impossible'.[5]

Which brings us back to the scandal Virginia Woolf denounced two centuries later: how difficult it was for women to enter into the order of letters and knowledge. But Madame du Châtelet aims far beyond a mere observation of this difficulty. She specifically emphasises the vital importance of letters for a portion of humankind to whom they are refused by a terrible irony of fate. Her observation is truly tragic, and one doesn't need to know Émilie's and Virginia's appalling fates to be moved by it.

Think of the many scholars who could have populated our books and memory and instead wander between library shelves as absent ghosts, brushing over with empty gazes and transparent fingers the volumes they never opened in their harried lives as wives and mothers. Their minds were only ever exercised on conversations at market; their vision was dulled by counting the stitches of their knitwork rather than deciphering alphabetical characters; their hands turned red from the washing but were never stained with the inkpot's black liquid. A tribute is due to this invisible half of the scholarly world, to these beings forever lost to the heights of knowledge.

Yet despite it all, the work and names of women scholars have miraculously survived to reach us from so many eras and different worlds: Marie de Gournay, Christine de Pisan, Hypatia of Alexandria... Bless their parents for giving them the education and space indispensable for scholarly work, often despite the opposition of their family circles.

To have 'a room of one's own': according to Virginia Woolf, this is one of the conditions necessary for a woman to become a scholar. She must also be able to create a space for herself where she is cut off from the contingencies of domestic life. A place and also, one should add, a time. For Sei Shōnagon, a court lady in the imperial court of Heian around the year 1000, this space was a bed or, more specifically, a pillow: a little square object made of wood or ceramic on which one rested one's head, the inside of which served as a box. The time was night, when Princess Sadako's lady-in-waiting took from inside the box the bundle of paper the Empress had given her to write down her daily impressions. This was the genesis of *The Pillow Book* (*Makura no sôshi*), one of the most beautiful books in the world.

But it's impossible to keep a space only for yourself for any extended period of time. One day, a handsome soldier came to visit Sei Shōnagon. He noticed the book laying on a mat and took it away. And so the world came to enjoy this secret work.[6]

Yet despite this forced publication experienced as a rape,

Sei Shōnagon continued to keep a space for herself that no one could take away from her: writing. As a woman, and despite the fact that she was the daughter of the great poet Kiyohara no Motosuke, she did not have access to classical and official literature, which was in Chinese; she only knew Japanese and syllabic writing; she had next to none of the titles or knowledge that would have entitled her to call herself a scholar. She had no choice but to create her own poetic world, a world marginal to male scholarly culture and composed of superficial anecdotes of court life, detailed descriptions of clothing, romantic intrigue, not to mention the close observations of nature throughout her writing – trees, landscapes, birds, insects...

The woman scholar must often create for herself a specific form or area of knowledge, independent of men's knowledge. For Sei Shōnagon, that space of intellectual freedom was in the sensations and experience of daily life, while Émilie de Châtelet found it in Newtonian physics, which at the time were scorned by most French scholars. By doing so, Voltaire's mistress laid the groundwork for her lover's triumph in France, and the humble lady-in-waiting to the empress served as an unsurpassed model for a Japanese literature that was barely coming into existence in her lifetime.

When scholarly tradition is forbidden to women, their paradoxical good luck is the opportunity to invent a new one. They are offered a different way of giving birth. Gender difference does exist, even among scholars. But at the cost of so much suffering and such frustration.

IV

Schedule

Ars longa, vita brevis.[1] It is no coincidence that the Hippocratic corpus opens with this aphorism. In just a few words, it evokes a fundamental aspect of the scholarly life: the incommensurability between knowledge and knower, or the impossibility of adapting the capacities of the scholar to the full scope of knowledge. How could it be otherwise when, as a matter of principle, the scholar aims to embrace all the knowledge accumulated by previous generations? You cannot gather in a single life the content of several others, however long-ago and distant, the way you might hold a mountain on the distant horizon between your fingers.

The succession of centuries certainly wears out knowledge more than is desirable: manuscripts are lost, texts are corrupted, comprehension is fragmented, rocks become sand and are scattered in the sea, the peaks become blue and dissolve in the sky. Inevitably, things are lost. But the scholar's job is precisely to resist being tricked by perspective and to take realities for what they were in their own time, not for how they appear to us now. The pieces must be put back together, even if that means letting yourself be crushed by the rock thus reconstructed. This is the scholar's drama – or his tragedy.

The problem is primarily a practical one: How do you make the substance of so many lost days fit into a single workday? The first solution consists of setting your watch back a few centuries, to let the past govern the present and put yourself in book time, without worrying about the necessities of the moment. This was the approach taken by Victor Cousin, the French philosopher who was reported by one of his disciples to live with the most extreme irregularity: he lunched 'at no set time', eating 'a cutlet' and 'a spoonful of jam with a glass of reddish water'; only went to sleep when he could really no longer postpone that dreaded moment (he was in the habit of saying, 'I step up to the gallows when I go to bed'); went to the bookshop at dawn, in the heart of winter, without a coat – or in the rain without an umbrella, or with the umbrella folded beneath his arm; paid no attention whatsoever to his toilette; was entirely absorbed in his thoughts and books, and his books and thoughts never left him a moment to himself.[2] A non-autonomous life, subjected to the paradoxical urgency of a timeless knowledge.

At the other extreme, one finds Kant, rising at five minutes to five, leaving to teach his course at the university at seven, copiously lunching at one, taking a stroll from five to six, reading from six to a quarter to ten, retiring to bed at ten, and asking himself, after having meticulously 'bundled himself up' (*emballiert*) in his blanket 'as if in a cocoon' (*gleichsam wie ein Kokon eingesponnen*): 'Can a man be healthier than I am?'[3] This went on day after day, with metronomic punctuality and following an immutable ritual. It would be impossible to lead a life further removed from Victor Cousin's chaotic existence. Kant's life was so extraordinarily regular that it inspired one of his contemporaries to write a comedy;[4] his existence was so imperturbably organised that it was never disturbed by the merest accident. Yet was this scholar's life monopolised by reading and thinking better attuned than the French philosopher's to the specific nature of time, which is all spontaneity and adjustment to circumstance? That's far from certain. The excessive orderliness of Kant's days does not denote a lesser scorn for ordinary contingencies than the disorder inherent to Cousin's life. The daily return of the same activities is a way of ignoring the vast power of change in the flow of time. In both cases, it is an alienated existence, entirely devoted to texts from the past, back turned on the present.

Kant and Cousin did not live in everyone else's time, nor even in their own time, but in that of culture and books, which arrange in the infinite corridor of the succession of past, present, and future for a secret door opening onto an elsewhere outside of time. A library is a machine to exit the world and smash the excessively narrow framework of everyday temporality. One should not hastily assume that the reader who goes to the library every day at the same time is merely obsessive: paradoxically, timelessness likes fixed-time appointments. In fact, that's the only way of taming it. If you do not choose to give it a well-defined portion of your day, it will swallow it all up. Anyone who does not follow this rule, like Cousin, risks seeing his life turn to chaos or, worse, destroyed.

By its very nature, the life of the scholar is eccentric or, to be more specific, it is elsewhere than the centre, arranged in relation to another centre: the texts that impose their laws upon it. The stakes of this arrangement are high: if you change the texts you read, you change life – at least your life. Conversely, you can only change what you read by changing lives. It is therefore not surprising that schedules were one of the most discussed subjects in Renaissance humanism. Considering new texts – which were 'new' because they dated from antiquity – implies making room for them in the course of the day. The daily schedule reflects this requirement. Passing from the Sorbonne's scholastic yoke to the humanists', Gargantua sees his day become excessively long: he no longer gets up between eight and nine, but at four. Not a minute is lost: he studies from the moment he gets up, while getting dressed, eating his meals, and even while moving his bowels, for which he appropriately saves 'the more obscure and difficult points'.[5] The giant's day is a giant day, as open-ended as the vast fields of knowledge to be explored. And what goes for Gargantua goes for every erudite person of the Renaissance – up to a point.

Some thirty years later, Pierre de Ronsard defended himself from accusations leveled against him by minutely describing his daily schedule.[6] Upon rising, he read for four or five hours, went to mass, lunched, took a walk with a book in hand, played games or exercised. Though less packed, the poet's day was fundamentally no different from the giant's. It implicitly defines the existence of a hypothetical opponent who loafs in bed, wastes his time with claptrap and balderdash, and stays cooped up or, strictly speaking, *cloistered*. Indeed, for Ronsard the epitome of this opponent is the fanatical Calvinist preacher and for Rabelais the uneducated monk, whose entire life is squandered in useless and repetitive religious services: matins, lauds, terce, sext, nones, vespers, compline.

The humanists responded to the canonical organisation of the day with a counter-model of a schedule based on a certain balance between study and physical activity. Though prayer still had a place in this schedule, it largely shared its prerogatives with the reading of secular texts. The Book was succeeded by books, which were not intended to dethrone the former, but to complete it: the very act of studying and knowing was now granted an importance previously reserved for ritual. For if God reveals himself in his creation, the study of man and of the world is no longer a simple pastime: it is the most sacred of duties, the one that Aristotle followed Plato in calling 'contemplation' (*theôria*).

During the Renaissance, this change in the scholar's status was far from unproblematic: it demanded not only an upheaval in religious institutions, but also a major change to a well-attested, essentially Roman tradition according to which reading was merely a leisure activity. How could the Ciceronian *otium* be transformed into *negotium*? In other words, how could relaxation be turned into a full-fledged occupation? How could it be turned into an *officium* as worthy as an ecclesiastical office? This was precisely the role played by descriptions of schedules: by organising the entire day around study, they elevated what had previously only been a leisure activity to the dignity of a profession, even a mission. The new cleric was born, to whom the old clericity of the convents and presbyteries would soon yield its dignity. The free man no longer demeaned himself by devoting himself to letters, which could occupy him just as well as a merchant's or artisan's work: one simply needs to know how to use one's time.

V

Education

It is a painting at the Museum of Fine Arts in Bordeaux. A painting so dark you could easily breeze by without noticing it: darkness cloaks nine-tenths of its surface. But the canvas's subject is no less obscure than its appearance.

Two characters are distinguishable. An old man with a salt and pepper beard looks toward the viewer, his head turned three-quarters to the left. He holds a large rectangular object upright, a little tilted back, a kind of black hole resting on the picture's lower edge, which appears to feature a table.

Visible in profile from the chest up, a child carefully examines the object in question, which proves to be a mirror. Four or five books are stacked behind the mirror. The image's only components consist of an old man, a child, a mirror, and a few books. No matter how hard you look, nothing else appears.

Nothing else, aside from the very fact of appearance, or what makes it possible: light. Indeed, the painting's most striking feature is not found in a simple list of its elements. It is elsewhere, in the radical treatment of chiaroscuro, in the best tradition of Caravaggio.

The light enters the painting from its upper-right corner, emphasising a few specific elements: the man's face, which is rendered in a realist manner, with deep wrinkles and weathered skin; his left hand, with pronounced creases and red joints, holding the top of the frame; his right hand, with the forefinger resting on the mirror, pointing either to the mirror itself or to the image reflected in it; the child's head, of which only the forehead, eye, nose, and ear are lit. Everything else, including the lower part of the child's face, is left in half-light, if not in total darkness, with the exception of the child's right hand, which rests on the table, while his other hand helps to hold up the mirror.

Juan Do: *Un maître et son élève* [A teacher and his student]
Musée des Beaux-Arts de Bordeaux.

The painting is attributed to Giovanni (or Juan) Do, a Spanish painter born in Valencia around 1604. He spent his entire career in Naples, arriving in the city in 1623 and dying there in 1656. Giovanni Do is not well-known. In fact, no painting has been definitively attributed to him.[1]

If a visitor to the museum in Bordeaux does not lean in to read the wall label, he may spontaneously think he recognises the hand of Jusepe de Ribera, the great Spanish painter of Naples, in whose circle Do did work. The old man's craggy face is particularly reminiscent of the little Spaniard's style.

In an even more specific way, the painting's two figures curiously evoke other sitters for Ribera: the man could be the one who posed for the *Diogenes* (1637) now in the Dresden State Art Collections and the *Astronomer* (1638) at the Worcester Art Museum in Massachusetts. The boy's profile is identical to Jacob's in the *Jacob and Isaac* at the Prado, which also dates from 1637.[2] The similarities are unsettling: while they don't necessarily mean we have to consider Ribera as the artist behind the Bordeaux paintings, since models could have been shared between his studio and a fellow painter's, they do force us to date it to the same period.

But the question of the artist is secondary here. The real problem it raises lies elsewhere: What is its subject?

Happily, the enigma is quickly resolved, for the Bordeaux museum has been good enough to affix a plate to help the viewer understand the image.[3] According to the official exegete, the painting is an allegorical representation of education. The teacher is showing his student a mirror in which the young boy observes the truth of the world. Relegated to the background, the books have been dismissed by the adult: the child is invited to discover life for himself, in the most direct way possible, through his personal perception of the world and the reflection of his own consciousness.

According to this interpretation, the painting praises a pedagogy of immediate experience, which rejects the traditional mediation of texts, manuals, and treatises. This is a beautiful – and oh so prophetic – lesson for today's teacher. One shudders to imagine classes of students visiting the Bordeaux museum with their teacher – a teacher necessarily well-versed in all the latest pedagogical novelties – collectively marvelling over this pictorial representation that puts the book back in its place at the bottom of the ladder.

In fact, the museum's interpretation is even too timid. Let us go a little further along the path to modernity: Does not the foregrounded mirror herald the coming reign of the image? Does not its rectangular shape foreshadow the computer screen now replacing the book? Such curious evidence of the artist's prescience would allow this *Triumph of Modern Pedagogy* pride of place in teacher training courses.

Unless, unfortunately, a certain number of external and internal arguments forced one to reconsider the painting's historical significance and call into question the museum's suggested reading.

The first argument is a historical one. A good way to legitimate the official interpretation would be to anchor it in the seventeenth-century history of ideas; the author of the wall label did not explicitly focus on this, probably to avoid being incomprehensible to middle school students, but we must now do so in his place. This pictorial praise of personal experience versus book culture and the ancient masters can only truly be understood in the context of the European spread of Cartesianism.

The dismissal of books was the first order of business in the *Discourse on Method*:

[...] as soon as I reached an age which allowed me to emerge from the tutelage of my teachers, I abandoned the study of letters altogether, and resolving to study no other science than that which I could find within myself or else in the great book of the world, I spent the rest of my youth in travelling, seeing courts and armies, mixing with people of different humours and ranks, in gathering a varied experience, in testing myself in the situations which chance offered me, and everywhere reflecting upon whatever events I witnessed in such a way as to draw some profit from them. For it seemed to me that I might find much more truth in the reasonings which each one makes in matters that affect him closely, the result of which must be detrimental to him if his judgement is faulty, than from the speculation of a man of letters in his study [...].[4]

In this case, the flat, empty mirror would quite aptly stand for the clean slate from which the student must start in order to get rid of uncertain knowledge. That would be the second part of the *Discourse*: 'as far as all the opinions I had hitherto accepted were concerned, I could not do better than undertake once and for all to be rid of them[.]'[5]

Finally, the gaze fixed on one's own reflection would represent the individual cogito fundamental to any real science: that is the third part of the *Discourse*. Here, the painting would transcribe the principles of Cartesian philosophy in an original plastic form.

It is certainly an attractive interpretation. The problem is that from a chronological perspective it does not hold.

Descartes's *Discourse* was published in Leiden in 1637, in French. It would reasonably take several years for the text to spread around Europe and reach Naples. As we have just seen, the painting itself couldn't have been painted much after 1637, when the models represented were working for Ribera and his circle. Given that the child does not appear to have grown much since the *Jacob* signed and dated in 1637, the Bordeaux painting cannot have been executed much later. In short, it is hard to believe that in so little time – before 1640, let's say – a painting inspired by Descartes' thought could have been produced in Naples – on top of that, by a painter who was more familiar with commissions on religious subjects than illustrations of philosophy of dubious reputation.

This historical argument could, however, be put into perspective if the museum's commentary was coherent with the principles that governed seventeenth-century image interpretation. But that is not the case.

Since the painting presents itself as an allegory, it must be read according to the corresponding rules. The museum's exegete seems to believe, in particular, that there is an axiological antagonism between the only two objects represented in the painting: the mirror, which has a positive connotation, and the books, which he claims have a negative value. But emblematical representations, which provided painters of the time with a repertoire of symbols, did not function this way. In an emblem, the components of an image generally add up: the signified functions through equivalence or synergy. In other words, the allegory does not practise irony: everything it stands for is true and participates equally in the definition of the object concerned.

For an element to be subtracted from the general meaning of the whole, the very act of subtraction must be represented, in the clearest manner possible, so that this act is itself endowed with a positive nature. For example, if the book were perceived as contrary to real education, one would need to see it lacerated by a knife, trampled beneath the teacher's feet, or burning in avenging flames.

The painting does not depict anything of the sort: the books on the Bordeaux canvas are simply in the background of the image. For instance, when Jean Baudoin represents the 'Desire to learn' by 'a woman, who is shown holding a mirror in one hand, & a little dog with the other', it doesn't mean that the dog is intended to be the mirror's antithesis: it's much more like its complement or its equivalent. For, as Baudoin explains, 'since the Mirror represents the Images of things that are its opposite, the Mind still retains the Ideas of what it is shown; from which one can say that the Dog is still a symbol, particularly since it easily lets its Master instruct and train it'.[6]

If a dog isn't the opposite of a mirror, a book certainly won't be! On a majolica dish dating from about 1555, Prudence is represented by a double-headed woman holding in one hand a mirror in which she is reflected, and in the other a book resting upright on the ground.[7] This does not at all suggest that the book means nothing to her. On the contrary, given that Prudence's other face is that of a bearded old man turned toward the book, an equivalence is clearly found between, on the one hand, the mirror, the usual symbol of truth, and on the other, book knowledge.

In his famous *Iconologia*, Cesare Ripa suggests two possible representations of science as a woman holding a mirror or a woman holding a book:[8] One could not find a better expression of the two objects' interchangeable nature. Indeed, as Ripa explains: 'The open book shows that, in books, the truth of things resonates: It therefore signifies the study of sciences.'[9] As for the mirror, 'it teaches that truth is in its perfection only when [...] the intellect conforms to intelligible things, in the same way that the mirror is good when it renders the true form of the thing that is resplendent in it.'¹⁰

Clearly, there is no doubt about the painting's general meaning as interpreted by the museum: it is indeed an allegorical representation of education.

Ripa invites one to imagine education as 'a man of magnificent and venerable appearance, in a long frock coat, full of magnanimous gravity, holding a mirror, inside of which will be found a plate with the words: INSPICE, CAVTVS, ERIS.'¹¹ 'Look inside, you will be safe': indeed, the mirror 'allows us to understand that all our actions must be weighed and measured in relation to others' actions.'¹²

Jean Baudoin suggests a slightly different interpretation of the same image, but one that perfectly matches our painting: the man 'seems to warn us to our attention to our own flaws, so that when we find stains on ourselves, we erase them if possible, like those who use a Mirror to clean dirt off their faces.'¹³ Isn't this exactly what the child does by concentrating on his own reflection?

As for the books, it goes without saying that far from clashing with the mirror, as the present-day exegete believes, they complete its function. Indeed, according to Ripa, 'without books, with only the Teacher's voice, it is difficult to take in and retain a great number of things, for they engender in us knowledge and science.'¹⁴

But there is really no need to dive into sixteenth- and seventeenth-century emblem anthologies to understand the meaning and value of the bound volumes depicted in the Bordeaux canvas: an attentive examination of the pictorial organisation will suffice.

As we have seen, light plays an essential role in the picture's significant structure. Everything light lands upon is immediately given a positive value: the teacher's illuminated face and hands, worn by time, are symbols of experience acquired; the young student's illuminated forehead, smooth and clean, bears witness to a still virgin consciousness; the boy's illuminated eye, nose, ear, and right hand are favoured instruments of the intellect and the distanced perception of the world and actions, while the mouth, an organ of material contact and a sense considered inferior, remains in shadow.

But there is a last element accentuated by light, though probably too subtly for certain observers: it is the open page of the top book on the pile, behind the mirror and partially hidden by it, as if it were its equivalent or substitute.

For the painting to be properly understood, it is fundamental for the book to be open, and not closed: clearly, it is still in the process of being read at the moment when the mirror is presented. This reading by the student also provides the key for reading the entire picture: the teacher, staring out at the viewer, seems to do nothing but invite this viewer to follow the child's example, to follow the same process, to let his gaze invincibly drift toward the open page in the lower right corner of the frame.

For if this page that more or less coincides with the painting's horizon is reduced by the play of perspective to a thin white line, the white mark shines with such a pure brilliance that it clearly imposes itself as the most luminous point in the entire painting, the one against which all the other elements are measured: not as the actual source of light, but that which reflects it in the most perfect way. Could one hope for a more beautiful and clearer allegory of the knowledge found in books than as a reflection of a foreign light come to illuminate our dark world?

Granted, this painting is an image, but an image that paradoxically rejects the omnipotence of images to, on the contrary, celebrate the power and necessity of texts, when it is a question of teaching and transmitting. This is what Juan Do, Ribera, or their Neapolitan contemporary sought to teach us. This is also what the exegete at the museum in Bordeaux did not understand or did not want to understand, for even when it is unconscious, the hatred of books has the power to blind us. In that, at least, the museum label proves instructive and exemplary, perhaps, of an entire era.

VI

The Examination

You cannot be a scholar by yourself. Of course, nothing prevents you from enjoying literature on your own, but there is nothing scholarly about that pleasure: it is the pleasure of the autodidact, who differs from the scholar in at least this respect. The pleasure specific to the scholar is a social one, even if by chance the scholar winds up stuck on a desert island or high on the slopes of a mountain, thousands of miles from civilisation. The pleasure specific to the scholar is in representing civilisation all on his own. Representing it and, especially, knowing that he represents it. Wherever he goes, the scholar recognises himself as a member of a community, invested with its legitimacy, if not its strength.

The examination provides so much assurance: it is a rite of entry into the community, of which it is often the most visible external manifestation, since as a matter of principle the neophyte does not have access to the group's internal life. A strange power of transmutation is invested in this rite: it transforms the disciple into a teacher and the teacher into a peer. At the very least, this is the power of the final examination, the one beyond which there are no more examinations and of which all the others are a more or less degraded image. Bachelor's, master's, certification: to this day, these titles' etymology expresses the authority enjoyed by their bearer or the fact that they belong to a new community. But both the authority and the community are paradoxical.

On the twenty-third day of the third month in 870, Sugawara no Michizane took his examination in Heyankiô, the 'capital of peace' now known as Kyoto. He was only twenty-six years old, while the other candidates were often in their thirties or forties. Locked in a room, he had to write two essays on set topics. The first essay was on the origin of the names of obscure families; Michizane began by describing how the first Chinese emperor legislated on surnames, then proceeded to elucidate the names required. The second essay dealt with earthquakes: the assignment was to explain why the earth moved, and to give the Chinese and Indian interpretations of this phenomenon. Judging by the essays – which by an archival miracle have survived to this day – Michizane rose to the occasion of both exercises, admirably blending historical knowledge and Confucian, Taoist, and Buddhist doctrine, all in the particularly convoluted style of classical Chinese, as was the custom of Japanese scholars. Also in keeping with this custom was the profession of humility with which the second essay concluded:

> I, Michizane, gaze in awe towards the Yangtze and Han rivers, but am ashamed of my inability to span the broad ocean. I wish to master the art of clear expression but get lost on the path amidst the clouds. How can I deal with the dark mysteries or discuss what is beyond my sight and hearing? I have not the leisure to visit the land of the Duke of Chou and Confucius, or let my spirit wander with Chuang-tzu or the Buddha. Unable to solve all the difficulties, I cannot avoid error.[1]

Michizane was not being excessively humble: indeed, at twenty-six, he had never crossed the sea to visit the continent; his knowledge of Chinese civilisation was no less bookish than the awareness of ancient Greek culture among the European humanists of the Renaissance. What Michizane did not yet know at the time he took his examination was that he would never go to China. Indeed, once he reached the high government position that was to be his, Michizane refused to go on a diplomatic mission to Japan's powerful neighbour, thus putting an end to Sino-Japanese diplomatic relations for many years. It is said that Michizane only refused because he was afraid he would give away that he was unable to express himself orally in Chinese: he allegedly didn't want to lose face in front of the mission's other members. This explanation isn't particularly convincing: however limited his gift for spoken Chinese, Michizane was the best China scholar of his generation and knew at least as much Chinese as all the previous ambassadors. The reason was more likely a political one: with the Tang regime sinking into civil war, sending a diplomatic mission would not have benefited Japan, without mentioning the dangers such an expedition would face even in less troubled times.

It is also permissible to think that as the future patron of scholars, Michizane did not particularly want to be confronted with the real China, which would have permanently spoiled his inner China, the one he had created for himself by consulting countless scrolls, with its philosophers flying astride the clouds and its poets playing the lute on a moonlit terrace. In the scholar's eyes, text is world enough, though fragile: the slightest contact with reality could shatter this glass pagoda. While Socrates knew that he knew nothing, Michizane knew that he knew little. This nuance shows the distance between the philosopher who is only comfortable with extremes and absolutes (everything, nothing, good, evil etc.) and the scholar familiar with compromise. Scholarly knowledge only knows its limits because it knows itself first as knowledge: unlike the philosopher, the scholar cannot accept that his knowledge could be nothing more than an appearance of knowledge – and even less self-knowledge. But not doubting yourself is sometimes a strength, sometimes a weakness.

Two months after the examination, Michizane received his grade. According to the system of evaluation in effect, an A recognised essays in which both style and reasoning were of a superior level, a B those in which one was superior and the other average, a C those in which both were average, and a D, those in which they were merely passable. Michizane received a D, the examiner having found errors, solecisms, and imprecise passages. Does such a grade seem contradictory for a man who would posthumously be glorified as the god of literature under the name of Tenjin? Or on the contrary, is it consistent with a being of divine nature? While some gods die on a cross surrounded by robbers, others are classed among the dunces: to each his particular infamy. In fact, there is a simpler historical explanation: in the ninth century, all candidates who took the examination invariably received a D, regardless of their level. This was probably the best way to remind these brilliant individuals of their duty to be humble.

When one of his teachers congratulated him on his success, Michizane replied with the following verses:

In good times, passing the examination makes one's name.
Treading in my father's footsteps, I will not break with tradition.
Fortunately, I do not return home a failure to become a frustrated old man.
Unexpectedly, I am ranked among the clouds in the blue sky.

> Your congratulatory note deeply touches me,
> But I wipe my eyes when with dismay I look at the criticism of my essays.
> Do not say I have succeeded and shall receive noble office.
> I must apologise to my father for breaking off only a worm-eaten branch of the cassia.²

In the Chinese poetic tradition, breaking off a branch of the cassia growing on the moon means passing the competition to become a civil servant; when the branch is worm-eaten, as it is here, the achievement is obviously less glorious. There is no bitterness, however, in Michizane's words, but the expression of a modesty that only befits the scholar's position: modesty towards his mother who, in a poem celebrating her son's impending adulthood, had hoped to see him break the celebrated cassia branch; towards the father, despite the fact that he too had probably only gotten a D on the examination; towards the teacher whose compliments were on principle unmerited. In other words, Michizane was not calling into question the examiner's judgement. His consternation was the necessary formulation of a knowledge conscious not only of its limits, but of the possibility of one day surpassing them.

When properly understood, the examination only aims to reveal the incompetence of those who successfully passed it. The form of the competition is in essence more philosophical than a mere examination, since while a student risks receiving deceptive assurance from an examination based on an absolute standard, the winner of a competition only ever wins because there was not a better candidate. This explains the scholar's paradoxical strength: he admits not to his total incompetence, only to his inadequacy.

VII

The Study

Voyage of a statuette.

    Due to some unknown crime (perhaps deciphering a forbidden secret on a scroll), the scholar's clothes, hair, and even his skin suddenly turned green, a beautiful pale green creating an illusion of transparency and depth. At the same time, his fingertips hardened, his hand joints became rigid, the tip of his goatee stuck to his chest, and his wide silk sleeves grew unfathomably heavy, leaving the figure frozen in mid-movement, with his head raised to the right and his left arm bent up to hold one of his braids between his thumb and index finger. The petrification only took a moment to set in, and now light caresses the precious jade reliefs at leisure, while the figure, reduced to a more modest scale (less than six inches), is embedded in a delicate interlacing of reddish wood scrollwork, forming an entirely openwork frame. Put all that on a pedestal carved from the same wood, and you have an elegant table screen, the perfect ornament for intellectual labour.[1] Though the person represented here looks in every way like a scholar or a sage, even a god, we will probably never know his name and exact function. What we do know, however, is that he saw the light of day in nineteenth-century China, under the Qing dynasty, to take his place among the possessions of another scholar. Scholars love to surround themselves with their fellow scholars and use them to decorate their studies.

The study contains three categories of objects. First, those called 'the four treasures of the scholar's study' (*wenfang sibao* in Chinese), which are indispensable to the activity that defines this space, namely, writing: ink (*mo* in Chinese; *sumi* in Japanese); brush (*bi* in Chinese; *fude* in Japanese); paper (*zhi* in Chinese; *kami* in Japanese); and inkstone (*yan* in Chinese; *suzuri* in Japanese). As eminently perishable resources exhausted through the very act of writing, the first three of these treasures are all the more precious: ink spreads into characters; sheets of paper succeed each other; the brush inexorably disintegrates, silk after silk. In an abundantly apparent paradox, writing provides a record for the future and protection from the assaults of time, but can be seen as the great consumer, the devourer par excellence. It is carried out through the perpetual sacrifice of animal and vegetal offerings, both solid and liquid, intended to appease the insatiable divinities of transmission and oblivion. To write is to expend against loss. Both flat and hollowed, the inkstone where the inkstick is ground with a little water is the only writing tool designed to weather daily use. It serves as an altar or a grail: the black libation daily prepared inside it is to be used for a king who is not a fisherman, but a reader.

In a lower category than the 'four treasures', one finds writing accessories, which are like the instruments of sacrifice: the inkwell, brush pot, brush washer, and brush holder. Though these tools are necessary for the ritual's harmonious performance, they are not at its centre. Then comes all the rest, that is to say the ornaments of the ceremony. The noblest of these is the seal, which certifies the scholar's identity: as the only irreplaceable and unreproducible sign, it transposes its bearer's face and voice to the flat and colourless world of written characters. Such an eminent function justifies the rich sculptures (animals and humans both real and imagined) that sit atop this small stone block: they symbolically deploy into three-dimensional space the authority that the seal imprints on the two dimensions of the page. Naturally, the use of red ink is reserved for the seal. Other objects evoke the arts to which the scholar is devoted. As early as Confucius, the scholar needed to be an accomplished poet, calligrapher, and musician. After Wang Wei (701–761), who invented a specific kind of 'scholars' painting' (*wenrenhua* in Chinese; *bunjinga* in Japanese), the scholar was also required to master this form of painting, as attested to by the several scrolls scattered around the room in various states, along with several lutes and zithers. A little messiness does not go amiss in the work of the mind.

However small it may be, the Far Eastern scholar's study in no way matches the predominant Western idea of this room as a closed-in, finite space. In the summer, the scholar enjoys working in a thatch-roofed pavilion open on all four sides, built near the water or a cool mountain hollow, as depicted in the landscape scrolls inspired by Wang Wei's poems and paintings. A waterfall echoes in the distance; stopping at the edge of a precipice, a visitor brushes the pine tops with his sleeve; a cloud crosses the painting, like a momentary barrier between the scholar's retreat and the rest of the world. Nothing is immobile: the movements specific to this world are palpable all over the image, if only through its oblong shape, which forces the gaze to constantly range over the entire space by failing to provide it with a centre of gravity on which to rest. The serenity to which the scholar aspires isn't that of retreating into himself, but one of a dynamic exchange with the world that surrounds him: less a station than a 'path' (*dao* in Chinese; *michi* in Japanese; readers will recognise this as Lao Tzu's 'Tao'). In a not dissimilar way, the critique of what he considered an excessively essentialist and paralysing Western metaphysics drove Martin Heidegger to follow 'forest paths' (*Holzwege*) that lead nowhere, if not to the heart of things and their mysterious presence: what finer revelation of the prolific nature of being than the landscape's continuous emergence over the course of a stroll or the unexpected appearance of a clearing? This could also serve as a definition of reading and writing understood as journeys.

When the season does not lend itself to such wandering, the scholar still has a garden, a miniature figure of the world, onto which his study affords a view. A window in the shape of a bell or a full moon opens onto a chosen scene (a venerable tree, a distant pavilion, a curiously shaped rock) whose limitation is underlined by the frame. There are no imposing perspectives here, no privileged point of view. Like the river, the hill, and the mountain, the garden never entirely reveals itself. All that is accessible are fragments of the garden irreducible to one another. The landscape always suggests both the possibility of a complement still hidden from sight and the impossibility of a completeness that would bring the visit to a close and enclose the space. The awareness of elsewhere remains on the surface of the here and now.

What is true of the garden is even more so of the study: it is only ever closed in appearance. Even when entirely enclosed, it opens onto other times and places, with which it secretly communicates. The scholar is not where one thinks he is: you see his body, but the text he's reading has transported his mind elsewhere, leaving only an empty simulacrum in his place. The fundamental alterity in words shifts and dismantles everything it touches. The scholar's study is the vehicle for this journey: the objects it contains aren't there for what they are, but for what they represent, the world to which they lead through the cracking of a hidden door. This is what distinguishes the scholar's collection from a collection gathered purely for aesthetic reasons: a painting on the wall needs no other justification than the pleasure it provides its owner and his visitors. Objects placed on a desk, however, must meet a multitude of sometimes contradictory obligations: they must be inconspicuous to avoid hampering the work of reading and writing, but not so inconspicuous as to be invisible to the gaze that briefly seeks respite from the page. And they must encourage the return to the intellectual labour momentarily interrupted.

Stone has this power. Or rather, stones, since no two stones are the same: they are the triumph of the singular. The porous Taihu stone, the twisted Lingbi stone, the coarse, crystalline Jun stone, or the Dali marble that forms a picture in a wood frame:[2] each has the power to transform before our eyes and to become a tree, a cloud, a mountain, or a dragon, depending on its shape or the mood of the person who contemplates it. There are 'dream stones' (*mengshi* in Chinese) the way there are typewriters, and in both cases these are tools to lead us elsewhere. Whatever it takes to help the scholar wander. This withdrawal from the world has in fact become one of the commonplaces of Chinese iconography: since the fourth century, there have been countless visual and poetic representations of the *Seven Sages of the Bamboo Grove* (*zhulin qixian* in Chinese), seven scholarly aristocrats gathered on the property of the poet Ji Kang (223–262) to talk, drink, meditate, and play music – in short, everything except deal with literature.[3] To all appearances, at least, since literature is precisely the power that allows us to extract ourselves from the whirlwind of things to become present to ourselves: being offers itself to those who know how to escape the game of political and social illusions to enjoy the sovereign freedom of leisure. In different climes, Cicero referred to this retreat as *ottium literarum*.⁴ At least one thing Western scholars have in common with Eastern scholars is that their studies have the structure, function, and ideal of a garden, unless it's the garden that takes the shape of a study: here, relaxing, working, and growing is all one thing. The word 'culture' expresses nothing if not a certain increase of being, common to plants and the mind.

The jade man mentioned earlier may be one of these seven Chinese sages. His informal pose, dreamy demeanour, and the amused gaze he seems to cast upon the world – everything here indicates the scholar on a stroll, having deliberately arrived on another scholar's desk to serve as a diversion in his moments of relaxation. But for reasons unknown, through some unknown path, his stroll took him so far away from the Celestial Empire: beyond the Great Wall, beyond the great plains and the mountains in the West, to a country populated with barbarians, on the work table of a scholar and healer of souls, a book collector and art enthusiast named Sigmund Freud. In the photographs Edmund Engelman took in Freud's Vienna apartment in May 1938, a few days before the psychoanalyst and his family went into exile, the table screen is perfectly visible on the desk, surrounded by a large quantity of collectibles:⁵ Chinese funerary figurines, Etruscan warriors, a head of Osiris, ancient bronzes in all sizes, Roman and Egyptian deities, Venus, Mercury, the mummy of the god Ptah, Sekhmet with her lion head, the cat head of the goddess Bastet, Isis nursing Horus... With these thirty or so artifacts placed in front of him, placidly staring back at him with their empty eyes like so many listeners, Freud selected a choice audience for himself: nothing less than a pantheon at his personal beck and call, to serve every purpose. Even when on a mountain vacation in Berchtesgaden, Freud made sure to take a few idols along in his baggage: 'My old grimy gods, for whom you have so little respect', he wrote to his colleague

Wilhelm Fliess, 'participate in my work as manuscript-weights.'[6] A scholar will only keep company with demons and divinities if he is at least on an equal footing. In fact, the psychoanalyst's collection wasn't limited to the objects on his table: the entire room he used as the office in which he received his patients was crammed with all sorts of statuettes and pictures, seals, amulets, engravings, bas-reliefs, papyrus, Coptic paintings, and fragments of Roman frescoes, hanging on the walls, resting on tables, and exhibited in display cases, filling the space with their silent and solemn presence and offering the patient on the couch the alternately peaceful and unsettling enigma of their millenary impassibility.

Freud was more attached to this collection of ancient objects than to any of his other possessions: he confessed to Stefan Zweig that he had 'made many sacrifices for [his] collection of Greek, Roman, and Egyptian antiquities', and had 'in fact read more archeology than psychology'.[7] Freud was probably exaggerating the extent of his reading in archeology, but it's certainly true that after the Anschluss one of his greatest consolations was that he could take all the treasures he had accumulated over the course of his life into exile with him in London (after the Nazis had collected an exorbitant twenty-five percent tax on their value, paid by Marie Bonaparte). To this day, a visitor to Freud's home lost in the verdant residential neighbourhood of Hampstead can still admire part of the collection, divided between the desk and the top of the fireplace.[8] After this final journey, still figuring prominently on the work table, the jade scholar once again taunts humans with his raised eyes. Yet in the vast, luminous residence where Freud lived out his days, one struggles to recognise the confined atmosphere of the Viennese apartment at 19, Berggasse: in that relatively cramped space, the accumulation of so many objects, imbued with a spellbinding presence disproportionate to their small scale, created a feeling of unease. Recalling the first time he entered this sanctuary of psychoanalysis, Engelman admitted that he felt 'overwhelmed by the masses of figurines which overflowed every surface'.[9] One might initially consider blaming the bourgeois aesthetic of an era inclined to decorative overkill and ostentatious accumulation. But as attested to by the photographs, the other rooms in the apartment weren't similarly decorated – or at least not to such a degree. Doctor Freud's office enjoyed a specific ornamentation.

Much has been said about the passion that led Sigmund Freud to do his weekly rounds of Viennese antiquarians who often saved their finest pieces for him.[10] Freud himself saw a metaphor of psychoanalytic work in archeology. His interest in Egypt has been interpreted as a quest for his Jewish roots (he even saw an Egyptian in the figure of Moses, legislator of the Hebrews and founder of monotheism).[11] Yet these interpretations legitimately connected to the psychoanalyst's work and personality have the drawback of considering Professor Freud's consulting room as a unique case, when it was in fact the distant successor to a composite tradition with a long and geographically vast history: inaugurated with the studies of Far Eastern scholars, the tradition found its western counterpart in the studies (*studioli*) of Saint Jerome and Saint Augustine, as circulated in iconography beginning in the mid-fourteenth century and depicted in great detail by Antonello da Messina and Vittore Carpaccio, among others.[12] In the sixteenth century, the scholar Gilles Corrozet would even design a coat of arms for the study.[13]

Writing instruments, books, scrolls, objets d'art, various curios: scholars of both continents sought every means possible to mark their work spaces and represent, less for others than for themselves, a demanding and difficult activity (reading, writing) that offered little for the senses to latch onto, and which they might otherwise risk turning away from entirely. The feel of fine paper and the sight of a beautiful object are perceptible compensations for the desiccating abstraction of the occupations of the mind. It is admirable to find such similarities at the two extremes of Eurasia in practices that evolved totally separately, without entering into direct contact or being exposed to a shared influence. Any culture of writing probably produces similar sacralisation of scholarly territory, which can be recognised as early as the Egyptian scribe. But these apparent resemblances mustn't mask the radical difference that arises between the two cultures. An open study in the one culture; a closed one in the other. While the Chinese scholar's collection opens onto the dimension of space and dream, manifesting a singular relationship with the world, which consists at once of presence and withdrawal, quiet and wandering at a time when the Far East was unaware of the classic Western antinomy between nature and culture, the European scholar's collection exists in time, the time of teachers and ancestors, precursors and models, of whom it simultaneously asserts the permanence and disappearance. From this perspective, Freud appears as one of the last Western scholars, for his work is specifically marked by an anxiety related to time: the vanished time of lost civilisations (Greece, Rome, Egypt), the obscure time of the formation of the ego and the unconscious, the incompressible time of the talking cure. Perhaps psychoanalysis simply transfers to the individual a temporal questioning specific to the scholarly enterprise.

As witnesses to vanished worlds that only the work of the scholar, archeologist, and psychoanalyst can resurrect, the gods arranged on Freud's desk accompany the European scholar's mourning with their silent cortège: though he does not know what he has lost, he doggedly tries to find it through studying, which has become both the end and the means of his intellectual quest. As it happens, this is exactly how Freud defines melancholia: like mourning, it is a 'reaction to the loss of a loved object' (*Reaktion auf den Verlust eines geliebten Objekts*), but 'an object-loss withdrawn from consciousness, in contradiction to mourning, in which there is nothing about the loss that is unconscious.'[14] Contrary to mourning, the work through which melancholia seeks to be resolved must constantly be started again, for the goal is out of reach. Studying the past is an infinite endeavour, which eludes the normal functioning of the world, and exceeds both the norms of political power and the laws of the market. But first it exhausts the powers of the mind.

This pathological excess is described in Albrecht Dürer's most famous engraving. While the scholar's study finds its ideal in Saint Jerome and Saint Augustine, it also has a nightmarish version: with his tools lying on the ground, his quill case toppled over, and the book closed, the sombre angel in Dürer's *Melencolia I* absent-mindedly toys with the compass between his fingers, succumbing to the horrifying weariness of intellectual labour that isn't achieving its aims. This study without walls, abandoned to the cold night and turned upside down, is the embodiment of the distress of the Western scholar overwhelmed by the passing of time.[15]

Here is where Professor Freud should probably step in and offer his cure, but also when a certain jade scholar should deliver the lesson of his ironic gaze: the Western scholar still has a lot to learn from the hedonism of his Chinese colleague, who knows how to find the Taoist freedom in the heart of Confucian ritualism and to make the in-depth study of culture a key to cosmic harmony among mountains and rivers. Thankfully, the Nazis were able neither to seize the precious jade nor to disperse the contents of the Viennese psychoanalyst's study nor – and this is the same thing – to put an end to the scholar's journey through time and space.

Albrecht Dürer: *Melencolia I*

VIII

Economy

To be a scholar, to read and write books, you must free your mind from the difficulties of everyday life. Juvenal observed as much in his day: 'It calls for a lofty spirit', he wrote, 'not one that's scared of buying a blanket, to have visions of horses and chariots, of immortal godhead, to limn the Fury that once confounded the Rutulian Turnus. For if Virgil had not had one slave-boy and a fairly comfortable lodging, all those snakes would have dropped from the Fury's hair, her grave trumpet would have been voiceless.'[1] The allusion here is to the passage in *The Aeneid* in which the deity of vengeance appears to the warrior Turnus, then blows into her horn to stimulate combat. The lesson is clear: a scholar's work, a philosopher's speculations, and a poet's lyrical flights are directly tied to their standards of living.

Each verse, each poetic image, and each episode of a narrative has a price, which can be precisely evaluated: today's sociologists apply themselves to the task in a slightly less rudimentary and far more systematic way than the Latin satirist did.[2] A little house, an odd-jobs slave: that is what the twelve pounds in Virgil's epic could buy. It was hardly too much to ask from a patron like Augustus – or Maecenas – whose resources were, so to speak, unlimited. If the scholar doesn't have a personal fortune at his disposal, whether familial or recently accumulated, like Cicero and Pliny the Elder, he must give writing a directly lucrative dimension or put himself in the service of a benefactor, like Varro to Caesar or Livy to Augustus, thus entering into a standard commercial exchange: 'You give and I write.' Free writing or venal writing, living to study or studying to live: these two economic models have always coexisted, including in a single scholar's life, in which reversals can be constant. Aristotle opened a school and wrote, Lucian gave lectures and wrote, Plutarch officiated as a priest and wrote: which half of these lives served the other?

The life of the scholar subverts every economic category. Work, rest, retirement: these words do not have their ordinary meaning in the scholar's case. His official occupation only serves to pay the bills, and leisure time serves to study, which is to say to do the real work: before it referred to studying or school, the Greek *skholê* meant to rest. Such a temporal structure fits a view of the world and society in which only slaves and serfs work: they are assigned the utilitarian arts and techniques, while everyone else enjoys the so-called 'liberal' arts (*artes liberales*), worthy of free men. Only a free man has the vocation and capacity to fulfill what Aristotle considered the ultimate human vocation: contemplative activity (*théorêtikê*).[3] The Stagirite also declared that pure knowledge emerged 'first in those places where men had leisure'.[4] In other words, the scholar's occupation is located outside the normal circuits of economic exchange: it is an 'autonomous' (*autarkês*)[5] field, with its own values and rules.

It would be vain to think that this autarchy is exclusively tied to certain historical, now outdated social structures specific to aristocratic, unequal worlds. In fact, beyond the vicissitudes of history, what Aristotle so precisely described in the fourth century BC is simply a constant of life dedicated to the accumulation and production of knowledge: the scholar creates around himself a sphere distinct from that inhabited by his contemporaries and even his kin.

The life of the scholar is necessarily a scholarly life, different from ordinary life: there are so many books to read and comment upon, as well as so many books to be written, that the task can easily fill – and overwhelm – a single life. A single library is worth as much as any family, with its headaches. For better or worse, a child grows alone; all he knows is how to grow, for that is his nature. But the nature of the book is to die on each page in order to be reborn, should the reader or writer want it to, on the next page or in the following sentence. Reading demands time, effort, and application: it consists of transcribing in your mind what someone else wrote on paper, to provide your own life to someone else's words, to use your own lungs to breathe life back into words expired. Contrary to an excessively popular belief, one does not devour books: they devour you, they suck your blood, feed on your being and energy, cut you off from the world to transport you into their own, eat up your space and time, overflow from your shelves, shorten your nights and days, shrink your houses and apartments, ruin you while enriching you, make you theirs when you thought they were yours.

To live as a scholar is to live a double life. First, your books' life; then your own, for which time is always lacking. Family duties and housekeeping do not get taken care of by themselves: they are quick to monopolise your attention. To live a double life, you must either be doubly rich or starving. No half measures: the scholar is either funded or cursed.[6] The history of the scholarly condition constantly oscillates between these two poles. It is all too easy to see the connection between intellectual autonomy and financial marginalisation. Contrary to appearances, nothing is less immaterial than a scholar's existence. It doesn't simply consist of the luminous crest of all social activity, a slight bubbling of foam at the crest of the wave: to have foam, you must first have a wave. There is an economy or rather a meta-economy of the mind in the most material sense of the term: finances, a budget, a cheque-book. Even in contemporary democratic societies, where private income is no longer the norm, Aristotelian autarchy must be recreated artificially: it is up to the scholar to create an economic niche for himself that allows him to absorb and produce words and ideas. No need to transmute gold to do so: regular currency or a minimum of comfort will do.

The church, which for centuries secured spiritual power on a temporal basis, has always known that the immaterial was closely tied to the material. Which long made it the scholar's refuge: before Julien Benda secularised the term,[7] the modern clerk was preceded by the clerk plain and simple. He wasn't always a priest, but at least had a tonsure, which afforded him his share of ecclesiastical benefits. Yet the scholar's needs sometimes contradicted evangelical rules. In 1672, Bossuet was forced to defend himself after agreeing to supplement his 16,000-livre income from the priories of Gassicourt and Plessis-Grimoud by accepting an appointment by the king to the abbey of Saint-Lucien in Beauvais, which would earn him an additional annuity of 22,000 to 25,000 livres. From a strictly legal perspective, his situation was beyond reproach: so long as the income did not involve spiritual leadership or residential obligations, canon law authorised the holding of several offices at once. Moreover, Bossuet had just given up the diocese of Condom, with its 50,000 livres in revenue, to take on the difficult position of preceptor to the Dauphin: he needed to find a source of financial compensation.[8]

On a spiritual level, however, a different conclusion could be reached: How could you reconcile the Christian exhortation to poverty with a clerk's accumulation of wealth, however illustrious the clerk? This was the observation made to Bossuet by the Maréchal de Bellefonds. The reprimand must have been all the more difficult to take given that it came from a lord to whom the bishop practically served as a spiritual adviser: for once, the roles were reversed. Bossuet spared no effort in trying to justify himself to his correspondent. First, regarding Saint-Lucien:

> The abbey that the king gave me relieves me of a difficult situation and attention that cannot long be compatible with the thoughts that I must have. Do not fear that I will increase my expenses with sociable activities: the table fits neither my state nor my temper. My kin will not enjoy the benefits of the church's goods. I will pay off my debts as soon as I can. Most of them have been contracted for necessary expenses, even in the ecclesiastic order: these are bulls, ornaments, and other things of that nature.[9]

This probably reassured the Maréchal regarding the bishop's austerity, though Bossuet opened by stating that he did not 'expect any shared joy about the fortunes of the world from those whose eyes have been opened by God to reveal its vanity':[10] exiled to Tours by the king, Bellefonds was attracted to the abbot of Rancé's infectious asceticism. But Bossuet felt he further needed to justify his financial situation:

> As far as I know, I have no attachment to riches, and may perhaps be able to do without many conveniences, but I don't yet find myself skilled enough to find everything

that is necessary, if indeed I only had what was necessary, and I would lose more than half my mind, if I was hemmed in by my domestic affairs.

And once again: 'I like regularity, but there are certain states in which it is very difficult to keep it so narrow.'[11]

One could initially interpret Bossuet's defense of himself as a guide for the perfect prebendary, unscrupulously using all the resources of casuistry to justify the accumulation of sources of revenue: since he cannot live without a certain number of conveniences, since wealth is indispensable to him, it could hardly be refused him. However, the prelate had nothing to gain from picturing himself to his correspondent in such a Machiavellian light. On the contrary, his argument must be taken seriously. In a later public debate, Bossuet would justify the plurality of benefits, in his particular case, by citing as evidence his duty of charity toward the converted Protestants who had come from all over Europe to seek his protection.[12] But here, in a private context, addressing a trusted and informed interlocutor, the explanation is entirely different: in his eyes, the justification for so many different sources of income is his intellectual activity, which could not be practised without a certain level of material comfort. Bossuet was a priest, admittedly, but he was above all a theologian and a scholar of the first order, who put his vast erudition at the service of Christian apologetics. At the very time when he took on the heavy responsibility of educating the Dauphin, he began writing three major treatises: *Discours sur l'histoire universelle* (Discourse on Universal History); *La Politique tirée des propres paroles de l'Écriture sainte* (Politics Drawn from the Very Words of Holy Scripture); and *Traité de la connaissance de Dieu et de soi-même* (Treatise on the Knowledge of God and of Oneself).[13] A hermit or an Abbott,

Albrecht Dürer: *Saint Jerome*

Rancé, founder of the Trappists, would be unable to carry out such a long-term endeavour. Bossuet countered the evangelic commandments of poverty with those no less legitimate commandments of another order of realities: the mind and science, a field in which clericature prevailed over Christ. It was clerk versus clerk, within the very institution: letters have their reasons, unknown to the Gospel, but not dismissed by the Church, which welcomed knowledge and its pressing necessities.

Far from the pompous official portrait Hyacinthe Rigaud painted of Bossuet at the end of his life, the Bossuet of 1672 more closely resembles, *mutatis mutandis*, Dürer's Saint Jerome, bent over his writing case, in a paneled cell bathed in sunlight, with the cardinal's hat hanging from the wall, slippers carelessly left on the floor, and plump cushions under the windows and on the benches: however arduous his labour, in every scholar there lies dormant a prelate wishing to be cosy, jealously guarding his comfort and rest. Along with the blanket and Virgil's little slave, these are the true emblems of the scholarly household.

IX

The Home

The scholar's home contains the books that contain the world. But what place can contain this home? Certainly the world isn't sufficient. The home must therefore be located outside the world, or at least on its margins. The scholar's residence turns its back on the world. It is a cosmos unto itself, organised as such, with spaces assigned well-determined functions: for reading, the library; for working, the study; for relaxing, the garden; for resting, the bedroom. The scholar finds strength and courage in structure: structure is what we call habit when it is transposed from time into three-dimensional space and creates the scholar's abode. Carefully adjusted schedules require equally well-defined premises.

Ernest Renan once ventured a theory of the scholar's home. This was in Paris, in mid-June 1889, shortly after the opening of the Paris World's Fair. The French President Sadi Carnot, later to be assassinated at another fair in Lyon, was for the moment content to spend each day visiting a different part of the fair in Paris. Visitors to the Eiffel Tower rushed to its staircases – the elevators were already in operation, but were still being used to remove rubble from the monument's upper floors. Special trains had been chartered to run from the provinces, but once travelers from the provinces reached the capital, they had to continue to the fair on foot for lack of carriages – the coachmen had been on strike for several days. This merry commotion was the context in which was held the annual congress of Paris and departmental scholarly and fine arts societies. The general assembly was convened in the great amphitheatre at the Sorbonne, under the presidency of the Minister of Public Education and Fine Arts. Minister Fallières arrived at 2 p.m., and Renan opened the session with a speech that turned away from Parisian obstacles to ask a burning question: 'Can one work in the provinces?'[1] Given the setting, scholarly work was naturally the only subject of discussion. Among all the positive arguments put forward (the example of illustrious scholars, the underuse of provincial libraries etc.), one in particular held the attention of the Collège de France's old administrator: the scholar's home.

It provided the occasion for a lovely reverie:

> A nice house on the outskirts of a big city; a long workroom garnished with books, covered on the outside by Bengal roses; a garden with straight walks, where the flowers can for a moment distract you from conversation with your books: none of all this can be overlooked to achieve the health of the soul necessary for work of the mind. Unless you are a millionaire (which is rare among us), good luck finding it in Paris, on a fourth floor, in banal residences built by architects who didn't once consider the possibility of a scholarly tenant! Our libraries, in which we would so dearly love to stroll through the variety of our books and thoughts, are dark studies, attics where our books pile up without producing a scrap of light. Paris does have the Collège de France: that's enough

for me to be attached to it. But if the Collège de France were like an abbey at the time of Saint Bernard, lost deep in the woods, with long avenues of poplars, oak groves, streams, rocks, a cloister to walk in when it rains, rows of unnecessary rooms in which long tables would display new inscriptions, new casts and engravings, one would wait for death more quietly there, and the establishment's scientific production would be superior even to what it already is; for solitude is good inspiration, and the value of the work we do is proportionate to the calm with which it is accomplished.[2]

One could certainly join Renan in daydreaming about the scholarly retreat he so appealingly describes. One could also notice that he dwells far longer on the scholarly house's surroundings than on the house itself. Paradoxically, the 'long workroom' is no less desirable for the 'Bengal roses' that cover its outer walls than for the books it contains. Around the same time, Larousse published a *Grand dictionnaire universel* that defined this variety of roses as perennial and extremely prolific. Also referred to as the dog rose, the rose hip, and the China rose, they are, according to the dictionary, 'very fecund in flowers and their blossoming lasts a very long time.'[3] The names of its subvarieties have an old-fashioned charm: Ajax, *canari*, Ninon de Lenclos, *abricoté*, *amour des dames*, *gloire de Dijon*... It is the rose for low-maintenance gardens, which leaves plenty of time for intellectual labour.

This flower with a gently Oriental connotation provides a counterpoint of sorts to another kind of exoticism: the more worrisome one applied to the house's contents. While all books don't necessarily transport you to imaginary destinations, they certainly all come from somewhere else. The book is foreign by nature; it is otherness embodied in ink and paper. And this otherness is irreducible: whatever you do, a book is unlike a flesh and bone interlocutor in that it will always be true to itself. It demands nothing but submission. So much otherness and negative power are exhausting: the home's function is to make less arduous the work whose difficulty cruelly tests the scholar. According to Renan, it is a question of 'more quietly [waiting] for death' in a kind of retreat or, as it was called in the seventeenth century, a desert. At this point in the speech, such words are unexpected: Could one possibly find a clearer way to say that libraries are tombs not only for books, but for readers, and that scholarly work is in league with death? Reading texts by dead authors and writing about them is not without its fatal consequences.

Renan was acutely aware of this. He had for several years spent his summer holidays in Brittany, at Rosmapamon, a bourgeois house whose hortensia-bordered terrace offered a view through the trees of the bay of Perros-Guirec (this was the house where the young Maurice Barrès paid Renan a famous visit),[4] but once he felt his days were numbered, he didn't want to die anywhere but his apartment at the Collège de France, surrounded by his books and papers. A hasty departure from Renan's beloved native soil was organised, and the master died in Paris two weeks later, on 2 October 1892, at 6:20 a.m.[5] The library is the real land of the dead, and if books are guides for souls, scholars gladly also entrust them with their bodies, as to infernal Hermes.

A reader who wants to set foot in the Bibliothèque Nationale, France's national library, is certainly aware of this when he climbs the immense windowless pyramid, truncated at the top, that anchors this mausoleum-like structure. The Collège de France imagined by Renan was lost in a vast forest; the library designed by Dominique Perrault includes the forest in the middle of the building. In both cases, the scholar's home is at one with nature. A centre of knowledge and the most advanced outpost of the mind, it symbolically represents humanity's fundamental tension: the deeper culture gets, the wilder nature becomes. The peaceful garden of the provincial man of learning, with its domestic roses and meticulously raked straight walks, is met with the dark forest of the professor at the Collège de France, scattered with rocks and traversed by streams, with only long avenues of poplars to remind one of the existence of humankind. Difficult work demands more than simple conversations with flowers; that is what long escapades through the woods are for. Here, the antithesis between nature and culture is resolved in harmony: isn't the wild man the one who chooses to lock himself up with books rather than spend time with his fellow humans?

The true scholar has no other home than the books in which he exhausts himself. The rest is whatever walls are appropriate to the moment, libraries he roams around the world, cramped studies, bedrooms in which his nights are always too brief. Whether lost in distant provincial suburbs or hidden in deep woods, his home simultaneously withdraws from the world and opens up to the earth. According to Heidegger's beautiful phrase, 'in the things that arise the earth presences as the protecting one.'[6] Both in this withdrawal and this opening, there resides the secret of the scholar and the essence of the individual, the former gaining access to the latter through the difficult clearing offered by the book. As a tenant of a home as invisible as the cage of air in which Merlin lets the wise Viviane imprison him, the scholar neither beds down nor sits to eat anywhere but the very abode of being.

X

The Garden

The tree of knowledge was in the first garden, but it was forbidden to touch it. When the first humans ate its fruit, they were chased from the enclosure. Knowledgeable, but cast out. And the first knowledge with which they were endowed was precisely the memory of this garden from which they had been excluded. Earlier, they had not known the garden, since they were its inhabitants. They identified it with bare existence; they were an integral part of it in a complete and successful fusion. Once they left the garden, they realised that contrary to what they believed it was not the world. It became a simple object, placed before them (*objectum*). Or rather behind them, which is practically the same thing: one merely needs to turn around. And this object was of memory and regret, in other words, of knowledge. For this is how knowledge works: we only know that from which we are separated by a sufficient distance, however unfortunate.

These were the beginnings of history. Since then, humans have never stopped yearning for a return to the garden. But would they really want to go back to ignorance, if that was the cost of return? Nothing is less certain: the ideal would be to return while retaining before them the knowledge that had gotten them chased out in the first place. The scholar has come close to achieving this ideal, having kept for himself a personal garden consisting of all the gardens that preceded it: each one is a palimpsest. The tree of knowledge is always the garden's principal ornament, a distant successor to the first of the line.

Already the gardens of antiquity were not valued primarily for themselves, but based on an illustrious model which they sought to reproduce. The Academy garden in Athens was intended to revive the memories of Socrates's conversations with Phaedrus under the plane trees on the banks of the Ilisos. Aristotle's Lyceum garden recalled Plato's Academy Park. In the garden of Cynosarges, Antisthenes and the Cynics attempted to recapture the original Socrates's rebellious spirit. Epicurus wanted to outdo all his predecessors: for 80 mina, i.e. 90 pounds of silver, he bought a garden that lent its name to the sect he founded.[1] The Romans were not to be outdone: in a more or less systematic fashion, Cicero set his dialogues in enchanting gardens, located either at his home in a villa at Tusculum, for example, which would find its way into the title of his *Tusculan Disputations*, or at the homes of his characters, Scipio (*The Republic*) and Crassus (*On the Orator*).[2] These gardens were inspired by Greece, but their comforts were wholly Roman: while Socrates lay on the ground to talk to Phaedrus, Crassus ensured that his guests had seats and cushions (*pulvinos*) to sit on;[3] senators weren't hardy youths or tramps, after all.

In antiquity, the garden wasn't simply a question of nature. Not only did it contain a gymnasium with all its components (palestra, portico, hexahedron), but the oldest gardens, such as those of the Academy, the Lyceum, and the Cynosarges, were initially solely gymnasiums. Keen to recreate the Greek gardens as accurately as possible, the Romans had these edifices imported from Greece built on their own estates.[4] This did not exclude intellectual activities. On the contrary: it was precisely because the gymnasium, as a place for physical exercise, was frequented by young people that it began to make increasingly more room for education and mental exercise. One was made into a citizen here, but was not yet a citizen. While commerce and politics triumphed on the agora, the gymnasium and, as a consequence, the garden could therefore be devoted to activities not as directly linked to the city's most immediate interests. Admittedly, the body exercised here was that of a future soldier and the mind that of a future assemblyman, but in the meantime a space of freedom opened up where philosophy set in. The Academy is the ancestor of every university campus.

In Rome, the separation between the forum and scholarly space was even more distinct: gardens were simply located on large properties outside the city. Laelius and Scipio 'used to become boys again, in an astonishing degree, as soon as ever they had flitted from the prison of town to rural scenes.'[5] No game was too puerile for them, including collecting stones and seashells on the beach. Remember that one easily moves from play to study, the ultimate 'leisure' activity (*skholê*).

Christian humanist tradition finds part of its inspiration in this Roman validation of the countryside: the garden is suitable for letters because it is the absolute antithesis of a city condemned for depravity. Petrarch always contrasted these two ways of life:[6] all the cities are called Babylon, all the gardens, Eden. But these are strangely populated Edens: in his praise of the solitary life, the poet of the Sorgue draws on thousands of examples from ancient Rome, from Horace to Seneca, and from Cicero to Scipio.[7] Despite appearances, the scholar is never alone in his garden: his studious solitude is visited by ghosts escaped from history and books.

The development of humanism progressively brought a

change to the garden's status. Once negative, it became positive: the garden was no longer a mere refuge from the world, but an alternative city-state, built entirely by the scholar and inspired by ancient treatises. Alberti gave an enthusiastic description of the 'villa', or farm, considered as an ideal site for economic experimentation. The farm alone, he wrote, 'seems reliable, generous, trustworthy, and truthful. Managed with diligence and love, it never wearies of repaying you. Reward follows reward. In spring the farm gives you a multitude of delights, greenery, flowers, aromas, songs. It tries to please you, it smiles and promises you a magnificent harvest, it fills you with good hopes as well as sufficient joy in the present.'[8] Alberti reviewed the other seasons in similar style. Fall, winter, spring – each contributes countless fruits and satisfactions. The humanist garden had become a farm. But make no mistake about it: it was no less scholarly. The model had simply changed, from Horace and Cicero to Virgil's *Georgics* and Xenophon's *Oeconomicus*. Another book is opened in the library and suddenly the garden changes faces.

The last step in the process was for the garden itself to become a book and source of knowledge. In one of his *Colloquies*, Erasmus meticulously describes an enchanting domain, where the plants speak through labels that express their properties. For example: 'Stay back, pig! My perfume is not for you.'[9] An erudite marjoram, doubly cultivated: both Lucretius and Aulus Gellius mention the pig's disgust for this plant.[10] The Erasmian garden is perpetually on display: under its porticos, it displays paintings of identical gardens where each tree, each blade of grass, and each animal expresses a Latin or Greek proverb. Knowledge is everywhere, under each leaf, behind every bush. While others want 'sumptuous' (*opulentas*) houses, the scholar likes his home to be 'full of words' (*loquacissimam*) in order to avoid the feeling of loneliness: a far cry from the secluded life celebrated by Petrarch. As a meeting place and the object of conversation between friends, the garden is simply the library's double.

Justus Lipsius, the most horticultural of the humanists, admitted as much in no uncertain terms: 'Aside from books, I have two distractions or consolations: the garden and my dogs.'[11] Lipsius had three dogs, Scottish terriers and Brittany spaniels, whom he loved passionately: Mopsus, Mopsulus, and Saphyrus.[12] As for tulips, he could never have enough of them, and constantly asked his correspondents to send him more: 'These choice tulip bulbs you send me', he wrote to one of his suppliers, 'are more precious to me than if they were nuggets of gold or silver. People won't believe me? I say what I think, how I think it. I am profoundly grateful to you; I am grateful and must be, eternally.'[13] In a painting now in the collection of the Palazzo Pitti in Florence, Rubens astutely depicted the famous scholar surrounded by his friends and disciples (including the painter and his brother), books, tulips, and one of his dogs (Mopsus, apparently).[14] Flowers and books: here is the programme of scholarly wisdom.

In his treatise *On Constancy*, Lipsius contrasts two panegyrics of the garden. The first, spoken by the author himself, is all sensuality:

> O true source of joy and pure pleasure! O residence of Venuses and Graces! May my rest and my life be in your shade; may I be allowed, far from the civil wars, to roam among these plants, among these plants of the known world and the unknown world, my gaze gaping with joy and admiration; to let my hand and my face wander first to this leaning plant, then to this one standing tall, and to

stave off through a kind of vague reverie all my worries and sorrows.¹⁵

The second panegyric, which he attributes to his friend Charles Langius, is all rationality and wisdom:

> Do you see these wise elders? They have lived in gardens. And the learned and scholarly souls of today? They enjoy themselves in gardens, and most of the divine writings we admire and that no passage of time or great age will abolish were forged in gardens. To this verdant Lyceum we owe so many dissertations on nature; to the shaded Academy, so many others on mores; and the fruitful streams of wisdom that spread everywhere, which we have drunk, and which through an ample deluge have happily drowned the entire Earth, flow out of the walks of gardens. And certainly the mind rises higher and stands for elevated things when freely and without obstruction it sees its sky than when it is locked away in the prisons of houses and cities. You poets, sing me a poem here destined to last! You scholars, do beautiful research and write here! You philosophers, debate here about tranquility, constancy, life, and death! This, Lipius, is the real use and real end of gardens: rest, I say, the place where one retreats on one's own, the place for meditating, reading, and writing, and yet as if it were relaxed and playful. And like painters with eyes weary from having stared too long in one place look in a mirror or at some greenery to gather their strength, here we do so with our tired or wandering mind. And why would I hide my habits from you? Do you see this arbour made of greenery? This is my house of the Muses, this is the gymnasium and palestra of my sapience.¹⁶

Langius counters his friend's voluptuous, melancholy reverie with a more determined attitude: the vocation of the scholar's garden is to become a new Lyceum or Academy. The Venuses and the Graces on one side; the Muses on the other. But the dialogue's very movement goes beyond this overly stark contrast: Lipsius is no less right than Langius. The Muses can only come to settle where the Venuses and the Graces have already set up residence – or, at least, nearby: the ones under the arbour serving as an intellectual palestra and gymnasium, the others among the beds of marvellous flowers from all over the world. Lipsius systematised this alliance in a parodic 'Law' that he had displayed at the entrance to his own garden, following the model of the Roman laws, and of which articles III and IV answer each other by completing each other:

> III. No CONVERSATION outside of the law.
> It is permitted to JOKE.
> It is permitted to NARRATE;
> It is permitted to ASK;
> But nothing SERIOUS.
> This place belongs to the GRACES.
> IV. However, everything in STUDIES that relates more to PLEASURE,
> While STROLLING,
> Expound it, teach it, study it,
> This place also belongs to the MUSES.[17]

Law and leisure, meditation and reverie, writing and reading, work and play: none of these terms is exclusive of its counterpart. The garden allows for opposites to be gathered in a typically scholarly utopia; not at the antipodes, but at the library doors, whether to exit or to enter. Here is the place where natural knowledge grows like a plant, without effort, and is absorbed by all the senses, in a diastolic movement that follows the rhythm of the mind. The ghosts of countless scholars flutter around here like butterflies, in an endless conversation between the living and the dead. Inside the library, the tree of knowledge's leaves rustle in the wind. And when night falls outdoors, Lipsius's tulips sometimes open like books. .

XI

The Animal

Animals are even more closely tied to books than humans are. Physically, of course, as cruelly attested to by parchments and gilded leather. But aren't animals also as silent and faithful as books? Only someone who has never seen a cat lovingly slip between the carefully arranged volumes on a bookcase could doubt it.

For example, take Mademoiselle de Gournay's cat – or rather her queens, the subject of too many jokes endured by the good woman over the course of a long life that straddled two centuries. For it was not easy to maintain a balance between the sixteenth and seventeenth centuries. Indeed, there are two Marie de Gournays. The sixteenth-century Marie de Gournay was Michel de Montaigne's publisher and 'covenant daughter', as she signed her letters, proudly using the title she was given in the second volume of the *Essays*[1] (unless she herself introduced the appellation in her edition – some doubts remain). She was also a correspondent of the great humanist Justus Lipsius and the niece of a poet who was a friend of Ronsard.[2] The seventeenth-century Marie de Gournay is an entirely different specimen, a ridiculous bluestocking, a passionate advocate for words fallen into disuse, an old biddy mocked by fashionable young poets, and the last living vestige of a freedom of tone and mores that had become most unusual in Richelieu's France: 'one day when she was asked whether pederasty was a crime, she responded, "God forbid I condemn what Socrates practised."'[3]

The change of era and aesthetic was rather severe for the damsel whom Lipsius called his 'sister' (*soror*)[4] and Montaigne referred to as 'one of the best parts of [his] own being'.[5] When Marie de Gournay was born in 1566, Henri Estienne had just published his *Traité de conformité du langage français avec le grec* [Treatise on the conformity of the French language with Greek] and Ronsard hadn't yet composed *La Franciade*. When she passed away in 1645, Malherbe had been dead for close to twenty years, Richelieu for three, and both Corneille's *Le Cid* and Descartes' *Discours de la méthode* were approaching their tenth anniversaries. For her, the transition from the wars of religion to Mazarin's government, from humanist erudition to Descartes's tabula rasa, and from the triumph of the Pléiade to that of the Académie française was a turbulent one.

By an ironic twist of history, this learned spinster's publication of an edition of Montaigne's *Essays* considered definitive for more than two centuries contributed despite her best intentions and much to her chagrin to a devaluation of scholarly knowledge. Montaigne became the handbook for an entirely new class of readers: in the seventeenth century, merry abbots, pretty ladies of the nobility, and well-bred pipsqueaks looking for adventure all referred to an ideal of the honest man paradoxically modelled after the author of the *Essays*. Scornful of erudite ponderousness, this new class of readers was satisfied to cultivate knowledge as amateurs, avoided ever flaunting it, and made far more noise about the pleasures of a conversation in high society than the silent and solitary company of the Ancients.⁶

In a world that gleefully fell into step with Malherbe and rejected the old poets' scholarly prolixity to provide itself with a simple and pure language (that of modernity), Marie de Gournay's desperate championing of archaisms and uncommon metaphors made her seem like a monster or a circus freak. She even dared to entitle her major work *L'Ombre de la demoiselle de Gournay* [The Shadow of damsel de Gournay] on the grounds that like a shadow any work reflects its author and survives her.⁷ Malherbe's disciples were not convinced by her explanation: in their eyes, such bizarre imagery indicated nothing but a shameful decadence of language.

And what of the damsel's cat? Here it comes – or rather here comes one of her cats, since she apparently had a whole flock of them, of whom two lucky creatures, Donzelle and Minette, were treated to two poems.⁸ We owe the following anecdote to the most gossipy of the century's memorialists, Tallemant des Réaux. One day, Marie de Gournay's mischievous friend Boisrobert 'took her to see Cardinal de Richelieu, who gave her a compliment entirely composed of old words he had taken from her *Ombre*. She could tell the cardinal was having a laugh: "You're laughing at the poor old woman", she said, "Go ahead and laugh, great genius, laugh; everyone must contribute to your amusement." The cardinal, surprised by the spinster's presence of mind, asked for her forgiveness and told Boisrobert: "Something must be done for Mademoiselle de Gournay. I'll give her a two-hundred-crown pension." – "But she has servants", said Boisrobert. – "Which ones?" replied the cardinal. – "Mlle Jamin", answered Boisrobert, "the bastard of Amadis Jamin, Ronsard's page." – "I'll give her fifty livres a year", said the cardinal. – "There's also my dear Piaillon", added Boisrobert, "that's her cat." – "I'll give her a twenty-livre pension", replied his eminence, "on condition that she is fed tripe." – "But, Your Eminence, she had kittens." The cardinal added a pistole for the kittens.'[9]

This dialogue is less insignificant than it appears, for it features a crucial moment of the life of men (and women) of letters of the period, though one rarely described in such a direct fashion: the one in which an authority determined a writer's pension – and often his only source of revenue – in this era before royalties. No one was fooled by the notion that this interview with Richelieu was for the mere pleasure of conversation, and one could hardly blame the spinster for taking advantage of Boisrobert's social skills to try her luck with the cardinal. What exactly was being sold in this negotiation? First, a witty remark, apt repartee, which is certainly worth two hundred crowns. Yet that's not enough: one has to haggle, as is the custom. But haggle over what? A name, the past, prestige. The allusion to Marie de Gournay's hired help is handy, because the servant's father was none other than that famous poet who was Ronsard's secretary and friend and the dedicatee of so many of his poems – or so the spinster liked to have her guests believe. Notarial deeds have since irrefutably proved that Nicole Jamin was not Amadis' daughter.[10] No matter: by cleverly playing on a mix-up between surnames, Marie de Gournay got close to a ten percent raise, or fifty livres.

Then there's the rest, which is to say everything that cannot be monetised or haggled over, everything in scholarly work that escapes commerce – every kind of commerce – that of money, society, and the world. Beyond a certain threshold, the knowledge of books exceeds ordinary human exchanges. For example, an individual can buy as many books as he wants, within his financial and spatial means, but when he needs to consult twenty folio volumes to write a single line, even the richest scholar has no choice but to go to a library made available to him more or less free of charge by powerful public and private institutions. Erudition is priceless – or worthless, which comes down to the same thing. Inestimable, thus underestimated. In *The Miser* (II, 1), a pile of useless old stuff is valued at two hundred crowns; the old terms championed by Mademoiselle de Gournay aren't worth anything more. Strictly speaking, they are actually worth nothing: since the old woman's claims to fame rested only on words – those by which Montaigne declared her to be his 'covenant daughter', those she saved from oblivion, and those she assembled into archaic sentence structures – how could she hope for a pension that was anything but a bonus, granted only by the cardinal's good graces?

Mademoiselle de Gournay's cat is like the piddling sign of this exchange of two incommensurable values, money and scholarly knowledge: backed into a corner by Richelieu's stinginess, Boisrobert is reduced to invoking the spinster's favourite companion cat, the one which the Abbé de Marolles reported 'was never once driven out of her bedroom at night to go running in the gutters or on the tiles like the other cats, in twelve years that it lived with her.'[11] Twenty livres for dear Piaillon and a pistole, i.e. an additional ten livres, for the kittens is not a fortune, but it's something. Anyhow, the cardinal would not go any higher. For once in her life, without even leaving her mistress's home, Mademoiselle de Gournay's cat had leapt over a wall: the limit beyond which scholarly work can no longer be converted into hard cash.

There are two orders of presence here. Pascal would have said: the measures of the mind and those of the world. Let's make a little adjustment: the order of books and that of man.

With all due respect to humanists, there is something in books that may not be inhuman, but is certainly extra-human. The scholar does not live with his fellow man: his works, values, and ambitions are distinct. The domestic animal so often by his side in representations does not refer to anything other than this portion of inhumanity that is the scholar's non-transferable lot. The earliest such animal was Saint Jerome's lion, not a domestic animal but a domesticated one, which only underlines the break with humanity. The story is well known, as immortalised by Vittore Carpaccio in an admirable series of frescos at the Scuola di San Giorgio degli Schiavoni in Venice. One day, a lion came limping into the monastery where Saint Jerome had withdrawn. All the monks ran off at the sight of the lion (Carpaccio depicts them scattering like swallows), except the saint, who stayed to remove a thorn from the animal's paw. From that moment on, the lion became the most faithful companion to the patron saint of scholars, or at least to his portraits: whether lying down, sitting, standing, asleep, or watching over the saint, the lion is there, always dependable, even – and especially – in Jerome's study. One can question the realism, if not the practicality, of the lion's presence. But what better way to represent the reader's unsociability? The more feral of the two is not the one you might think: remember Jerome's proverbial fits of anger. The animal is as domestic as the scholar can't be. At the very heart of the library and its apparently civilised shelving, the lion contributes a little silence and sand from the Desert of Chalcis where the saint spent three years in utter solitude: from the hermit to the scholar, the distance is not so great. The only reason the question of what book one would take to a desert island has become so trivial is because books are islands in and of themselves.

Vittore Carpaccio: *Saint Augustine*
San Giorgio degli Schiavoni (Venice)

As small and docile as it might be, every scholar's animal is descended from Saint Jerome's lion. Carpaccio himself initiated the process of transformation in the last of his frescos depicting the saint. One recognises Saint Augustine at his writing table, his eyes looking up at the radiant sunlight coming in through the window: just as he was preparing to write to Jerome, Augustine is learning through a supernatural revelation that his friend has died, at that very moment, one thousand leagues away, and is entering into paradise.[12] In a direct extension of a virtual line that connects the top of the window to the saint's head, one finds a tiny white dog sitting on the ground in an empty space at the picture's extreme left, with its head also raised, toward its master and the divine light. Is the allusion to the sense of smell? Probably: the legend says that the room was then filled with 'the most ineffable, unnatural fragrance' (*ineffabili inauditaque odorum omnium fragrantia*).[13] A symbol of faith and fidelity? Of course. But there is no doubt that the Maltese Bichon lost in the middle of the immense room also carries the symbolic legacy of Saint Jerome's lion, as well as that of Saint George's formidable dragon, likewise present in this cycle of paintings: it serves to create a subtle continuity between the series' elements. There is no real hiatus between the dragon and the Bichon: while the knight George triumphantly dominates the fierce monster on the Venetian church's left wall, the mere silhouette of Augustine's dog on the right wall, so small in the vastness of the surrounding space, represents the silent asocial behavior that must be adopted by the scholar. On the one side, an animal wild by nature is tamed by man; on the other, a member of society becomes wild through an excess of culture: this chiasmus says a great deal about the power and danger of books.[14]

Much later, Baudelaire was right to recognise in the cats curled up in libraries the attitude 'of desert sphinxes sprawled in solitude' ('Cats').[15] Indeed, whatever its shape, size, or fur, from Saint Jerome's lion to Augustine's Bichon, from Petrarch's cat[16] to Mademoiselle de Gournay's dear Piaillon, the domestic animal offers nothing more or less than the mystical advantages of a four-legged desert: a scholar's portable hermitage.

XII

Sexuality

Like angels, scholars are not gendered. Which comes down to saying that the scholar has something of both sexes. The entire community of scholars lives on this paradox.

Few places are more chaste than a library. Yet few are more torrid: day after day, the same readers encounter each other at the same tables, observe and brush past each other, without knowing a thing about each other. No one is less known to library-goers than their fellow readers: name, background, and profession are utter mysteries. Silent and secret, a library neighbour's existence is limited to the scratch of pen on paper, the clicks of a computer keyboard, the sound of a page turning or a pen being placed on the table, the little manifestations of organic life – a cough, a breath, a throat cleared – and the tilted face lit by a lamp as night begins to fall. The neighbour is an apparition: he has no body or rather he is nothing but body. A pure body, immobile, concentrated, voluminous, *perinde ac cadaver*.[1] The only thing one can know about him with certainty and relative ease is which books he consults. A treatise on angelology, an outsize atlas, yellowing newspapers, or a thick folio volume with an emblazoned binding: anything can serve as an ID card here. This identity is as complex and mysterious as the succession of books on the table is numerous and diverse. One might suspect that some readers are posing by asking for certain books – aiming for the effect of a provocative low-cut neckline or a roaring motorcycle on the street. Inside a library, sexual signals are so muffled, subdued, and indirect that everything that would go unnoticed outside immediately feels like a forceful invitation. No need for fishnet stockings, skin-tight jeans, or over-the-top makeup: a book will do the trick, and it doesn't even have to be erotic. The originality of one's reading material is a powerful spur to libido: nothing makes an exegete of judicial codes fantasise more intensely than a high-flying metaphysician or a reader of Renaissance poetry, and vice versa. Since the scholar's body disappears behind the book and the book is his real body, whoever is reading a different book inevitably belongs to a different sex. In the library of Babel, there are as many sexualities as there are books.

Communities of scholars have always put into practice this bookish sexuality, narrowly overtaking bodily sexuality to the point that it has replaced it: books read and written are very good at making love by themselves. This reality is accurately captured in the Rabelaisian myth of Thélème: in the hexagonal space of this imaginary abbey where men and women live side by side and court each other while studying the arts and letters, 'the great beautiful reading rooms' (or libraries) 'well stocked with books in Greek, Latin, Hebrew, French, Italian, and Spanish' take up an entire side, along the boundary between the ladies' bedrooms and the gentlemen's. Facing them, by way of a symmetrical border, are 'beautiful galleries, large and open, painted with scenes of ancient heroism, episodes drawn from history.'[2] The parallel between the galleries and the libraries has a double meaning: it may well contrast the space of the image, stroll, and conversation with that of the text, sojourn, and study to highlight the equivalence between the two activities. Could architecture be any more explicit in expressing that like galleries, libraries are places of desire and encounters, and that *libido sciendi* is an exact counterpart to *libido amandi*? But this is precisely where the power of allegory stops: Thélème is a utopia not only because of the colossal nature of the project (a hexagonal castle nearly 2000 feet in diameter, with 9332 rooms, etc.), but also, in a subtler manner, because of its claim to a possible coexistence or complementarity between bodily sexuality and scholarly knowledge. This scholarly knowledge, as a sexuality in its own right, has a tendency to take up all the room and exclude physical love. In the real world, a Thelemite who was both gallant and scholarly would not survive: he is a chimera.

For a long time, scholarly communities institutionalised this purely bookish sexuality by trying to keep any carnal business outside. One thinks of Benedictine monasteries, as well as those peculiar monasteries known as Oxford and Cambridge, universities that for centuries imposed celibacy upon their professors ('fellows'), who were all ordained clerics, but didn't enjoy Anglican priests' right to marry. The rule did not have a strictly religious origin: it was due to a necessity of scholarly life, which was alleged to demand a monastic existence. Marriage for Oxbridge fellows was only authorised in 1874.[3] Until the interwar period, students' sexual activity was closely monitored, through a system of supervision of which a young William Empson bore the consequences in 1929.

At twenty-two, Empson was one of Cambridge University's most brilliant students. A poet and mathematician, he was finishing a dissertation under the direction of his professor I. A. Richards that would lastingly mark the history of twentieth-century English-language criticism: an ingenious classification of every type of ambiguity (a total of seven) that can be encountered in a literary text.[4] Not only had Empson recently seen his achievements recognised by an English prize from Magdalene College, but he had been unanimously elected an Associate Professor, or Bye-Fellow, of the same College on 15 June. A prestigious academic career awaited the young prodigy. Five weeks later (nearly as many weeks as ambiguities), everything collapsed. On 22 July, the general assembly of professors abruptly announced the following decision: 'It was resolved that William Empson be deprived of his Bye-Fellowship and that his name be at once removed from the College Books.'[5] No other information was provided to explain the decree, and for good reason: it being essential to hush up a scandal that would otherwise tarnish the university, official advertisement was out of the question.

Only outside accounts permit us to reconstruct what actually happened. During the academic year, Empson had lived in a College residence, where he had behaved in an extremely free manner that included hosting a young woman in his room. After his election as a Bye-Fellow, he was invited to live in the College's principal building. It was during his move that a servant discovered a condom in his drawer. Empson's landlady, Mrs. Tingey, who despised him for his dissolute life, messy room, and three-a.m. baths, needed no better excuse to take revenge on her debauched lodger. The rumour grew and reached the ears of the Master, who knew no rest until he had gotten rid of the black sheep. 22 July, the feast of Mary-Magdalene, the College's patron saint, proved to be the day of repentance; had Empson been so disposed, he would have had his whole life to regret his expulsion. Though it certainly did not stop him from becoming one of the most important critics of the twentieth century, it shattered what otherwise promised to be an illustrious career, by limiting him to relatively marginal positions in Tokyo, Peking, and Sheffield.

Unfortunately for Empson, his mentor I. A. Richards was unable to intervene on his behalf: he was travelling in China at the time, and didn't learn about the affair until two months after the fact. His disciple was understandably bitter when he told him what had happened:

> The Master (with an air of melancholy conviction) told me that anybody who had ever touched a French letter, no matter when or why, could never again be allowed with safety in the company of young men, because he was sure in some subtle way, however little he himself wished it, to pollute their innocence; and this in spite of the fact that his own intellectual powers would have been destroyed. As an act of grace I was allowed to poison the air of Magdalene for a day after my exposure, and this gave time for several of my judges to come and explain that I must mind and not bear a grudge, or that what they had done would be the best thing for me in the end, or that 'personally' they thought their own actions a Great Pity, or that though they were not addicted to Those Particular Vices (I wept with rage when this was said to me) I was to understand they had extremely Broad Minds.[6]

Behind Empson's rancour and the comedy of cowardice and puritan hypocrisy he delights in unmasking, the Master's words also reveal two distinct layers in the discourse about scholars' sexuality. On the one hand, a moral condemnation of adultery, which is aggravated by the fact that the culprit, as a teacher, must live in contact with young people. But the most salient point lies elsewhere, in a few words in a single sentence. It could be summed up as follows: in and of itself, in whatever form it takes, sexual activity is considered destructive of 'intellectual powers'. The argument no longer makes the slightest moral claim; it is purely pragmatic. At worst, it perpetuates the old criticism of onanism put forward by Doctor Tissot in the eighteenth century;[7] at best, it reveals a kind of deontology of the scholar. The Master merely alludes to it, as if he were ashamed to continue to refer to the old monastic tradition of university life: given the incompatibility of scholarly life and sexuality, chastity is of the essence.

Or at least a certain kind of chastity. The irony of the story is that Empson was kicked out of Cambridge for sleeping with a woman, when he spent most of his student years desiring one of his classmates, a tall and handsome young blond man to whom he sent poetic missives made profoundly hermetic by his erudition and the density of his cultural and scientific references. The seven ambiguities to which Empson devoted his first academic paper indicate an eighth ambiguity, of a sexual nature, which was to be a characteristic of his entire life: much later, once he married, Empson eagerly introduced his wife's young lover into their couple and may also have enjoyed his attentions.[8] The same ambiguity can be found both in Shakespeare's sonnets, which are sometimes unclear as to whether they are addressed to a male or a female, and in the poetic letters Empson modelled after them:

> Where is that darkness that gives light its place?
> Or where such darkness as would hide your face?
>
> Our jovial sun, if he avoids exploding
> (These times are critical), will cease to grin,
> Will lose your circumambient foreboding;
> Loose the full radiance his mass can win
> While packed with mass holds all that radiance in;
> Flame far too hot not to seem utter cold

    And hide a tumult never to be told.[9]

One could call it non-obscure obscurity, in the manner of Empson's beloved metaphysical poets, since this astronomical poem's hermeticism implicitly describes the desire that cannot be clearly named and that lastingly stimulated the brilliant student's poetic and academic work. Despite how worrisome it was to the young man, this particular desire never troubled the university, because it had the intelligence to disregard ambient puritanism and recognise in that desire one of the crucial forces driving study and one of the scholarly community's strongest bonds: generalised sexuality, sexuality without gender, in signs and on pages, the voluptuousness of knowledge specific to books and libraries, like the one in which I am writing at this very moment.

XIII
Food

Traditionally, the scholar has a choice between two apparently contradictory menus, which also define two cultures: asceticism and the banquet, depending on whether spiritual nourishment is considered to be in competition or, on the contrary, complementary with terrestrial nourishment. This antagonism between the two types of nourishment is primarily due to cultures in which religion is a dominant feature; their coexistence is due to more secular practices. Yet the difference between asceticism and the banquet is not as great as one might imagine.

Where there is competition, the food of the mind, or more precisely that of the soul, is supposed to replace that of the body. The ideal would be for the scholar to sustain himself with 'herbs' (*holera*) and water, according to a recipe once given to the widow Furia by Saint Jerome.[1] This is the entire menu for the ascetic or hermit eager to diminish the power of concupiscence, for whom grilled salt, three olives, five chickpeas, two prunes, and a fig are already a feast fit for a king, the very one that Abbot Serenus served to Saint John Cassian when he paid him a visit.[2] Yet by seeking to reduce the *libido amandi*, one risks putting an end to *libido sciendi*. No doubt there are scholarly ascetics – Jerome, generally depicted in an advanced state of gauntness, is the most convincing example – but in practice few scholars are ascetics. In fact, the anchorites of the Thebaid left a reputation, whether deserved or not, for virtuous ignorance in everything except spiritual matters; it is attested to by Rancé's commentaries or, in an entirely different, distinctly anticlerical category, the novels of Alfred de Vigny and Anatole France.[3]

Conversely, lay knowledge does not provide a solution offering radical continuity between the realms of the body and the mind: an empty belly means an empty mind. When it isn't serving religious interests, a scholarly culture best develops in a world or social class that satisfies the basic needs of existence. Far from being the enemy of knowledge, food is its auxiliary or necessary condition.

When Hegel travelled to Paris at Victor Cousin's invitation in 1827, he wrote extensively to his wife about his diet. 'We did not dally long over lunch (that is to say we had cutlets at eleven with a bottle of wine)',[4] he wrote on 3 September, the day after his arrival. Quite quickly, he was faced with the little challenges encountered by an ordinary tourist, philosopher or not. Since he had trouble ordering from 'the enormous list on the menu' ('*die enorme Liste der Charte*') without his friend's help, he found refuge at a '*table d'hôte*' where the dishes on offer were displayed, making it easier to choose.[5] A few days later, he was plagued with stomach pains: he was prescribed 'enemas, fomentations, and herbal teas'.[6] He blamed the water of the Seine and Cousin's eccentric habit of eating at improbable hours like five in the afternoon. Once he recovered from this indisposition, Hegel decided to return to the usual German schedule, taking his main meal at one or 1:30 p.m., even if it meant leaving Cousin to dine alone:[7] such was the price of good digestion, even for the author of *The Phenomenology of the Mind*.

Hegel's stomach was more Kantian than his mind. In the last years of his life, the master of Königsberg insisted that his lunch be served at one p.m. on the dot. Kant ate only once a day. At 12:45, he called his cook, who brought him a glass of hot wine. He then went down to the dining room, where his guests awaited him. Never less than two and never more than five, since the number of guests was not to be inferior to that of the Graces nor superior to that of the Muses.[8]

Now Kant's friend Borowski will take over:

> His meals consisted of three dishes, along with butter and cheese, and in summer, fruit from the garden. The first course was always a meat soup, often veal, with rice, barley, and vermicelli. He was used to putting little pieces of bread in his soup, which he sliced over the plate, in order to make it heartier. The second course either consisted of variously seasoned dried fruit, dried vegetable purees, or fish. The third course was a roast, but I don't remember ever eating game in his home. He put mustard on nearly every dish; he was also very fond of thick butter with vegetable dishes and meat, and he himself pondered the best way to prepare this thick butter with carbonic acid. Butter and cheese provided him with a dessert he held dear. And since he personally liked cheese so well, he appreciated it if his guests were also cheese connoisseurs. This is why he also joked with my brother about his inability to say anything about two important subjects of conversation, namely cheese and tobacco. He liked to eat a tasty and thin twice-baked rye bread. Sometimes finely grated cheese was on the table. Of every kind of

cheese, he liked English cheese best, but not the reddish kind, which seemed to him to have been coloured with marsh beet juice that slightly altered its taste, but the white kind, which is rarer. When the table was crowded, another dish was added, as well as a cake. Kant's favourite dish was cod. One day he assured me that even though he was completely full, he could eagerly have eaten a whole plate of cod.[9]

So much for food. As for beverages, Kant didn't drink beer, which he considered too nourishing, but 'a light red wine, generally a Médoc'.[10]

Beyond the particularities of Kant's diet – the nearly immutable order of his meals, his immoderate taste for English cheese and cod, his mistrust of food colouring – Borowski's account highlights but doesn't dwell on what made these three- or four-hour lunches so appealing, and may even have been their main ingredient: conversation.

The scholar is not meant to eat alone. Leopardi later observed as much: 'there are many people, who, since they devote themselves to study or seclusion for some other reason the rest of the day, only converse at table, and they would be *bien fâchés* [very annoyed] to be alone and silent at such a time.'[11] For the scholar as with the Gospel, that which comes out of the mouth is at least as important as that which goes in.[12]

As it happens, Kant was a first-rate chatterbox. He and his guests talked about everything, starting with what appeared before them on the table: butter, cheese, tobacco, and favourite foods were the leading subjects of conversation. Woe to those who were unable to join the fray, like Bokowski's brother. Since each dish could serve to display a specific bit of knowledge, the scholar's meal quickly became a scholarly meal, where the order of discourse paralleled that of the courses. There was no separation here between nourishment for the body and for the soul.

This brings us to a venerable tradition of scholarly culture: the banquet. The nineteenth century had its own banquets, including those legendary feasts enjoyed by some of the leading intellectuals of the Second Empire, all enthusiasts of the pleasures of the table: Sainte-Beuve, Taine, Flaubert, Renan.[13] However, the greatest number of literary accounts of banquets is found in classical antiquity: along with Plato and Xenophon's two famous dialogues and Epicurus's lost one, there are Plutarch's *Dinner of the Seven Wise Men* and *Table-Talk*, Lucian of Samosata's *The Carousal Symposium, or the Lapiths*, and Macrobius's *Saturnalia*. To tell the truth, in the banquets the most faithful to Greek tradition, such as those described by Socrates's two disciples, food seemed to be far less important than drink: guests started by having a moderate meal, followed by libations and hymns, after which the drinking began. It was only during this second part of the meal that conversation flowed freely. The ceremony described by Plato is even more precise: a guest's turn to speak corresponded with the passing of the cup from one guest to another.

In one of Plutarch's dialogues, Mnesiphilus the Athenian explains this process to the seven wise men:

> When such men as you, whom Periander has invited here, come together, I think there is no need for a cup or an oenochoe: the Muses place discourse (*logon*) in the midst of you, like a krater without wine, in which pleasure, jest, and seriousness combine, and with this they awaken, foster, and dispense gaiety, allowing the ladle for the most part to lie untouched atop the krater.[14]

The Greek banquet in the Platonic mode is primarily concerned with *logos*, seen as the true wine of the intellect, and of which the wine pressed from grapes would only be considered a pale imitation. As paradoxical as it may seem, the ideal would be the sober banquet, where one doesn't drink: asceticism, as we see, is not far off.

The Roman preference for the *convivium*, in other words for the feast, where guests come together to eat over the *symposion*, or gathering of drinkers, led to a cultural revolution. The meal now imposed an order on discourse: each new dish was the opportunity for guests to show their knowledge, to contribute a curious explanation or a rare quotation. Is varied food easier to digest than simple food? Are truffles produced by thunder? Why don't Jews eat pork? What makes figs so sweet? What is Homer's intention when he defines salt as 'divine' (*theion*)? Why do weddings always have so many guests?[15] A single meal allows for a multitude of questions on the natural sciences, medicine, social customs, the history of religion, and literature: a banquet is an encyclopedia. The masterpiece of the kind, at least in terms of scale, is unquestionably the monumental volume by a Greek rhetorician of the third century BC: *The Deipnosophists* – or *The Dinner Scholars* – deals with every subject imaginable and is the most considerable compendium of knowledge passed down from antiquity. Nonetheless, the 15 surviving volumes are only a summary of the 30 originally composed by Athenaeus: it's not a meal, but a library.[16]

Unless every library is itself a pantry. Naturally, the narratives of the banquets in ancient literature shouldn't be mistaken for the historical reality of these meals: they are primarily literary works, essentially fictional ones, and the reason so many scholars, *pepaideumenoi*, and *philologoi*[17] chose this form to pass down their knowledge was primarily that they wanted to imitate Plato. But perhaps they also thought that knowledge is structured as a *symposion* by its nature and function. The academic tradition of colloquiums – or symposiums – got its name here, if not its origin. Plutarch himself seems to indicate as much when he observes in his *Advice about Keeping Well* that intellectuals who devote themselves to study and the Muses easily let themselves be distracted from the dinner table if they are given 'a mathematical problem to solve, or some pamphlet or musical instrument':[18] they see them as helpful ways to control their appetite.

Here we recognise knowledge in all its ambivalence: it accompanies the meal, but it could just as well replace it. It isn't content with seasoning the meal: it nourishes. Thus the scholar constantly oscillates between the banquet and asceticism, like between the two faces of a single reality. The book sometimes opens onto the world and sometimes replaces it; it is sometimes a mere sign, sometimes the site of a real presence; an affirmation and at the same time a negation. The index (or language) lands on things either to show them or to hide them: the table is full if the text is empty – and vice versa.

XIV

Melancholy

The day Aristotle dictated the few pages that make up *Problem* XXX to a slave or one of his disciples, he may have been under the spell of one of those 'daily despondencies' (*kath'hêmeran athumias*) he mentions in the text. 'Often', he explains, 'we are in a condition of feeling grief, but we cannot say what we grieve about; and sometimes we are feeling cheerful (*euthumôs*), but it is not clear why.'[1] Few passages offer such an intimate view of the philosopher's inner life, though it avoids any superfluous outpourings. Perhaps the mode of scientific enquiry allowed him to fend off the turmoil that afflicted him that day? What he certainly couldn't imagine was that at the very moment he purified himself of his melancholy through reflection and writing, he was bequeathing it to a multitude of subsequent readers who would find in his words the very definition of their condition – for better and for worse. There is a communion of scholars as there is one for saints, involving the sharing of and compensation for sorrows and merits.

In fact, *Problem* XXX's initial statement immediately elevated it to a universal level:

> Why is it that all men who become outstanding in philos-

ophy, statesmanship, poetry or the arts are melancholic, and some to such an extent that they are infected by the diseases arising from black bile, as the story of Heracles among the heroes tells?[2]

Heracles's name comes as a surprise in these remarks primarily intended for intellectuals: the robust hero who defeated the Nemean lion hardly distinguished himself as a bookworm. But it has always been validating for a scholar to be racked by the same turmoil as the first and most beloved of heroes, however ignorant he may have been: few are those who would hesitate if given a choice between Michel Foucault's baldness and Zinedine Zidane's. What Aristotle's text is surreptitiously doing is claiming equal dignity for colossuses through their body and colossuses of the mind, with a range of more or less legendary names like Lysander, Ajax, and Bellerophon serving only to introduce the adventurers of the intelligence:

> Many other heroes seem to have suffered in the same way as these. In later times also there have been Empedocles, Plato, Socrates, and many other well-known men. The same is true of most of those who have handled poetry.[3]

As for the account of melancholy's deeply entangled causes and symptoms, this is basically what Aristotle has to say: since wine has identical properties to black bile, the latter's effects are comparable to drunkenness. It follows that in the same way that a man who drinks starts by becoming more self-confident and eloquent before ultimately losing his mind and retreating into silence, an abundance of black bile, which is the essence of melancholy (from *mélas*, black, and *kholê*, bile), subjects those it affects to alternating episodes of agitation and dejection, depending on whether the bile is respectively hot or cold. The melancholy temperament therefore oscillates between two extremes: genius and madness. It is an inebriation 'not pathological, but natural' (*ou dia noson, alla dia phusin*), which produces beings who are necessarily 'outstanding' (*perittoi*).[4]

As soon as it takes hold, melancholy scrambles all preexisting boundaries. While it isn't strictly speaking a 'disease' (*nosos*), it does cause a certain 'weakness' or 'infirmity' (*arrôstêma*); it turns 'stupidity' (*môria*) and 'excitement' (*mania*) into the two faces of a single reality; its manifestations sometimes arouse admiration, sometimes contempt. In short, it is characterised less by positively analysable symptoms (an outbreak of fever or a sudden rash) than by a rather complex and abstract kind of personal or social inadequacy. A person suffering from melancholy is not identified by a particular state, but by the alternation of contrary states; its definition is not expressed in absolute terms, but only in a relative manner, in comparison to the social sphere or the average person.

The question of melancholic distress can therefore only be raised in the context of a crisis of medical and philosophical doctrine: it forces the stable ontology of essences and ideas to make way for a more dynamic, indeed more dialectic, view of reality. An Aristotelean 'problem' of melancholy could only exist because from the outset there was a malaise in the concepts themselves. It is no coincidence that from the beginning black bile was considered characteristic of scholars and thinkers, in other words those whose work and very existence destabilise thought by bringing the unthought to light.

Such precariousness of meaning quickly contaminated all those who somehow refer to melancholy. So it goes with Cicero: in the *Tusculan Disputations*, he jokingly reminds the reader that 'Aristotle says that all intelligent (*ingeniosos*) men are prone to melancholy' and that he himself 'can easily bear being relatively slow-witted (*tardiorem*)'.[5] From a historical perspective, this explicit reference to the Aristotelean theory of melancholy is the major philological argument that makes it relatively probable to attribute *Problem* XXX to Aristotle himself. But this is the only certainty the reader will find here: What exactly does Cicero mean? That he prefers to be slow-witted than to be subjected to all the inconveniences of intelligence and melancholy? Or on the contrary that his slow-wittedness is not incompatible with intelligence, given that Aristotle claimed stupidity is a symptom of melancholy? In the first case, melancholy appears as a disease to be avoided; in the second, a sought-after status. The two interpretations are not compatible, though both elevate intelligence to the rank of a dubious privilege, the advantages of which may not be worth the price paid. This dual status of the intellectual as both cursed and sacred (in Latin, it's the same word: *sacer*) was established as early as classical antiquity. Later centuries would merely play with this ambivalence by accentuating it.

If Aristotelean melancholy bears little resemblance to the vague feeling of sadness we now refer to by the name, it is due to black bile's tumultuous two-thousand-five-hundred-year history, a history that underwent radical transformations of meaning before ending up with the current semantic blandness. It is a history also inseparable from that of scholars. In the Middle Ages, few people were afflicted with melancholy: once the moral and theological point of view supplanted physiology, one only found individuals afflicted with 'acedia',[6] and thus guilty of the worst sin, disgust with life. Significantly, melancholy's resurgence in the fifteenth century coincides with the emergence of a new class of humanist scholars, close readers of the recovered ancient texts and, in particular, of Aristotle. The key date is 1489, when Marsilio Ficino published his treatise *On Life* (*De Vita*), a kind of handbook for good health primarily aimed at intellectuals. Reissued throughout Europe over the course of two centuries, the book would be immensely successful. Ficino begins by raising the inevitably melancholic character of scholars. The chapter titles emphasise the point with somewhat tedious repetitiveness: 'Learned people (*litterati*) are subject to phlegm and black bile (*atrae bili*)'; 'How many things cause learned people either to be melancholy (*melancholici*) or to become so'; 'Why melancholics are intelligent (*ingeniosi*) and which melancholics are so and which are not'; 'How black bile makes people intelligent (*ingenio*)'[7] etc. In 1514, Albrecht Dürer depicted the dark angel of *Melencolia I* ready to come out of one of these books practically fully armed. 'Melancholic fury' (*furor melancholicus*) became the Renaissance scholar's latest 'snobbery'[8] and the mysterious key to all wisdom. In an elegant rewriting of the dictum *Post coitum, omne animal triste*, itself inspired from a sentence in *Problem* XXX, an obscure scholar from Rouen hammered home that 'The end of love is but melancholy'.[9] Shakespearean characters including Hamlet suffered from this fashionable disorder, when they weren't simply pretending to be afflicted with them (such as Jacques in *As You Like It*). Doctors offered endless clinical descriptions and indications for remedies. In 1621, Robert Burton's monumental *Anatomy of Melancholy* marked the peak of the world's melancholisation: in this pseudo-medical, satirical summa that surrounds the question of black bile with every possible glimmer of knowledge, melancholy is no longer considered a mere physical affection among others, but as the universal driving force for human actions, the dizzying, monstrous hearth in which the entire globe burns. Perhaps the first manifestation of the scholar's disease was simply the proliferation of discourses.

This was the extraordinary fate of Aristotle's *Problem* XXX:

what began as a mere accident of ancient thought ultimately occupied a central place in modern civilisation. Yet this process's apparent linearity should not obscure the radical mutation undergone by melancholy. While every thinker did indeed connect an excess of black bile with the scholar's vocation, the situation gets more complicated in the details: Does one choose to study because one is melancholic, or does one become melancholic by studying? According to Aristotle, the former hypothesis prevails without contest: since black bile warms the middle of the body, that is to say the seat of thought, melancholics are necessarily fated to become extraordinary thinkers.[10] But after considering the stars' influence on the matter, Ficino offered a murkier answer. The mechanism is organised around a subtle play of interactions: planets such as Mercury and especially Saturn incline a person towards intellectual labour; the physical immobility and mental concentration associated with this kind of work provoke a state of dryness analogous or favourable to black bile – which through its own action leads to a contemplative state.[11] Intellectual labour and melancholy reinforce each other. In Ficino's neo-platonic world, the harmony of microcosm and macrocosm is so powerful that cause and effect are difficult to separate: study and melancholy are the two indissociable sides of a single reality. As for the dignity of the scholarly condition, halfway between the stars and the humours, it is never called into question.

Late sixteenth-century medical discourse took an entirely different approach. Since study was considered the principal cause of melancholic states, the first remedy was purely and simply to abandon it or, at the very least, to attenuate its intensity: 'above all, spare your brain any study, or reflection.'[12] In his *Treatise of Melancholy*, Timothy Bright specified:

> Of the labours of the mind, studies have great force to provoke Melancholy if they are vehement and deal with difficult matters and high mysteries: and therefore they are above all to be avoided.[13]

If that proves impossible, 'a subject of study is to be chosen that requires no great effort, but is able through a certain moderation to unbend the stress of the mind subjected to that overvehement action, and bring it contentedness and a feeling of joy.'[14]

A severe prescription, but Robert Burton didn't stop there. In his eyes, study brought about melancholy not only through an internal physiological process (the effect of black bile), but also through the external action of society. While in Aristotle black bile was a sign of the election of a few great men, and appeared less as a disease than as a blessing, it now struck an entire class of penniless and disenchanted intellectuals, on whom Alberti had already published a humorous panegyric one century earlier.[15] Burton's assessment is more bitter. In one of his long chapters, he provides a pitiful description of 'the misery of scholars' ('the Misery of Schollers'), busy in the best of cases pleasing uneducated protectors or aspiring to modest ecclesiastic income, when they didn't have to be satisfied with teaching undisciplined children their ABC's. At fault was a university system that would still benefit from a critical examination today: the lack of recognition of talent; the devaluation of degrees, granted without discernment by venal universities; the appeal of professionalising studies (law, medicine, theology) to the detriment of liberal arts curricula etc. Also at fault is the world, which can't distinguish between real merit and vain claims to fame:

we can make *Mayors* and officers every year, but not Scholars: Kings can invest Knights and Barons, as *Sigismond* the Emperor confessed; Universities can give degrees; and *Tu quod es, è populo quilibet esse potest*; but he nor they, nor all the world can give learning, make Philosophers, Artists, Orators, Poets.[16]

In short, the real cause of melancholy is not physiological: it is moral, social, and political. Like the folly to which Erasmus gave *Praise*, but with less gaiety, melancholy now imposed itself as the symptom of a collective crisis, the purely negative consequence of the general toppling of values. The scholar suffered from his maladjustment to the world, but what was truly ailing was society.

Melancholy had come a long way from the neo-platonic harmony dreamed up by Marsilio Ficino. And even from Aristotle: two thousand years after the Stagirite, with the connection between mind and body having loosened, the affects were now detached from the corporeal structure and had been moralised and spiritualised. A short time later, melancholy would become what it is today, namely, little more than a mere variation on a feeling, a sadness without content, and without the slightest physiological anchor. Simultaneously, the classical ideal of balance at every level, both internal (between the humors) and external (between the individual and the world), would lose any pertinence. Chaos triumphed on all fronts, and the scholar's relationship to society has principally become critical. One can already feel in Burton the curse that would soon strike poets and intellectuals. Later, Leopardi, Nietzsche, Valéry, and Benjamin, to name only them, would not hesitate to use melancholic feeling as the driving force of their thought and their relationship to the world.[17]

Initially 'outstanding' (*perittos*), then marginal, and ultimately cursed: there is a certain logic to the scholar's path from Aristotle's *Problem* XXX. Aristotle had said as much in his own way, on that memorable day when he was feeling despondent: melancholy is not so much the scholar's illness as it is his nature, and less his nature than his situation. Or else, in other terms, it is less an excess of being (*huperbolé*) than a defect of order (*anômalia*),[18] and less a defect of order than a disturbing relationship to the world.

XV
The Soul

Does the scholar have a soul? The question might seem surprising, yet it was the source of virulent debate within Christianity. No doubt it wasn't expressed in such abrupt terms. Like every human being, the scholar is born with a body and soul; no one could doubt that, so long, of course, as one accepts the existence of souls.

But can the scholar succeed in keeping this soul – and in keeping it as pure as it was at his baptism? Doesn't he lose his soul by studying? More generally, can anyone who devotes himself to study achieve salvation? This final question was answered in the negative by *The Imitation of Christ*:

> Why not take a rest from this exaggerated craving for mere knowledge which only has the effect of distracting and deluding us! People are so fond of passing for learned men, and being congratulated on their wisdom – yes, but what a lot of knowledge there is that contributes nothing to our souls' welfare! And there can be no wisdom in spending yourself on pursuits which are not going to promote your chances of salvation. All the talk in the world won't satisfy the soul's needs; nothing but

holiness of life will set your mind at rest, nothing but a good conscience will help you to face God unashamed.[1]

Here we recognise the wariness in 'modern devotion' (*devotion moderna*) for established knowledge.

In general, many Christians were highly suspicious of scholars. Take the Blessed Pietro Pietroni of Sienna: on his deathbed, he made a host of predictions and exhorted Boccaccio and Petrarch to give up the study of poetry to save their souls. Petrarch had to be brilliantly persuasive to convince his poet friend to ignore this advice and not give in to fear; the examples of Saint Jerome and Saint Augustine proved useful.[2]

Yet this didn't settle the problem. At the tail end of the seventeenth century, the issue cropped up again, pitting against each other two exceptional protagonists who were major figures of the Church and French monarchism: Armand Jean de Rancé and Jean Mabillon.[3]

Versailles never had a more inspired guru than Rancé, who is remembered thanks to the biography by Chateaubriand and perhaps more indirectly thanks to Molière: the character of Alceste, the Misanthrope, is said to have borrowed some of his moral contortions. This spiritual father's story certainly makes a lasting impression on anyone who hears it. The gallant abbot Rancé frequented high society and denied himself no pleasure. Until his mistress the Duchess of Montbazon died suddenly of a malignant fever. He converted before her dead body, and died too – but only to the world he had loved so much. He settled in a ruined abbey at La Trappe, where he soon instituted an extremely rigorous way of life, turning the abbey into the in place for the court aristocracy to withdraw from society. Along with more bona fide devotions, it's likely that those who came to La Trappe did so to see for themselves whether the rumour that the grieving lover kept his mistress's skull on his desk was true.

For Rancé, monastic life was to be reduced strictly to prayer and mortification of the flesh. All the rest – studying, reading – only distracted the cleric from the straight path to salvation. Rancé did not rest until he had imposed this severe reform of Benedictine rule on his entire order.

But in doing so, he directly thwarted the interests of a considerable institution: founded in 1618, the Congregation of Saint Maur had indeed put study at the heart of monastic life. The congregation aimed to serve as the kingdom of France's bureau of history by classifying and studying its archives. With three thousand monks, 170 monasteries, and as many inestimable libraries, the congregation's numbers succinctly express the power of its work. Under the direction of the erudite clerics working at the heart of this system in Saint-Germain-des-Prés, the Maurists produced volume after volume of annals of the Benedictine order and of the history of France and literature, preserving for generations of historians to come countless documents whose originals were later often lost to successive revolutions and wars. In the nineteenth century, French historiography would make the most of all the treasures accumulated by this distant ancestor of the Centre National de la Recherche Scientifique (National Center for Scientific Research).

The greatest scholar among the Maurists was Dom Mabillon, the genius inventor of the art of diplomatics. Mabillon was the first to set the rules for the study of old documents, providing the ways to authenticate them and evaluate their age. This indefatigable scholar travelled to all the monasteries in Europe to collate deeds and diplomas. Some two hundred monks worked under him. Like his brothers devoted to works of the mind, he was dispensed by his superiors from attending service and doing the manual work required by the rule, so that he could dedicate himself to his scholarly duties without any distractions.

Among the Maurists, study was as individual as it was collective. In the second half of the eighteenth century, an effort to promote competitiveness among monks and rekindle their ardour for intellectual labour led the congregation's 'Bureau of Literature', which had been established at the abbey of Saint-Germain-des-Prés, to hold competitions on the most diverse topics. Even a non-exhaustive list of these topics creates an impressive picture of the diverse fields of knowledge in which the Maurists laboured: scripture ('Is it apparent, as the Rabbis claim, that Balaam is the author of the passage in *Numbers* in which his story can be read; & that Moses inserted it in his Book, as he inserted a few books of the *Book of wars of the Lord*?'); ritual ('What was the Liturgy observed in the Monasteries of France from the establishment of the Order of St. Benedict to Pepin & Charlemagne?'); civil law ('Are there proofs that Vassals of Vassals owe to their death, with sovereign rights and without appeal, either to the King or to the great Vassals?'); without forgetting morals ('What are the greatest obstacles that Truth finds in the heart of man? Show, through striking examples drawn from sacred & profane antiquity, that envy, the mortal enemy of merit & virtue is of all the passions that which produces the most evils in the Universe').[4]

The secular world was no less a subject of research than biblical history. A few questions even dealt explicitly with the relation between pagan mythology and Revelation:

> Could one prove that the Fable originates in part in misunderstood Scripture & who are the most ancient

> Peoples whom one could suspect of having drawn their system of Fable from Scripture?

Rather audaciously, the Maurists attempted to offer a unified vision of the era's dual culture – mythological and Christian – by reconciling religion with the popularity enjoyed by aesthetics and pagan legends in that period of triumphant neoclassicism.[5]

In any case, this list of questions was only intended as a guide:

> Since everyone has the right to choose among the printed questions & even to focus on another subject of erudition & of literature, the Bureau will be pleased to receive everything it is sent.

The field of research was therefore unlimited.

It might strike one as strange that a congregation of regular monks organised a competition among its members. Was that really compatible with the spirit of charity? According to the Bureau of Literature, the answer was self-evident:

> There are means of rewarding those who will have better dealt with the question suggested, without departing from the Laws, nor the propriety of our state: the Bureau is disposed to use them in the most honourable manner for they will have received the suffrage & applause of the Assembly.

The nature of these means isn't difficult to guess: dispensation from doing manual labour or participating in the service in order to better devote oneself to labour of the mind; assignment to Saint-Germain-des-Prés for monks who distinguished themselves;[6] research trips to foreign libraries etc. The announcement was categorical: 'All talented Members of the Community are urged not to miss this opportunity to be recognised &

distinguished.' Organisations today have not surpassed the Maurists in rewarding the most deserving researchers.

But the reforms initiated by Rancé threatened the entire structure. Published in 1683, his treatise *De la sainteté et des devoirs de la vie monastique* [A Treatise on the Sanctity and the Duties of the Monastic State] couldn't be more lacerating in its criticism of the abuse of scholarly work by monks. The study 'even of holy things' leads to every 'excess' and every 'passion' of the mind: 'pride, vain glory, presumption, uneasiness, envy, contempt of others, and curiosity.'[7] The Maurists felt themselves targeted by a covert but no less violent attack in many of the book's passages. Then the news came that the Abbot of Trappe had forbidden the nuns at a certain convent to read the Ancient Testament.[8] The context itself was not favourable: the scandal sparked by Spinoza's *Tractatus theologico-politicus* in 1670 hadmade it delicate to defend historical studies of religion. The exegete Richard Simon would bear the consequences of this generalised suspicion.

The Maurists had to react, sparking an epic controversy. To reply to Mabillon, Rancé started to write a voluminous *Traité des études monastiques* [Treatise on monastic studies]. Backed by friends in high places, the Abbot of La Trappe had Mabillon spied on and used every possible means to prevent his book from being published. It was no use: Mabillon's *Traité* was published in 1691. Rancé wasted no time: his retort came out with a bang in 1692, in an edition published by the king's printer. The magnificent in-quarto copy in the collection of the Bibliothèque nationale de France, bound with the royal library's coat of arms, is indicative of the powerful support the abbot enjoyed. Mabillon did not allow himself to be intimidated: his *Réflexions sur la réponse de M. l'Abbé de La Trappe au "Traité des études monastiques"* [Reflections on the Abbott of

La Trappe's response to the 'Treatise on monastic studies'] was published the same year.

Would the opposing parties come to blows? Only if one overlooked the magnanimity of these two clergymen, who always made certain to conduct their interactions in the most respectful manner, adopting the courtesies appropriate to their positions. A meeting was organised to facilitate a reconciliation. Mabillon travelled to La Trappe. The two men exchanged signs of mutual respect. Eight days later, Rancé would write: 'The interview took place as expected; it would be difficult to find more humility and erudition in one person than in this good father.'[9] And that's where they left it: Rancé decided not to publish another response. Both men stood their ground and gave up on waging war on the other camp.

Beyond the disagreement between individuals and institutions, only one question ultimately remained up for debate: What value does studying have for the soul's salvation? According to Rancé, none at all, and that's in the best of cases, if the search for knowledge isn't in fact harmful: it inflates the soul, diverting it from its real duties and exposing it to error and heresy. 'Science', Rancé wrote, 'is a nourishment foreign to the condition of Monks [...] it can only do them harm, disturbing their heart, leaving on them impressions of death & ruining that core of piety, simplicity & purity to which their sanctification is tied.'[10]

Mabillon dismissed these reasons for concern with a wide range of arguments. One was historical: while Rancé shrugged off the examples of learned monks as mere exceptions to the rule, the Maurist could easily point to the fact that since its foundation, the Benedictine order had by vocation never stopped devoting itself to study; monasteries could thus provide weapons against heresies rather than leaving themselves wide open to them. The Abbot of La Trappe's imprudent theory was no match for the cleric of Saint-Germain-des-Prés's irrefutable erudition and accumulation of citations and references.

The other argument was moral and psychological: it relied on the nature of the spiritual and intellectual principle present in every man. 'Reading is the food of the soul', Mabillon wrote. 'If the latter is not provisioned enough, it will suffer from hunger and be weak in everything. No kind of practice, no physical labour will have the slightest appeal, nor even the holy services themselves, if the mind has not recovered through the use of pious reading. It will make the heart dry and arid, the urge to spiritual things will lose all vigour, going out like a flame, once they have been deprived of the oil and sustenance of reading.'[11] A beautiful image, which creates a mysterious link between the monk reading in his cell and the flickering flame of his lamp: to deprive either of them of their favourite food would be to extinguish the light with which they shine. It is far from certain, however, that only the scholarly reading practised by Maurist monks is being championed here: spiritual reading is too.

Yet of all Mabillon's arguments, one theological and semiological approach is even starker in its opposition to Rancé. The abbot only allowed his monks to read the New Testament and a few lives of the saints, with a view to contributing to their edification. As he saw it, these texts set out the paths to salvation in the most direct manner, without any risk of error. Yet Mabillon showed that the divine message was only so simple in appearance. Even the easiest texts do not provide a prefabricated meaning offered to the reader as is. They reveal themselves only through work and study. This is exactly what Christ means when he enjoins us 'to carefully examine the Scriptures to find him there'.[12]

Subject to exceptions, Revelation is not the fruit of unconstrained communication between God and the Soul. It must be earned. It is obtained through the scholarly examination of the sources. A text is not an idea. That would be too easy. It is only a means to the idea, and it is the scholar's role to know the text according to the nature of his own means, when so many naïve readers are taken in by the message's illusionary immediacy.[13] We all think of ourselves as good readers, and that's exactly where we are wrong: reading is a job, which is learned like any other job. Mabillon cites Saint Jerome:

> Each of us deals with his profession without applying himself to anything else. Holy Scripture is the only thing which everyone claims to understand. *Sola scripturarum ars, quam sibi omnes passim vindicant.*[14]

This is the root of so many heresies or, at least, misinterpretations, so damaging to religion and truth. Faced with a fundamentalism that holds that texts speak by themselves, whether in the eighteenth century or today, Dom Mabillon reminds us that no text, of whatever nature including divine inspiration, simply gives the reader the keys to its contents. The interpretation of the text is always to be constructed and this construction cannot be achieved without rules. In these matters, prudence and science are recommended.

Thus the monk of Saint-Germain-des-Prés ultimately defended the practice of study among monks by responding to Rancé with a reflection on the hermeneutic regime of texts in general and of Scripture in particular. Far from distancing the soul from God, study brings it closer to Him.

Let us go even further: isn't it possible to recognise in the effort of study the very dynamic of charity? For these are the words with which Mabillon ends his *Traité des études monas-*

tiques, quoting another magnificent meditation by the patron saint of scholars, Saint Jerome:

> We die every day, our life changes at every moment & yet we believe we're immortal. The time I take dictating, rereading & correcting what I write is all taken away from my days. We write, we write replies: our letters cross seas; & the waves that the vessel that carries them excite by splitting the waters are like as many moments of our lives passing. The only advantage we have left is to remain united with each other through the love of Jesus Christ.[15]

To trace a line with a quill or to sacrifice a little of your life is the same thing. Is not the movement that brings us to texts to humbly understand them from the inside the very one that drives us to other people in a spirit of charity? Are not commentaries simply letters written to great works? For the texts offer themselves to us like our fellow man does, as creatures to be loved and served. This is how the scholar's soul will be saved.

XVI
Religion

The scholar's gods will always be in a fragile position, subjected as they are to the perpetual examination of the texts and documents that revealed them. It might even be said that as a general rule, scholarly knowledge doesn't go well with religion. As powerful as the institution may have appeared in the Middle Ages, the Catholic church struggled to survive the shock of nascent humanism: this tradition uninterrupted for more than 1400 years, claiming to be of divine origin, suddenly found itself rather helpless to fight against a handful of philologists armed with nothing but their ability to read Greek. From Catholic humanism to the Reformation, from the Reformation to free enquiry, and from free enquiry to atheism, an implacable movement was set in motion. Who can resist the power of the texts?

However religious the scholar might be, he can't stop himself from honouring gods other than that of the common people. Hence the danger he poses to established religion. Even the greatest poet of medieval Christianity has a constant whiff of sulfur: *The Divine Comedy*'s theology is neither Marian nor Christian, and even less papist, for it is above all centred on the beloved, subsequently lost female figure of Beatrice. This relative independence from dogma is in all likelihood the basis for the universal attraction of Dante's poem, which the secular world probably has less trouble accepting than the Christian one. In fact, literature could probably be defined as what in one way or another escapes the historical and ideological conditions of its production.

From every text, including the most sacred, there emanates a subversive power that doesn't easily tolerate religious authority. Beginning at the dawn of time, the generations of Brahmans who learned the hymns of the Vedas by heart to ensure the slightest vowel or shortest aspiration wouldn't be lost wound up inventing grammar and forever setting the rules that governed the 'perfect' language of Sanskrit (for that is the meaning of the word). They became the servants of language at least as much as they were the servants of the gods of sacrifice over which they had custody. Would anyone dare to claim that the gods weren't jealous?

The rabbis were even more daring, if that's possible. In 68 AD, when Yohanan ben Zakkai, the head of the Sanhedrin, went to see General Vespasian, whose troops were besieging Jerusalem, to ask his permission to withdraw to Yavne and run a school for sages there, he laid the foundations for Judaism to undergo a transformation more radical than any experienced by any other religion: from a religion focused on the Temple, it became a religion of the text; under the direction of the scholars of Yavne, the study of the Torah replaced sacrifice.[1] Yes, the Temple of Jerusalem was destroyed by the Romans, but the ritual it contained was fully transcribed in the commentaries that form the Talmud. Not a detail was lost. In place of a completely vanished form of worship, another emerged, entirely devoted to preserving the memory of the former: liturgical knowledge replaced the carrying out of the liturgy itself. Judaism thus became the only religion where, at every level, in the yeshivot and in the synagogue as within the family, commentary, annotation, and scholarly discussion are the fundamental rite. This left the Kabbalah to bring the movement to its logical conclusion: here the sacred text is endowed with truly divine properties and powers, as the image on earth of the infinite and absolute.

The sacred text's first effect is to kill the god who pronounced it. If one dared, one would like to give potential divinities and demons lacking ambition a piece of friendly advice: 'Do not speak, nor write, it would be in your best interest.' But since the gods are always too talkative and as a result exegetes are needed, textual religions confer an ambiguous status upon these official scholars: no one is more closely watched than the guardian of the treasure; his power is carefully controlled. In fact, he often has no power at all; what may be missing from the close reading of the holy book, the commentaries, and the commentaries of its commentaries, as practised in certain yeshivot and Koranic schools, is that dash of freedom or heresy which distinguishes from strictly religious study, that scholarly leisure which led a ninth-century Benedictine monk to transcribe a passage from the Satyricon between a speech of Saint Athanasius against the Arians and a sermon of Saint Augustine on the Gospel According to John. The true scholar likes mixtures, which the Latins call *satura* or satire. Literature is the impure.

When religion doesn't rest on texts, there's no longer a need for a caste assigned to serve an immutable canon: the cleric returns to being a scholar. In the absence of a recognised holy book, any writing can serve as such: Homer and Virgil were the Old and New Testaments of ancient paganism – though not completely. In fact, the system functions differently: while literature and poetry are deployed where the religious text is lacking, they don't fully occupy the territory left vacant. Since the two spaces don't perfectly overlap, custom and oral tradition are left to fill the gap.

But if tradition itself comes to disappear, anxiety grows: the pagan is more dependent on the social sphere than the Christian, who doesn't belong to this world and for whom the Gospel acts as a society, if only a celestial one (the Sermon on the Mount presents social marginality as the best path to the kingdom of heaven). The pagan isn't so lucky: if the society of his time abandons him, he must find new support elsewhere, for example in scholarly knowledge, which might well form a kind of parallel society.

A significant part of Plutarch's work was born of the decline of the dominant religion, for which he had to compensate through the means offered by study, reading, and reflection. As a priest of the Temple of Apollo at Delphi, he could have discharged the duties of his position by peacefully enjoying its prestige. But the time had passed for that: at the end of the first century BC, the Pythian sanctuary was a shadow of its former self. City-states and kings no longer sent diplomatic missions there; they no longer asked the oracle grave political questions on which the futures of entire nations hinged; they no longer presented sacrifices or sumptuous gifts, like the solid gold lion mounted on a pyramid of 117 white gold bricks offered by Croesus, the king of Lydia, in the fifth century BC, in an admittedly gaudy gesture of piety. The time of theft had succeeded that of munificence: the sanctuary had been pillaged several times. The most recent predator, Nero himself, hadn't been the least avid. To decorate his new Roman villas, he didn't think twice about stripping the Apollonian compound of most of its treasures, the very ones that made the sacred path leading up to the temple the ancient world's most beautiful art collection. What remained of this lavish open-air museum was little more than a memory, though Rome attempted to return Delphi to a little of its former luster beginning under Domitian's reign.

While Plutarch was appointed in the context of this restoration of the oracle, he could hardly delude himself regarding the likelihood of its renaissance. The great age of Delphi was over. During the sanctuary's golden age, three Pythia had to take turns delivering the oracles, but a single one was now more than up to the task. Plutarch himself enjoyed certain advantages of the sinecure his job had been reduced to: as a priest on foot or on the back of a donkey, like today's turbo-teachers, he did not live in Delphi, but in his native city of Chaeronea, close to twenty miles away. It's likely he only left his home to travel to the sacred sites once a month, around the seventh day, when the Pythia was preparing to deliver her oracles.

The tranquil nature of Plutarch's sacerdotal life did not prevent him from seeing the decadence of the sanctuary for which he was responsible. He devoted the time he didn't commit to Apollo to studying and researching the causes of the oracle's obsolescence. This wasn't simply the relaxation of a mind unoccupied, but a case of absolute necessity: in a world where religious tradition was being lost, it was essential to preserve in written form all the knowledge that the last devotees would take to the grave. Here, the letter – letters – come to the rescue of the spirit. Plutarch was the Yohanan ben Zakkai of paganism: not only did he preserve the most complete, precise descriptions of the cult with which he was entrusted, but what he did for Delphi, he also did for the entirety of the ancient world. The historical and moral work of this citizen of Chaeronea and confidant to emperors probably accounts for the most prodigious accumulation of knowledge passed down to us from antiquity. Plutarch knew everything that a man of his time could know, but he did better than knowing it: he wrote it down. In Flaubert's correspondence, one finds this remarkable sentence later noted by Marguerite Yourcenar: 'With the gods gone, and Christ not yet come, there was a unique moment, from Cicero to Marcus Aurelius, when *man* stood alone.'[2] Plutarch was the witness to this unique moment for eternity: the scholar is the one who passes down a world.

The same is true of the gravedigger: more surely than oblivion, which does not prevent an unexpected return of the repressed, knowledge reduces its object to silence, suffocates it, then gives it the coup de grâce. The scholar is a passer then, but in the same way as Charon, the ferryman who escorts souls to the Underworld: even the gods don't get back on their feet from such a journey. It's no coincidence that Plutarch recounts the death of a god in one of the most mysterious and famous tales of antiquity. Rabelais gives an extremely faithful version of that story:

> Epitherses, father of the orator Aemilian, was sailing from Greece to Italy in a ship carrying an assortment of merchandise and a number of passengers, when one night the wind died down near the Echinades Islands (between Morea and Tunis) and their vessel was carried close to Paxos. Anchoring there, some of the passengers asleep, some awake, others eating and drinking, they heard a loud voice calling, from the island of Paxos, 'Thamous!' This terrified them. Thamous was in fact their pilot, a native of Egypt, but only a few of the passengers knew him by name. Then they heard the voice a second time, shrieking most horribly, 'Thamous!' No one answered; they all remained silent and fearful; and then the voice was heard a third time, crying out even more horribly than before. And then Thamous replied, 'I'm here, what do you want of me? What do you

want me to do?' At which the voice spoke again, even more loudly, and commanded him, when he came to Paloda, to publicly announce that the great god Pan was dead.

Epitherses tells us that, hearing this, all the sailors and passengers were stunned and terribly frightened. Debating among themselves whether it was better to keep silent or to make the public pronouncement that had been commanded, Thamous told them that he thought they should stay silent if a wind blew up behind them and swept them along on their way, but if the sea remained calm they ought to speak as the voice had commanded. When they were near Paloda, it happened that the wind was not blowing. So Thamous, climbing up on the prow, his face turned toward land, announced, as he had been commanded to, that the great god Pan was dead. He had not spoken the last word when deep sighs were heard on land, great lamentations and startled cries, not from just one person but from many, all together.

The news (because many people had by then heard it) was soon revealed in Rome. And Tiberius Caesar, then the emperor, sent for Thamous. Having heard him speak, he believed Thamous' tale. And when he consulted the learned men, then present in great numbers at his court in Rome, to find out just who this Pan was, he was informed that Pan had been the son of Mercury and Penelope.[3]

This is indeed 'an exceedingly strange tale', to quote its teller Pantagruel. So strange, in fact, that one might think it came from Rabelais's imagination. Yet that isn't the case: in Plutarch's original text, the event is reported by someone who heard it from Epitherses himself, and several listeners also confirm that they heard it from Epitherses's son, Aemilian. Given the number and quality of indirect witnesses, the episode's veracity is not to be questioned. Plutarch purposefully emphasises this point, for his aim here is less to explain the disappearance of the oracles through the death of the demons appointed to their operation (other less provocative, more reasonable hypotheses are provided later in the dialogue) than to confer on an unusual account from purely oral sources the authority of the written. This is one of the scholar's fundamental moves: to gather tradition to perpetuate it, to give a current and coming existence to what has been and that, for the single reason that it *has* been, is liable to no longer be. Contrary to received ideas, the future and the present matter to the scholar at least as much as the past.

From this perspective, Plutarch's enterprise was not unsuccessful: if the story of the great Pan's death has been preserved to this day, it isn't, as Pantagruel rather hastily claims, because it was 'recorded and vouched for by many learned and knowing historians'. In fact, we owe it exclusively to the author of the Pythian dialogues. Surprisingly, no other ancient text mentions the anecdote; one would have thought that after reaching Tiberius's ear, it would have left more traces. From Eusebius to Nietzsche via Rabelais and Hegel, there certainly hasn't been any lack of commentary: the death of a mere demon, of paganism as a whole, of the God of the universe (since *pan* means *everything* in Greek), even of Jesus Christ – all these interpretations have been given, along with many others. But these were only made possible because as the first century AD faded into the second, in a tiny city in Boeotia, a Greek scholar decided to write down what had happened. One can find no greater justification for the scholar's existence than the transformation of spoken words into text, event into knowledge, past into future. If, according to the probably inaccurate etymology given by Lactantius, religion indeed consists of 'linking' (*religare*),[4] then the scholar can know no other religion than the link to be established between two moments in history, two places, two cultures, two beings. Humanity hangs on that thread.

But this link stifles as much as it invigorates: it exhausts the present while putting an end, in a more discreet but no less effective manner, to that past it claims to perpetuate. In the normal course of things, oblivion makes the present the sole legitimate heir and natural continuator of the past: the absolute abolition of the past is the proof that it has given all it had to give; it lives totally in that present which nonetheless believes, through a wise form of ignorance, that it owes nothing to the past. By artificially reviving the past and forcing it to rise from the dead, the scholar turns the order of the world upside down. Far from recreating what has been – since, strictly speaking, what has been cannot be a second time – he gives us a figure of the past, a simulacrum. A ghost. And this ghost – or this ghost of a ghost, to be precise: that of Pan – is not reassuring for the living or the gods, and even less so for the divine Apollo, who presides over the Oracle of Delphi. By dying in Plutarch's narrative, the great Pan dies twice: a first time as a mere demon, under Tiberius's reign, and a second time as sign or symbol, to be forever interpreted and reinterpreted, dying a universal death from which even higher beings aren't exempt. This second death is to be feared far more than the first one, though in a subsequent part of the dialogue Plutarch acts as if he's laying down his weapon at the last moment by mentioning other reasons for the disappearance of the oracles. Regardless: rarely have the gods been so closely threatened. Nietzsche would remember it.

The gods must always fear what a scholar will say about them, including a priest of Apollo, even and especially in the case of a panegyric. Witness another one of Plutarch's Pythian dialogues, devoted to the mysterious epsilon suspended in front of the temple of Delphi. Over the course of this scholarly conversation, several more or less plausible hypotheses are put forward by the various participants in the debate in an impressive competition of their erudition and culture: E, the fifth letter of the Greek alphabet, is said to refer to the five wise men of the ancient world, or to the importance of the number five in the universe, or else to the conjunction *if* (*ei* or *e* in Greek) used by the faithful to consult the oracle: 'I would like to know if...' etc. But one interpretation ultimately prevails by its incontestable theological richness: the E, addressed to Apollo and meaning 'You are', shows that only the gods participate in true being, while mortals are pulled along by the dizzying flow of time whether or not they like it. The dialogue ends with one of the most powerful pages of prose in antiquity, an admirable meditation on being and the divine, which Montaigne, as a fine connoisseur of the beauties of language and thought, repeated nearly word for word at the end of his 'Apology for Raymond Sebond':

> We have no communication with being, because every human nature is always midway between birth and death, offering only a dim semblance and shadow of itself, and an uncertain and feeble opinion. And if by chance you fix your thought on trying to grasp its essence, it will be neither more nor less than if someone tried to grasp water: for the more he squeezes and presses what by its nature flows all over, the more he will lose what he was trying to hold and grasp. Thus, all things being subject to pass from one change to another, reason, seeking a real stability in them, is baffled, being unable to apprehend anything

stable and permanent; because everything is either coming into being and not yet fully existent, or beginning to die before it is born.

After having shown that human life is subjected to perpetual change, Plutarch returns to being:

But then what really is? That which is eternal: that is to say, what never had birth, nor will ever have an end; to which time never brings any change. For time is a mobile thing, which appears as in a shadow, together with matter, which is ever running and flowing, without ever remaining stable or to which belong the words before and after, and has been or will be, which at the very first sight show very evidently that time is not a thing that is; for it would be a great stupidity and a perfectly apparent falsehood to say that that is which is not yet in being, or which already has ceased to be. And as for these words, present, immediate, now, on which it seems that we chiefly found and support our understanding of time, reason discovering this immediately destroys it; for she at once splits and divides it into future and past, as though wanting to see it necessarily divided in two.

The same thing happens to nature that is measured, as to time that measures it. For there is nothing in it either that abides or is stable; but all things in it are either born, or being born, or dying. For which reason it would be a sin to say of God, who is the only one that is, that he was or will be. For those terms represent declinings, transitions, or vicissitudes of what cannot endure or remain in being. Wherefore we must conclude that God alone is –not at all according to any measure of time, but according to an eternity immutable and immobile, not measured by time or subject to any decline; before whom there is nothing, nor will there be after, nor is there anything more new or more recent; but one who really is – who by one single now fills the ever; and there is nothing that really is but he alone – nor can we say 'He has been', or 'He will be' – without beginning and without end.[5]

In Plutarch, the dialogue concludes with a luminous synthesis of the two famous mottoes displayed in the temple:

> But this much may be said: it appears that as a sort of antithesis to 'Thou art' stands the admonition 'Know thyself', and then again it seems, in a manner, to be in accord therewith, for the one is an utterance addressed in awe and reverence to the god as existent through all eternity, the other is a reminder to mortal man of his own nature and the weaknesses that beset him.[6]

What better tribute could be given to the god of Delphi? It would be impossible to more concisely articulate the most elevated theological reflection with the material realities of the sanctuary: immemorial rites, mysterious monuments, enigmatic inscriptions.

This may well be the problem. For according to Heraclitus, in a fragment preserved by Plutarch himself (this is the scholar's honour: to pass down the words of others), 'the Lord whose prophetic shrine is at Delphi neither tells nor conceals, but indicates.'[7] Wouldn't replacing the Apollonian sign, the humble E of the sanctuary, with philosophical discourse and conceptual reflection fatally betray that 'language [...] of all mute things'[8] by turning the god of signs into the god of language and logos? Immediately after his long quotation from Plutarch in 'Apology for Raymond Sebond', Montaigne seems to sense this difficulty, expressing his surprise at 'this most religious conclusion of a pagan'. Not that the priest of Delphi was in any way Christian, but there is in the cultured pagan a religion of the spoken word, of rationalisation and commentary that contradicts in an unsettling way the principles of the cult of which he is responsible. The eternal and immutable divinity of which Plutarch gives an impressive portrait is indeed far more like the single God of the philosophers than the god who was born in Delos and defeated the serpent Python before founding the oracle of Delphi. An immobile god could hardly have so many adventures. Plutarch himself was not fooled: his spokesperson in the dialogue advises the devotee who continues to believe that Apollo and the sun are one to elevate himself to a less naïve view of divinity.[9] Mythology had been left behind.

The scholar's philosophical and theological discourse certainly proves to be an even more effective means to kill the god of Delphi than the tale of the death of the great Pan, which despite everything was the occasion for a good story: indeed, a dead god will always leave behind a memory or a tomb, on which, with a little luck, miracles will still take place, while a rational and transcendent god no longer has much to do with human history. Plutarch's melancholy is probably due to the painful awareness that while a scholar might well strive to champion the established religion, he can do nothing but hasten the death of the gods.

XVII
Quarrel

Anyone who naively imagines the world of scholars as a space impermeable to human passions, a fragment of the original paradise free of corruption, or an island devoted to the peaceful conquest of knowledge and preserved from the conflicts that darken our world is in for a bitter disappointment. Nothing is less irenic than the life of a scholar. Granted, conflict between scholars rarely draws blood. Only ink is spilled with any regularity. But styluses are sharp weapons.

Far from softening interpersonal relations, spending time poring over great works in dusty archives and reading forgotten manuscripts seems to accentuate disagreement. When one lives in permanent contact with objects that transcend the human condition (such as texts, whose existence far exceeds a mere mortal's temporal limits), decides to participate in a debate passed down through immemorial tradition, or enters into conversation with the dead, it is to be feared that mere social propriety will be revealed to be futile. The respect for humans does not hold up in the face of the respect for books. Philological truth will not stand for moral compromise.

For those who live in the longue durée of scholarly knowledge, it is hard to place much importance on any concern for the present, for momentary alliances and childhood friendships: the society of texts takes precedence over that of humans. Spending time with books does not hone negative passions rather than check them, but it eliminates the social superego that tends to keep the individual within common boundaries, and replaces it with a feeling of extraterritoriality that isn't particularly favourable to ordinary sociability.

Saint Jerome, patron saint of scholars, was prone to proverbial fits of anger. It wasn't wise to venture that you disagreed with him: his old friend Rufinus and even the great Augustine felt the heat of his disapproval.[1] Insults rained down: one of Jerome's detractors was called 'Onasus',[2] a contraction of the Greek and Latin words for donkey (*onos*, *asinus*) and nose (*nasus*); others were accused of 'having no balls'.[3]

Could it be any other way? When you sacrifice your life to provide as faithful a Latin translation of the Scriptures as possible, based on the best Greek and Hebrew sources, anyone who rejects your titanic endeavour's results amply deserves being accused of preferring to drink water from 'a muddy streamlet' (*caenosos riuulos*) than from 'the clear spring':[4] Fussing over the text's exactitude is all the more inappropriate given that it was obtained through immoderate labour.

Exerted in the name of criteria beyond this earthly world, the scholar's anger isn't merely extraordinarily forceful and abrupt, it is a holy anger: it manifests that another reality has emerged, the transcendent reality of texts, which follow their own rules, unknown to the layperson. Even the founder of the Chinese scholarly tradition, Confucius himself, an apostle of good manners and universal harmony, had trouble suppressing a fit of rage when a sovereign didn't conform to the rules he inherited:[5] against every tyrant and enemy of civilisation, the essential counter-power of culture legitimates the use of anger.

Most often, the victims of scholars' anger are themselves scholars. To put it more precisely, they are *other* scholars, colleagues – or at least those who claim to be, for a scholar is always ready to consider that others don't fully deserve the title or might even have usurped it. While a scholar regularly meets individuals more erudite than himself, he more often has the impression that he lives in a world of false sages.

One of the most significant of these disagreements was the quarrel around Nietzsche's first book, *The Birth of Tragedy*. As curious as it may now seem, one of the major philosophical revolutions of the nineteenth century was sparked by a dispute among scholars.

Today the image in many of Nietzsche's readers' minds is of a thinker purely exalted and marginal, free from every principle and form of knowledge as he carried out a frenzied attack on every value and institution. While this reputation is not entirely unfounded, it flatters the somewhat facile and demagogical – and, in any case, perfectly anti-Confucian – idea that only individuals defiant of authority and detached from their cultural roots can effectively challenge the world. By contrast, it is agreed at least since Adorno that the in-depth study of culture is incapable of producing a real critique of the functioning of society.[6] One need only slightly exaggerate to say that the ideal contemporary revolutionary is the ignoramus.

As for the Nietzschean philosophical revolution, it took the reverse approach, since it was carried out in the name of a search for a historical and philological truth.[7] Naturally, one recalls the philosopher's appointment as a professor of classical philology at the University of Basel at the age of twenty-five. His appointment was no accident: even after he resigned his chair a decade later, in part for health reasons, Nietzsche remained obsessed with philological investigation for the rest of his life.

In Nietzsche's view, there was a direct connection between the study of ancient works and the critique of modern man. Not that antiquity had qualities in any way contemporary or similar to our current situation, as the traditional humanist believes. On the contrary, the real philologist recognises the aspects of the Greek world that are irreducible to our own values; he rejects the widespread lazy idea that there is a straightforward continuity between that world and our own. It is precisely because the philologist is disposed to perceive the ancient texts' radical alterity that philology can serve as an ideal tool for self-knowledge.

'So if we fully understand Greek culture, we see that it is gone for good', Nietzsche wrote in a collection of posthumous notes known as *We Philologists* (*Wir Philologen*). 'Thus the philologist is *the great sceptic* in our cultural and educational circumstances: that is his mission. – Lucky he, if like Wagner and Schopenhauer, he has a presentiment of those auspicious powers in which a new culture is stirring.'[8]

To this day, naïve champions of the teaching of Greek and Latin think they make their argument more convincing by demonstrating how much our society owes to antiquity. Yet in doing so, they unintentionally play into their adversaries' hands: if the classics interest us because they are like us, we might as well focus directly on ourselves, without using the Ancients as an intermediary, and read only news articles and sociological studies – already a common enough practice to make it unnecessary to reinforce this pedagogy of self-involved modernity with a clumsy defence of ancient studies.

In fact, what should be said is exactly the opposite: it is precisely because the Ancients are fundamentally unlike us that they deserve to be studied and read in a serious fashion. In a world convinced of living on eternal foundations or in which only superficial novelties are accepted (which would be the same thing), the philologist is the one who takes a closer look. He examines not only the ancient works, but ideologies and affects, to which he applies the rules for the constitution of scholarly knowledge and the same analytical methods used in philology: in the same way that the Hellenist looks for a text's sources, hunts down its errors, and determines its useful lessons, one must trace the genealogy of values, ferret out the false and misleading ones, and suggest how to rectify them. This was Nietzsche's sole objective, and *The Birth of Tragedy* marks the specific moment when philological research turns into philosophy.

However, this early work's ambition apparently remained limited. The book's original full title expresses its basic intuition: *The Birth of Tragedy Out of the Spirit of Music*.[9] According to Nietzsche, the essence of Athenian tragedy was musical; he set out to prove his point against all those scholars who had too long forgotten it. This constitutes the first, philological phase of his demonstration. The second phase is more philosophical and aesthetic: Nietzsche set out to prove that any real tragedy can only be musical and to use the opportunity to champion the Wagnerian revolution.

However, the title also states the relative failure of Nietzsche's undertaking: its anthropomorphic and metaphoric language (*birth*, *spirit*) does not belong in a philological study. Nietzsche himself would later recognise the feverish, quasi mystical character of his youthful essay, which suffers from a scant presentation of its arguments and doesn't meet the scientific criteria of traditional philology, though it claimed its place in that field.[10]

But before Nietzsche personally confessed to his failure, the academic community to which he belonged made sure to let him know – as bluntly as possible. The fact that this controversy unfolded among scholars shouldn't lead one to assume that it was characterised by the distinction and refinement associated with scholarly milieux. On the contrary, a giant wave of censure progressively swelled until its full strength was unleashed on the young scholar.[11]

Initially worried that his mentor and former professor in Leipzig, Friedrich Ritschl, had not acknowledged receipt of his book, Nietzsche wrote him to express his surprise. As courteous as Ritschl's reply may have been, it left no doubt about his feelings: the first book by his favourite disciple, the very one whom he had helped to secure a highly sought-after position at Basel, had profoundly disappointed him. The philosophical path that Nietzsche had chosen resolutely broke with the rigour of philology. For an old scholar like Ritschl, the hardest thing to accept was that Nietzsche only attributed the privilege of saving humanity to art – and no longer to knowledge.[12] Paradoxically, this volume which the new professor at Basel had conceived as his philological magnum opus ultimately proved to be very hostile to the positivist foundations of philology, which he contrasted with his praise for the powers of art.

While Ritschl was able to moderate the expression of his disappointment, the same would not be true of his fellow philologists. Nietzsche's betrayal of philology set off a kind of trench warfare. The two camps were markedly different: prestigious on one side, though low in numbers and without much scientific authority; more obscure on the other, but far more representative of the scholarly community. Around Nietzsche were gathered a few colleagues at Basel, including the famous Jakob Burckhardt; Erwin Rohde, his university classmate and also a philologist; and especially the Wagners, Richard and Cosima, who would loudly intervene in the controversy. Facing them was just about everyone else, that is to say practically every Germanic philologist, with a flamboyant spokesperson in Ulrich von Wilamowitz-Möllendorf, Nietzsche's former fellow pupil at Pforta, the venerable boarding school they had attended a few years apart.

The Birth of Tragedy was published in January 1872. The enthusiastic response from the author's close friends was soon followed by silence, broken only by rare rumours: one person, for example, was said to have declared that Nietzsche was lost to philology; others were said to find him ridiculous.[13] But where would the first attack come from? Would there even be one?

The first manifestation of hostility was indirect: Rohde had prepared a laudatory review; it was rejected by two newspapers, the *Literarisches Centralblatt* and the *Philologischer Anzeiger*. He wrote a second one: it was published in another newspaper, the *Norddeutsche Allgemeine Zeitung*, a purely political publication, devoid of literary influence.

Rohde's piece was published on 26 May 1872. From that point on, things began to accelerate. On 30 May, Wilamowitz's pamphlet *Future Philology!* was published in Berlin with the explicit subtitle: *A Reply to "The Birth of Tragedy" by Friedrich Nietzsche, Ordinary Professor of Classical Philology at Basel*.[14] On 23 June, Richard Wagner, whom Wilamowitz had implicated in the failure of *The Birth of Tragedy*, came to Nietzsche's defence in an open letter to the young author published in the *Norddeutsche Allgemeine Zeitung*. On 15 October, Rohde violently attacked Wilamowitz in an open letter to Wagner published in Leipzig. Finally, in February 1873, Wilamowitz published a follow-up to his initial pamphlet, directed against 'rescue attempts' [*Rettungsversuche*] for Nietzsche's book.

In this memorable controversy, which would lead to a lasting change in the direction of Nietzsche's intellectual evolution and in the history of philosophy itself, these distinguished Hellenists were not ashamed to use the two most traditional forms of polemic discourse: irony and invective. Wilamowitz makes liberal use of the former: with its exclamation point, his pamphlet's title openly parodies the slightly overexcited tone of Nietzsche's book.

What did the young philologist have against Nietzsche? The fact that he was simply turning philology upside down by interpreting ancient tragedy through Schopenhauer and Wagner, instead of following the 'historical-critical method' [*historisch-kritische methode*] and seeking only 'to grasp each historical phenomenon based on the sets of assumptions of its own time'.[15] This philology is only 'future' because it starts from the future to go back to the past, instead of following the opposite path. Wilamowitz invites Nietzsche to take full responsibility for his Dionysianism:

> Let him seize the thyrsus; let him move from India to Greece. But let him step down from the lectern from which he is supposed to teach knowledge. He may gather tigers and panthers around his knees but not Germany's philologically interested youth[.][16]

In other words, a 'future philology' without a future. The irony is flagrant, and Nietzsche would in many ways wind up realising the programme his young colleague set out for him: he would resign his chair, travel south (to Nice and Italy), and invent a new form of philosophical discourse.

Standing up for his friend's interests, Rohde proceeded to tear apart the young pamphleteer: while Wilamowitz's argument stuck to the substance of Nietzsche's book, Rohde had no qualms about responding with *ad hominem* attacks. Throughout his reply, Rohde referred to his opponent as the mere 'doctor in philosophy' (*Dr. phil.*) that he was: an expeditious though inelegant manner of discrediting him by comparison with the professors he was up against (Nietzsche and Rohde).[17]

Rohde wasn't afraid to be coarse. His pamphlet's title is an obscene play on words: *Afterphilologie*, that is to say *Backward philology*. Rohde's title insinuated that the field of knowledge Wilamowitz claimed as his own belonged to the past and was aimed at the past, as opposed to the Nietzschean 'future philology'. But in German, *After* is literally *anus*. This 'backward philology' is therefore also presented as a 'philology of the rear end' or, more violently, as a 'shit philology'. Which goes to show where the study of letters can lead.

But let's not be too hasty to condemn Rohde. Wilamowitz had preceded him in the flood of insults. After all, his own pamphlet's epigraph consisted of a few well-chosen verses from a lost play by Aristophanes that indirectly assimilated Nietzsche's work to a crude 'buttfucking' (*katapogusonê*).[18] The delights of extreme erudition (citing a practically unknown fragment of a great Greek writer) combine here with the joy of insults: an eminently scholarly pleasure, and a game at which Wilamowitz is incontestably the winner, since he was an unrivaled expert at scattering his slightest remark with erudite citations and allusions.

In fact, history would prove him right, since the little 'doctor in philology' of 1872 would soon become the most famous and respected Hellenist of his time, ending his career as the chancellor of the University of Berlin. By then, he would regret having let himself be dragged into a polemic as vain as it was vehement, against such an adversary.[19]

Perhaps his regrets were equally vain: if one finds a curious parallel between Wilamowitz's professional success and his talents as a polemicist, it is that it's difficult to have one without the other. Despite appearances, passions are at the heart of the scholarly life: disagreements and anger are its ordinary mechanism, with value systems and thresholds of violence that in no way correspond to those in effect in everyday life. One does not devote oneself to such arduous work, so foreign to regular life, without profoundly transforming one's relations to people and to the world.

On a deeper level, the scholarly life and quarrel are connatural, for if 'War is the father of all',[20] according to Heraclitus, it is also the father of all real knowledge, which only emerges through the confrontation of opposites. Yet for all that the opposite of knowledge is not non-knowledge: even to this day, one cannot have an accurate idea of Athenian tragedy without taking into account both Nietzsche and Wilamowitz, adversaries for eternity in a battle that is endless but certainly not fruitless.[21] There may be no such thing as just wars, but there are indeed scholarly ones.

XVIII

The Academy

On 7 December 1486, the Roman printer Eucharius Silber issued one of the most astonishing books in the history of thought. Strictly speaking, it wasn't even a book. Rather a long, very long invitation card, thirty-six in-quarto pages, without a frontispiece, beginning as follows:

> The following nine hundred dialectical, moral, physical, mathematical, metaphysical, theological, magical, and cabalistic opinions, including his own and those of the wise Chaldeans, Arabs, Hebrews, Greeks, Egyptians, and Latins, will be disputed publicly by Giovanni Pico of Mirandola, the Count of Concord.[1]

He added:

> The conclusions will not be disputed until after the Epiphany. In the meantime they will be published in all Italian universities. And if any philosopher or theologian, even from the ends of Italy, wishes to come to Rome for the sake of debating, his Lord the disputer promises to pay the travel expenses from his own funds.[2]

In principle, this invitation to debate was not completely

surprising: when a student was preparing to defend a thesis, it was customary to post his thesis on the university's walls. At the time, an entire thesis fit on one page.

In Pico's case, it wasn't one thesis, but nine hundred. Taken individually, each thesis is brief: no more than a sentence. It's clear, however, that despite each statement's concision, there are radical shifts of scale and category. The sum of these propositions borrowed from the scholastic theologians, Arab Peripatetics, Greek philosophers, esoteric Neo-Platonists, and Cabalists was supposed to reveal their shared foundation, that is to say the eternal philosophy underlying so many apparently antinomic doctrines.[3]

Giovanni Pico della Mirandola's title of Count of Concord was perfectly appropriate, for his work drew on the entire history of thought, from Iamblichus ('There is no force in the celestial stars that in itself is evil') to Avicenna ('It is impossible for the same species to be generated from propagation and from putrefaction'), from Hermes Trismegistus ('Nothing in the world is devoid of life') to magicians of every obedience ('To operate magic is nothing other than to marry the world'), from Christian theology ('If Adam had not sinned, God would have been incarnated, but not crucified') to the Cabala ('Anyone who knows how to unfold the quaternarius into the denarius will have the method, if he is skilled in the Cabala, of deducing the name of seventy-two letters from the ineffable name'), and vice-versa ('What the Cabalists say, that we will be beatified in the shining mirror restored to the saints in the future world, is exactly the same, following their principles, as that which we say, that the Saints will be beatified in the Son').[4] This collection of statements earned its author the reputation of having been, at the tender age of twenty-three, the most erudite man in history, a reputation that persists to this day.

These nine hundred theses were always scholarly, often mysterious, sometimes scandalous, but ultimately they presented a unified vision of the world. Pico's comparative study of every text generated by three thousand years of religious, esoteric, and philosophical tradition promised to lead to nothing short of the triumph of *philosophia perennis* and the revelation of the principles of the universe. To witness it, one only had to wait for the days immediately following Epiphany in the year 1487.

Unfortunately, this magnificent programme stalled at the planning stage. Eternal philosophy will forever remain unknown to us, along with the relative truth of each of its theses: Pope Innocent VIII decreed that the disputation of the nine hundred conclusions would not take place. A commission was quickly assembled and condemned thirteen of the nine hundred statements. Pico fled Rome. Arrested in Savoy, he was taken to Paris, jailed at the Château de Vincennes, then freed under pressure from the Sorbonne, which would indefatigably support the prodigy against the Holy See throughout the affair.[5] It must be said that the Count of Concord had himself always explicitly preferred to the flowery and somewhat vain eloquence of the Italian schools of his time the dry form of the controversies practised at the university in Paris, which emphasised knowledge in its rawest state.[6] Pico died in Florence a few years later, at the age of thirty-one, in obscure circumstances.

What survived of the author of the nine hundred theses' aborted project, however, was the idea that one never thinks alone, an idea that came in two complementary modes: one thinks with or against a tradition, and one thinks with or against one's contemporaries. Knowledge is a collective thing. It emerges progressively from a triple confrontation: between books and other books, people and other people, and people and books.

Granted, the Scholastics were aware of this, and Pico was certainly influenced by them. But with this erudite young lord's colossal undertaking, there emerged a need for another kind of scholarly community than that of the medieval university, the need for a permanent tournament of thought, a space open to free debates, where the collective search for truth would be subjected neither to outside pressures nor to the overly constraining formal rules required by the awarding of diplomas. A space as friendly as it was scholarly, and all the more friendly given that the questions debated would be of the highest importance: what Pico called, in the stirring opening speech he never delivered, a 'palaestra' or 'literary gymnasium' (*literaria palaestra*).[7]

Aristotle had theorised this point long earlier, in *The Nicomachean Ethics*:

> the wise man on the contrary can also contemplate by himself, and the more so the wiser he is; no doubt he will study better with the aid of fellow-workers, but still he is the most self-sufficient of men.[8]

The 'wise man' (*sophos*) must also be understood to refer to the scholar or man of letters. Paradoxically, the more people are with the scholar, the more he is autonomous: his 'fellow-workers' (*sunergoi*) increase his freedom. However, to see these collaborators as mere servants attending to their master's basic needs would be to diminish the originality of Aristotle's point. Having already dealt with the question of 'the necessities of life' (*ta pros to zên anagkaia*) a few lines earlier, Aristotle refers to something else here: what he has in mind is indeed a collective search for truth, as it was practised in his Lyceum and in his teacher Plato's Academy.

This model began spreading in Italy as of the late fifteenth century, spawning the Platonic academy in Florence, inspired by Gemistos Plethon and Marsilio Ficino, Il Panormita's and Giovanni Pontano's Neapolitan academy, Giulio Pomponio Leto's Roman academy, and Aldus Manutius's Venetian academy, to cite only a few examples. Pico della Mirandola could have had his own academy, but the Church decided otherwise.

The principle on which every academy is founded is courteous debate. Good manners don't prevent discussion; on the contrary, they enable it. Controversy can only freely develop if the opponents are guaranteed that no one will be mortally wounded. This rule of academic politeness is absolutely explicit in the statutes of the Académie Royale des Inscriptions et Belles-Lettres [Royal Academy of Inscriptions and Belles-Lettres], which was founded in 1663 under the name of Académie des Inscriptions et Médailles [Academy of Inscriptions and Medals] and was the epitome of the scholarly academy in France. Initially charged with writing the inscriptions on the kingdom's monuments and the mottos on its medals, the academy saw its activities expand over time to every field of humanist erudition: the study of languages and literature, history and geography.[9]

According to the very detailed 1701 statutes, the academicians, of which there were forty, met twice a week at the Louvre, on Tuesdays and Fridays, from 3 to 5 p.m., outside of holidays – in which case the assembly would take place on the previous or following day – outside of vacation periods, which lasted from 8 September to 11 November, and outside of the major religious festivals ('from Christmas to Twelfth Night', Easter fortnight, and the week of Pentecost). Outside of vacations, an academician could not be 'absent for more than two months for his personal business'.[10] Which goes to show the importance placed on these meetings that make up the main part of academic life.

In fact, the way these meetings are run has not changed much since the eighteenth century, and anyone who attends a session today can only be struck by their extremely ritualised nature. At each session, academicians are invited to take turns submitting 'a few writings of their composition'[11] to their colleagues' assessment: a formidable ordeal. This system can only really function in an atmosphere of mutual trust, far from any form of aggressivity. Paragraph XXIV of the statutes is very clear on this point:

> The Academy will very carefully ensure that on occasions when some Academicians have different opinions, they will not use any terms of scorn or bitterness against each other, neither in their speeches nor in their writings and even when they fight against the opinions of any Scholar at all, the Academy will exhort them only to speak to them with consideration.[12]

This rule of tactfulness even applies to anyone who reports on the work of individuals outside the Academy: he 'will make his report to the Company without criticising it, only observing if it features views from which we can benefit.'[13] The Academy thus presents itself as a pacified, codified world, in which widespread trust and respect allow for the free development of knowledge.

Unless this peace was an illusion, a soft veil thrown over the brutality inherent to the order of knowledge? Strangely, when the King decreed new statutes for the Académie des Inscriptions et Belles-Lettres in 1786, any mention of a rule of courtesy in debates disappeared. Article XXII read:

> Each Academician-Member & Ordinary-Associate will be required to bring a few Works of his composition each year to be read in the Academy's Assemblies. The Honoraries & Free-Associates will be invited to carry out the same exercise & each Academician present will be invited to make remarks on what has been read.[14]

Difficult to imagine a more blunt assertion of the academicians' freedom of speech: one recognises the administrative style of a cold technocracy whose advent was in many ways already announced by the reign of Louis XVI. Is that to say that after more than a century, the institution no longer needed to be reminded of a standard of courtesy that had become second nature? Or on the contrary, should one see in this decline of academic manners the prodrome, relatively speaking, of the revolutionary violence that would be unleashed a few years later? The second interpretation is more likely the accurate one: with the passage of time, science would ultimately have to impose its own demands against the protocol of aristocratic society. As a last resort, dispute and quarrel always win out over sociable discussion. The scholarly republic's evolution can only ever lead to a superficial pacification of relations, of which the academic institution is the most accomplished example.

To this day, when an academician corrects one of his colleagues' presentation in the magnificently wainscoted rooms where the Assembly's sessions are held, permitting himself to bring an error to the gathering's attention, no amount of tact or courtesy will dispel the intrinsic violence of such a statement: despite all his efforts, it remains a painful moment. Officially kept outside of the scholarly enclosure, the mechanism of conflict is always on the verge of being set off again.

As the utopia of a world closed off and preserved from external brutalities, entirely dedicated to the collective production of knowledge, the academy remains the useful, necessary mirage that Pico della Mirandola sought and failed to recreate. But it is a fragile mirror: one only needs to touch the tree of knowledge to be chased out of earthly paradise. This could have been the Count of Concord's 901st thesis.

XIX
Politics

There is a republic of letters only because letters are situated outside the republic. As a world apart, they provide themselves with their own laws. And this autonomy is unbearable to the state.

In *The Nicomachean Ethics*, Aristotle compares the politician's occupation with that of the scholar or philosopher, in other words of those who engage in 'contemplation' (*theôria*). The politician, he explains, enjoys the greater dignity, but his occupation nonetheless remains fundamentally self-serving. His goal in practising it is beyond the occupation itself, either aimed at his own advancement, or that of his fellow citizens – in other words at the happiness of the state.[1] The scholar's occupation is entirely different:

> Also the activity of contemplation may be held to be the only activity that is loved for its own sake: it produces no result beyond the actual act of contemplation, whereas from practical pursuits we look to secure some advantage, greater or smaller, beyond the action itself.[2]

What better way could one find to describe the scholarly profession's autonomy, compared to that of the man of state? In fact, what Aristotle means by contemplation probably doesn't exactly match with scholarly activity: it is perhaps less the study and search for truth than the actual holding of that truth, accompanied by a delectation close to mystical rapture.[3] Nonetheless, if the search for truth is a precondition to its possession, the characteristics of the one must inevitably be found in the other, though to a lesser degree. In particular, the quality of 'autarky', 'self-sufficiency', or 'independence' (*autarkeia*)[4] specific to contemplation. To work toward grasping the truth, as any scholar does, means to enjoy this self-sufficiency, or at the very least to be moving towards it with all one's might.

As it happens, the scholar's self-sufficiency – whether actual or desired, it doesn't make much difference – has two antithetical consequences. On the one hand, it implies freedom, in the political sense of the term, the very freedom associated with every citizen in full possession of his rights. Not that a slave can't be a scholar (in ancient times, many children's private tutors were slaves or servants; they were nonetheless scholars), but for those who have it at their disposal, the knowledge of letters necessarily opens up a space of freedom, even if they are in a servile condition: no scholar could be entirely a slave. Knowledge liberates, even if this liberty is only internal and of a purely intellectual order. This is especially true, generally speaking, when the scholar is also a free citizen: the superior freedom acquired by letters confers on him the ability to fully exercise his civic responsibilities and to work towards the good of the state in the most informed manner. In his biography of Apollonius of Tyana, Philostratus recounts how the Greek philosopher and his friends Demetrius and Musonius Rufus victoriously opposed tyrants like Nero and Domitian, who despite their many threats never managed to silence them:[5] the citizen scholar's freedom is more effective than the non-scholar's. Which explains the important role education plays in any political project, as Plato was the first to recognise in *The Laws*.[6] And this is even truer in a regime with democratic aspirations.

Yet the scholar's self-sufficiency also has a negative effect: it puts him on the margins of the state he belongs to. For if self-sufficiency is truly characteristic of any political body able to equip itself with its own laws and, particularly, if it defines the political operation of a free state, then it necessarily turns the scholar into a kind of small autonomous republic, endowed with specific objectives separate from the rest of the state's shared interests. Aristotle emphasises this point, as we have seen: the fact that scholarly activity finds its own reward in itself clearly sets it apart from political activity, which is always aimed at an external good. The scholar therefore finds himself in an eminently ambiguous position: his knowledge should give him every qualification to exercise power in the state, but this same knowledge tends to distance him from the state and prevent him from participating in its government. Worse, it makes him suspect to the state, which most often will not stand for the formation within it of micro-states unconcerned with the common good.

In the surviving texts, Aristotle does not completely resolve the problem: while he considers the scholar who abstains from participating in the state as reduced to living 'the life of an alien' (*bios xenikos*)[7] and consequently endorses a life devoted to politics, he nonetheless sees the individual who dedicates himself to contemplation as the happiest of men, without ever showing how a contemplative life could fit with that of the citizen. The philosopher's indecisiveness on this subject is remarkable.[8] But could he have done any different, given that he was torn between his admiration for the independent and democratic Athens of his youth and his allegiance to a dynasty of conquering Macedonian kings? It hardly bears repeating that Aristotle only arrived in Athens to found the Lyceum after the Battle of Chaeronea, that is to say after the Greeks were defeated by the Macedonians, which would make Athenians aliens in their own home. This troubled context probably explains these hesitations of a philosophical order between, on the one hand, the praise for an active participation in politics, which was a fundamental aspect of the Greek state, and, on the other, the admiration of the contemplative life, the only resource remaining to the citizen stripped of his powers by the invader. Since this fateful moment, the crucial question of the scholar's political engagement has been left unresolved, and has continued to poison the life of scholars to this very day.

For instance, Julien Benda was no more successful than Aristotle at clearing up the issue when he published a famous pamphlet criticising the 'clerks' or intellectuals of his time for being unfaithful to their mission by beginning 'to play the game of political passions'[9] and concerning themselves with practical interests. If one agrees with Benda in defining intellectuals as 'all those who seek their joy in the practice of an art or a science or metaphysical speculation, in short in the possession of non-material advantages, and hence in a certain manner say: 'My kingdom is not of this world','[10] in other words in embracing a particularly angelic view of the scholar, then yes, those intellectuals who get mixed up in the quarrels of their time have indeed committed treason. But it's far from certain that the definition proposed is the right one. One does not escape the world merely by saying: 'My kingdom is not of this world.' On the contrary, the world tends to feel threatened by those who claim to follow laws other than its own, and the call to order always comes fast, with a violence that the hypocrisy of the proceedings does little to conceal: Pilate may not sentence Christ, but he does nothing to oppose his crucifixion. The scholar's self-sufficiency is a highly dangerous position.

Furthermore, even Benda recognises the intellectual's right, if not duty, to appear 'in the public arena, if he appears to preach the religion of what is just and true and if he openly preaches them as non-practical values', in other words, 'devoid of any attention to selfish interests, whether of one's nation or one's class.'[11] He goes on to cite the names of Erasmus, Kant, and Renan. But the line between a position dictated solely by the great abstract principles and concrete engagement in the life of the state is less easy to draw than it appears, and in any event the state always has the ability to draw that line where it pleases, with consequences often fatal to the scholar.

Where lives a scholar, there is freedom and autonomy. In other words, the scholar is by nature a dangerous man. Consider an example from more than two millennia ago: Confucius's life consisted of endless peregrinations, from the kingdom of Lu to the kingdom of Qi, from Qi to Lu, and from Lu to Wei, all according to the unpredictable favour he enjoyed with the local sovereign. The father of Eastern scholars could never stop himself from criticising the governments to which he gave advice and comparing them with the great models from history, at the very risk of his life. The scholar's politics proceed from a permanent dissatisfaction with the present, yet never lead to a potential conquest of power: it is a politics of opposition.

In one of the most beautiful passages from the *Analects*, Confucius asks his disciples: 'I'm a few days older than you, but forget that for the moment. You are always complaining that no one understands you. If someone truly understood you, how would you proceed?' Each of the disciples then reveals his secret ambition to participate in the highest functions of the state. The Master merely smiles, then turns to Zeng Xi:

> Zeng Xi ceased strumming on the large zither and, as the last notes died away, set the instrument aside and stood up. My tastes are different from those of these three men, he replied.
> What harm in that? said the Master. Each person has simply to speak of his desires.
> In the late spring, said Zeng Xi, when work on the spring clothes is finished, I'd like to go with five or six older fellows who have been capped and six or seven young boys to bathe in the Yi River, take the air among the altars where they pray for rain, and come home singing.
> The Master gave a deep sigh and exclaimed, I'm with Zeng Xi![12]

The Master's approval is significant. Zeng Xi gives the answer most in keeping with what one expects of a scholar: unlike his fellow disciples, he does not want to command an army, administer a territory, or officiate in a big temple. Yet his answer is not the least political one. Clearly, the ideal expressed is that of a community of scholars where the master and his disciples join in deliberately turning their backs on the highest state offices to assert by their mere presence that some things surpass politics. Harmony, nature, poetry: the surpassing of politics also presents itself as another politics, in which the principles that govern the republic of letters apply. Confucius tells us that the scholar must aspire only to the contemplative life, without desiring politics for itself: politics will come anyhow, and soon enough there's no need to make it an end in itself.

This Confucian example provides the key to finding how the contemplative and the political life fit together, which Aristotle always left unsaid: contemplative life appears in and of itself as a political proposal, which the state will promptly observe, either to accept or reject it.

A certain simplification, or even a distortion, of Confucius's nuanced thought was therefore required when the first competitions allowing scholars to serve the empire as administrators were established under his egis four centuries later, under the Han dynasty. This recruitment system would last until the beginning of the twentieth century and was used in a large part of the Far East. Once the Jesuits decided to import it to the West, it even achieved global influence. Nonetheless, there remained a certain antinomy between the worlds of scholars and of power. It was sometimes expressed with extreme violence: in 213 BC, the first emperor of China ordered the canonical texts of the Confucian tradition systematically burned and had numerous scholars buried alive.[13] Had this undertaking been pushed to its logical conclusion, not only would Confucius's name have been forgotten, but no trace of the empire's past would have remained. This is the utopia peculiar to every revolution: the drive to start over from scratch, on completely virgin territory. Where such an ambition is found, the existence of scholars obviously poses a serious problem, which only an extensive campaign of eradication can resolve.

But the antagonism between power and scholars is rarely expressed in such an absolute manner: it more frequently focuses on a particular victim. This was the case with Sugawara no Michizane, the patron saint of Japanese scholars. A brilliant student, he was able to use his talent to rise to the coveted position of Minister of the Right at the court of Emperor Daigo, the highest attainable office other than the Minister of the Left, which was held by a young offspring of the powerful Fujiwara family. The latter family quickly refused to tolerate a mere scholar threatening its hereditary privileges: abruptly dismissed from his duties and relegated far from the capital, he died in exile two years later, in 903.[14] Such is the scholar's fate: even at the pinnacle of power, he remains marginal.

Michizane's story does not end with his wretched death, however. Immediately after his passing, Kyoto was hit with a succession of catastrophes – storms, fires, epidemics. These events were interpreted as the minister's posthumous revenge, and he became the object of a cult intended to appease his wrath. The years passed, but Michizane continues to be venerated in many of the archipelago's sanctuaries under the name of Tenjin, like the god of literature. The lesson is clear: it's easier for a scholar to achieve celestial immortality than to be appointed a minister of the emperor.

Boethius and Thomas More also bore the tragic consequences of a similar situation after being respectively appointed consul and chancellor. Both men were sentenced to death for high treason by the same government that had promoted them.

Scholarship is a continuation of – or preparation for – politics through other means. Everyone knows this, including Michizane's enemies and Cicero, who seemed to find refuge in philosophical activity after having been removed from power by Caesar's supporters. In his treatise *The Republic*, Cicero gave his own point of view on the relation between the contemplative life and the political life: it was absurd, the orator wrote, to ask the wise man to save the state when circumstances require it, if the wise man hasn't practically and theoretically prepared himself for the exercise of power beforehand. Cicero reminds the reader of his personal experience when Catiline attempted to overthrow the Republic:

> What could I have done at that time had I not been consul? And how could I have been consul if I had not followed from boyhood the career that would bring a man of equestrian birth like me to the highest office?[15]

This is a singular line of reasoning: by asking the wise man to commit to political life from an early age, Cicero seems to go against the entire Greek philosophical tradition, though he often claims to adhere to it. But the apparent paradox is linked to a difference of context: Cicero's reflection only makes sense in the context of a deeply hierarchical Roman republic, where government offices are accessible after a regulated career, while in Athens the democratic order theoretically gave every citizen the possibility of exercising power at any moment. If the Roman scholar is to come to the aid of the state in its time of need, he must already have successively fulfilled each of the steps of a political career.

Conversely, the wise man's withdrawal from political life after he has completed an entire career can only ever be provisional. This was certainly Cicero's view as he wrote countless scholarly treatises that definitively placed him at the forefront of Roman science and thought. Unfortunately for him, this was also the view of his adversaries, and particularly of Mark Antony, who was terribly annoyed by his series of *Philippics*: Antony relentlessly asked for Cicero's head and finally got it when young Octavius realised that the tired orator, who had promised him his support, in fact only aimed to exercise power himself. The ultimate cruel twist of fate came when the murderers arrived to kill Cicero in his villa and he was betrayed by an emancipated adolescent whom he had himself instructed 'in literature and the sciences'.[16] Cicero's sister-in-law later had the traitor horrifically tortured, forcing him 'to cut off his own flesh bit by bit and roast it, and then to eat it',[17] a living image of the very fate he had inflicted upon his master: Wasn't it his own flesh he had delivered to death by betraying Cicero?

Long after the last bulwark of the Republic had collapsed with Cicero's death, the state's new leaders did their utmost to remodel Latin literature and simultaneously introduced a new phenomenon to Rome by building one public library after another. The astronomically rich Asinius Pollio, a patron to Horace and Virgil, launched the trend, followed by the emperors Tiberius, Vespasian, and Trajan. As for Augustus, he built two libraries, beginning with the library at the Temple of Apollo on the Palatine Hill, right next to his residence. One suspects that with these libraries the prince still at the height of his glory was paying a discreet homage to the great writer whom he had abandoned to his death but for whom, if we are to believe Plutarch,[18] he continued to profess his admiration and respect. But what's certain is that in Rome and the Hellenistic world, as in France under Charles V, founder of the royal library, or the United States with its Library of Congress, libraries are the ornament of power and also serve as its instrument: since it's too dangerous to let scholars escape from the state, collections of books provide a good way of keeping an eye on them. Not without reason, for scholars are always traitors in the making.

Augustus was probably right to annex the library to his palace in order to always keep scholars under his control. Perhaps he remembered the name of the young man who pointed the assassins in the direction that Cicero fled. Plutarch mentions it in passing: his name was Philologos.

XX

War

No situation is less favourable to scholars. Nowhere is their knowledge more useful. By destroying culture, war reveals its value.

Yet we need to make a distinction. The wars of yesteryear weren't absolutely incompatible with study. Some people even went to war in order to study. Take the example of the Egyptian campaign, where Bonaparte behaved less as the leader of an army than the head of a laboratory: orientalists, antiquarians, geographers, geometers, naturalists, astronomers, and artists were this unparalleled expedition's real heroes. Having set out on 19 May 1798, the expedition returned in 1801: a short-lived conquest. But it spawned a monumental *Description de l'Égypte* [Description of Egypt] in nine volumes of text and eleven of plates, the publication of which would only be completed under the Restoration: knowledge is more precious and lasting than empires.[1]

Military men – or at least the best of them – have always known that conquests only last a limited time. What a good strategist has been able to do, another will be able to undo. On the other hand, books remain. War is destined to be written, to leave behind memoirs as trophies and accounts of a victorious campaign – at least temporarily. One must defeat the enemy, but above all time. There have been generals who were writers: Xenophon and Caesar were the very first, and far from negligible; their successors include Monluc and de Gaulle. In the lower ranks, the alliance of arms and letters proves to be more unstable. There have been fewer soldiers who were writers than writers who were soldiers: Stendhal, Kleist, and Vigny gave up their military careers rather quickly.

A special place must be reserved for Captain Paul-Louis Courier, a valorous battalion leader of the Napoleonic light artillery and an incomparable Hellenist. He took advantage of his various encampments in Italy to have the libraries opened for his use and to collate their Greek manuscripts. In Florence, he discovered eight previously unknown pages of Longus's novel *Daphnis and Chloe*. In Parma, it was Xenophon's *On Horsemanship*, appropriate reading for a cavalry officer: for Courier, the Greek author was not just another ancient writer – he was a soldier. 'I did not travel alone, but with my Xenophon, in other words in good company', he wrote to Monsignor Gaetano Marini, the prefect of the Vatican library. 'In Florence, I collated three measly manuscripts that rewarded me for my efforts only with the certainty that they didn't contain anything worthwhile. One of yours and one in Paris are the only ones that provided me with a few good lessons. With this help and my conjectures, I re-established a few passages, and I'm leaving few to be corrected. In a word, I think that I've done everything that a soldier could do, explaining to the scholars what they can't know, following the rule: *tractant fabrilia fabri*.'[2] Here we have a campaign narrative decidedly more philological than military. At least on the surface. The closing quotation from Horace emphasises as much: 'Artisans handle artisans' business.'[3] In other words, only a horseman can correctly edit a treatise on horsemanship. The scholar on horseback thus comes to the aid of scholars in their studies.

Soldier-scholars like to read their fellow soldier-scholars. Limited to only a handful of books, the soldier's portable library is transformed into a circle of companions in misery. What was true of old-fashioned war, where it was important to keep up elite appearances, is only more apt with modern and democratic war, where one does not like to burden oneself with the superfluous. Having become rarer, the opportunities for sanctuary are all the more prized.

'When I was forced to limit my library to what a soldier's bag can hold', wrote Albert Thibaudet, 'three books were enough for me (six volumes that in the end Azor and its procession of satchels always obligingly contained), a Montaigne, a Virgil, a Thucydides. A soldier in the war of 1914 could be a man who lived an important stage in history with poetry, and in the same way that at a stage on a journey you use your hand to draw spring water, mixed here with eternal essences, in Montaigne I drew the water of life, in Virgil the water of poetry, and in Thucydides the water of history. The three forms, Naiads, Nymphs, and Fates, French, Latin, and Greek, bound themselves like a perfect chorus around my bag, and an ingenious sibyl taught me that this library of three books, as a relic and witness to thousands of others, had a strictly higher value than the six and nine, the ten and one hundred, the one thousand and ten thousand now distant, inexistent, burned.'[4]

The allusion is to the Cumaean Sibyl, who responded to Tarquin's refusal to purchase nine books of prophecy predicting Rome's future by burning first three, then three more. The Sibyl was on the verge of burning the last three when Tarquin suddenly repented and decided to buy them for the same price as the initial nine. In 1919, 450 French writers were listed as having 'died for their homeland'.[5] In other words, far more than 450 books did not see the light of day. Alongside military cemeteries, we should build libraries of all the books that were never written and whose authors are resting beneath their markers. In fact, why limit ourselves to France? The situation was no different on the other side of the German border, without mentioning the Allies, led by the Russians, British, and Italians. In short, the First World War cut down several thousands of scholars in the prime of life. Nothing less was needed to bring into being the new century and create a culture detached from its memory. The Sibyl's six burned books seem nearly insignificant compared to this carnage.

But the three books that remain are all the more precious. They weren't chosen at random: Montaigne's writings came out fully armed from the wars of religion; Virgil from the civil wars; Thucydides from the Peloponnesian War. The soldier-scholar finds comfort in the experience of other scholars who were soldiers. But he goes even further: he writes, he writes to them. One must imagine Corporal Thibaudet in the cold and empty camp over which he has guard duty, bent over his three volumes and annotating their margins, writing on sheets of paper passed off to his fellow soldiers as letters to his family and friends (for it was not common, in this context, to write for yourself). In fact, he was closer to Thucydides than to his parents or friends behind the lines. Communities of scholars do not care about their period: war and ink form a tighter bond.

'I never scribbled on more paper than during those four years',[6] Thibaudet emphasised. The scholar on a military campaign experiences a singular sense of urgency: to write before the end of the world, as it were. Ludwig Wittgenstein composed the *Tractatus logico-philosophicus* on the eastern front, when he was posted to observe the Russian lines, then in captivity in Italy.⁷ The title's openly pedantic nature is not gratuitous: in the heart of combat, it proclaims with a hint of despair the permanence of a European tradition of thought that the bellicose madness of the nations seemed to be on the point of reducing to ashes. Likewise Alain:

> I was under the canvas of a supply carriage. The evening was hectic and noisy; the driver was scared, though he had imbibed alcohol. The horses were scared. In the dark under the canvas, I heard whistling and explosions; I could see frightening reflections through the cracks; the trouble is that in that position you deliberate about whether you'll jump out and finish the journey on foot. I didn't feel like a hero at all. The same way that believers say their prayers, I kept myself busy with a panegyric to Descartes, which I later wrote as is. It's in *Quatre-vingt-un chapitres* and I like it. I still feel the powder in it, but I don't feel the fear.⁸

This is how Alain wrote *Quatre-vingt-un chapitres sur l'esprit et les passions* [Eighty-one Chapters about the Spirit and the Passions], published in 1917. These were also the circumstances for his *Le Système des Beaux-arts* [The System of Fine Arts], based on 'postcards after Da Vinci, Michelangelo, and Raphael', which the philosopher asked friends to send to him.⁹ 'I remember that I wrote a chapter on sculpture in the middle of cabbage cores',¹⁰ he noted. Though doubtlessly less perilous than a supply mission, peeling duties were no less productive from a literary perspective.

But in the kitchen as on the road, in the camp as on the front lines, the soldier-scholar's ultimate guiding light is Descartes. Alain wrote an essay in praise of Descartes as the shells rained down around him. Thibaudet 'liked to convert his narrow shack made of boards into a Cartesian stove-room',[11] that famous stove-warmed room where the philosopher sought refuge in 1619 when the Duke of Bavaria's army took up its winter quarters. The 'principal rules of the method'[12] came into existence in this toasty environment. It was the scholar's study on the military campaign.

A paradoxical scholar, however. In fact, was Descartes really a scholar? According to his biographer, it seems more like he wanted to break free from 'the prejudices of his education & of books'.[13] Hadn't he 'given up' on books? Descartes chose to be a soldier specifically because it was the opposite of being a traditional scholar, confined in his study. His war was a philosophical war, taking as its target the knowledge found in books: 'By making up his mind to take up arms', Baillet wrote, 'Descartes resolved to encounter himself nowhere as an actor, but to find himself everywhere as a spectator of the roles that are played in all sorts of States on the great stage of the world.'[14] A spectator rather than a reader, then, or else a reader, but in that case of the only big book worth opening: the universe. There are no other books in the Cartesian stove-room, once this purely intellectual book-burning has been carried out.

But after being driven out of thought, books return in force through dreams, that is to say through the body: on 10 November 1619, shortly after having found 'the foundations of admirable science', the philosopher had three dreams in rapid succession. In the last, two books appear in a prominent place: 'a *Dictionary*' and 'a collection of Poems by different Authors, entitled *Corpus Poëtarum & c.*' The dream was interpreted as being eminently propitious and a decision was taken to 'compose a treatise', which Descartes hoped to 'finish before Easter of 1620'. He even planned to 'look for booksellers' to talk to them about the 'printing of this book'.¹⁵ A fine revenge on the man who thought he could do without books and who ultimately had to admit there was more depth in the poets than in the 'writings of the Philosophers'.¹⁶

Letters ultimately vanquished this soldier who had left to make war on them in his Bavarian stove-room, less of a retreat far from the front than a battlefield for thought: these are the only wars worth fighting.

XXI

The Coronation

The mystery of the two messengers.

Around 9 on the morning of 1 September 1340, a rider was announced at Petrarch's home at the source of the Sorgue. He delivered an official letter from the Roman senate asking Petrarch to come to the Eternal City to receive the 'poetic laurel' (*lauream poeticam*).[1] That same day, seven hours later, a second messenger presented himself at the great scholar's home with another letter: this time, the University of Paris was inviting him to travel to the capital of the kings of France to be decorated with the same laurel. A strange story, in truth: it's already exceptional for a scholar to be offered a crown of laurels, in the tradition of the competitions held in Ancient Rome, rarer yet to be offered it twice, but it's virtually miraculous for two cities separated by a journey of several weeks on foot to simultaneously make the same offer to one man in a period when communication was notoriously slow. Yet the story is reported by Petrarch himself in a letter he wrote that very day to ask his illustrious patron Cardinal Giovanni Colonna's advice about his decision. As proof of what he wrote, the scholar sent the two letters in question, accompanied by their seals.

It isn't hard to see why Petrarch's problem was so thorny. One even sympathises with him, for once the pure moment of satisfaction he must have felt for being simultaneously requested in two places had passed, he faced a choice between the old and illustrious capital of an empire that stretched to the ends of the world and the most powerful university in Christendom and the leading city of the West. Which entity would be less dangerous to offend? By asking for the advice of a cardinal of the Roman church, the Italian poet seems already to have made up his mind: he would go to Rome to collect his much-vaunted laurels. It was in Rome, after all, that were held the Capitoline Games instituted by Emperor Domitian. And it was here too that the poet Statius himself was widely believed to have been awarded the crown.[2] Petrarch would merely need to send a note to explain his absence to his friend Roberto de Bardi, the chancellor of the University of Paris. He would also endeavour to explain his choice at the coronation.[3]

But the most difficult remained to be done: he had to prove he was worthy of the crown he was offered. To guarantee his merit, Petrarch chose to be sponsored by the King of Naples and Count of Provence, Robert of Anjou, whose reputation for wisdom and scholarly knowledge he thought would serve as a bulwark against the envious. On 16 February 1341, the poet left Avignon; he travelled to Marseille, where he boarded a ship bound for the sovereign's court. There, for three days, Petrarch discussed poetry with the humanist king 'from noon to night',[4] first in private, then in public. On the third day, Robert of Anjou declared Petrarch worthy of receiving the laurel. The king would have liked to personally bestow the crown upon him in Naples, but Petrarch wouldn't hear of having his ceremony anywhere but Rome. Too old to make the trip, the king wrote a certificate and Petrarch was finally able to travel to the city he so desired, preceded by messengers, the precious document in his pocket, sure of himself and of his value.

The coronation took place on Easter Sunday, 8 April 1341. In Naples, the royal examination had already followed a paschal structure: just as Christ was resuscitated on the third day, Petrarch triumphed on the third day. If one is to believe the poet's account, his coronation in the senatorial palace's vast audience chamber on the Capitoline Hill in Rome could not have been more grandiose:

> Suddenly, upon the call, the noblest Romans assemble; a joyous murmur fills the Capitoline Hill; the walls of the ancient palace seem to participate in the celebration. Now the fanfares have rung out; the crowd squeezes together in disorderly rows and prevents everyone from seeing. I myself do believe I saw my friends with their breasts bathed in tears, breathless with emotion. I go up; the trumpets have fallen silent, the murmur has subsided. A few words provided at the beginning by our dear Virgil, and the speech can begin; I did not speak for long. For the law of poets forbids it, and one does not carelessly violate the sacred rights of the Muses: didn't I tear them away from the Apollonian peaks to force them to dwell a moment in the midst of the city, among the people? Then, with his great eloquence, Orso takes the floor. Finally, he rests the Delphic crown on my head, accompanied by the applause of the people of the Quirites.[5]

But that wasn't all: after another encomium by his lordship Stefano Colonna, Petrarch descended the Capitoline Hill to the cathedral, where he left his laurels on the altar of Saint Peter.

So solemn! Such emotion! You'd think you were back in the heyday of imperial Rome. But those days were long gone: since

1309, the popes had settled in Avignon, the old capital was a shadow of its former self, and the declining Senate would soon make way for a dictator, Cola di Rienzo. Petrarch's account describes an ideal triumph, but the reality was something else entirely. The plan was for the poet to be crowned by an eminent representative of the King of Naples, but after the representative was attacked on the road to Rome, Senator Orso dell'Anguillara was at the last moment recruited to preside over the ceremony. Later, after Petrarch had barely passed the city limits on his return journey, he fell into the hands of bandits and was forced to turn back and take shelter inside Rome's city walls; he was able to leave only the next day, under heavy escort.[6] What surer sign of decadence than a freshly crowned laureate narrowly avoiding getting his throat cut on his way home? The era of the great Roman peace was a thing of the past.

Yet in the middle of all this chaos, Petrarch only had one idea in mind: to make visible a new power, to put in place a new order of things, that of poetry. Granted, he was not the first in his century to receive the poetic laurel with great pomp. Putting aside the musical and poetic competitions of Antiquity, the humanist and man of state Albertino Mussato had been crowned in Padua on 3 December 1315.[7] But that ceremony had proceeded according to a rigid academic protocol, close to that used for doctoral graduation ceremonies. While it also appears that Dante and the grammarian Convenevole were granted the Apollonian laurels, this was only done posthumously, in the context of their funerals.

With Petrarch, the event took on an entirely different dimension. First, a royal one: the poetic crown visibly retained something of Robert of Anjou's majesty. While Petrarch could have received the prize solely under the authority of the Roman senate, he only wanted to receive it from a sovereign power. On the day of the coronation, Petrarch wore a personal robe belonging to the King of Naples, who had given it to him for the occasion: there could be no clearer indication, in the eyes of all and even in the absence of the monarch, of the extent to which the poet now glowed with the royal aura. As for religious symbolism, Petrarch emphasised that it was always indissociable from poetic ritual: while some doubt remains about the coronation's actual date, after the fact the poet systematically sought to associate Easter Sunday with his triumph. It isn't insignificant that the speech delivered that day followed the exact structure of a sermon, with the exception that in place of a sentence from the Bible, Petrarch chose to comment a line by the divine Virgil: 'But a sweet longing urges me upward over the lonely slopes of Parnassus.'[8]

The transposition from the lonely Parnassus to the crowded Capitoline Hill was far from pro forma: it implied a real reversal of values and imposed the triumph of a new power, that of a language inspired by the gods, ordered according to the past, and measured in time. 'On a path so difficult and, for me, so dangerous', the orator explains, 'I was not afraid to offer myself as a guide, with the idea that many would subsequently follow in my footsteps.'[9] One mustn't forget that the 'guide' (*dux*) is also the leader: the double nature of the laurel, 'as imperial as it is poetic',[10] serves as the speech's leitmotif. The poet relied solely on the power of his words to briefly bring the transcendence of a third order down into the Eternal City deserted by the kings and popes: when politics and religion have decamped, another system of the world becomes possible, where withdrawal guarantees presence; beauty, truth; rarity, wealth; and softness, power. Invested with the two routed legitimacies – the royal and the pontifical – poetry descended to earth for a moment on 8 April 1341.

Petrarch's coronation was unlike those that had preceded it. When they were crowned, Mussato was fifty-four and Dante and Convenevole were dead at close to sixty and seventy respectively. By comparison, Petrarch was only thirty-six. At that stage in his career, did he really deserve the laurels more than anyone else? It's far from certain. While he had already written some hundred poems in vernacular language, these couldn't be considered in support of awarding him the prize, at least not officially: only the Latin work counted. As it happened, Petrarch had only composed some fifteen poems in Latin at the time, none of which were of notable stature. It's likely that he was already circulating a preliminary draft of his great poem about Africa, and he had written profoundly erudite letters, but strictly speaking nothing justified his coronation other than his relationships with the rich and powerful and, in particular, with the Colonna clan.[11] For Petrarch, the 'desire for the laurel' (*vaghezza di lauro*)[12] long anticipated the realisation of the work, as is evident in numerous early poems written when he wasn't even thirty. Was it the desire for the laurel or the desire for Laura? The direction of the metonymy remains unclear. Much later, at the other extreme of his life, in his last letter to Boccaccio, the poet would bitterly regret his absurd youthful pride and a coronation that, all things considered, had brought him nothing but envy and hostility.[13]

Before this late show of remorse, Petrarch had made use of all his connections, which explains how two riders appeared in rapid succession at his door in the Vaucluse, or 'closed valley', on one fine morning in September 1340. At least that's how he tells it. One now understands that the reality must have been a little different: here lies the solution to the mystery of the two messengers. It's most likely that by dint of relentless pressure the poet initially received an invitation from the Sorbonne. He was undoubtedly dismayed, for he considered this university a last recourse. He therefore had to postpone his reply until the arrival – how many days later? – of a messenger from Rome. After that, it was simply a question of appearances and presentation. In keeping with his wildest dreams, the imperial and paschal coronation would finally be able to take place: a new age would begin – not golden, but green like laurel. Humanism would take its first steps and poetry would reign on earth. The year 1341 marked the beginning of a Petrarchian era that would encompass many centuries, stretching at least until the Renaissance and Romantic period, as well as the first signs of the triumph of literature. Forging such a powerful symbol and conceiving and orchestrating such a grandiose project by turning the hierarchy of the world and words upside down was certainly worth a branch from the tree of Delphi, even had Petrarch not yet written a word: to be anointed the prince of scholars, all he needed was to have read – a lot – and to believe in the power of language.

XXII

The Island

The scholar only appears to belong to the world – his domain is elsewhere; it is an island or a mountain. In fact, one can easily be turned into the other, and the metamorphosis does not cause insurmountable difficulties: the most important thing is that it should be a retreat.

On the day of his coronation, Petrarch quoted Virgil when he proclaimed, 'But a sweet longing urges me upward over the lonely slopes of Parnassus.'[1] Every scholar has his own Parnassus and his own Arcadia, both an unassailable refuge and a passage to a parallel order of reality, an open door to another world no less real than the first one: that of texts and books, Muses and teachers. A unique yet interchangeable destination, named Mont Ventoux, Milan, Venice, or Arquà, near Padua, to name only the poet's successive residences.[2] For what matters isn't the mountain, which is only the visible sign of an inner Arcadia, it's the book collection. In Petrarch's case, it was immense – he was the owner of the largest private library of his time.[3]

For lack of a mountain, the ordinary scholar will make do with a library: a stack of books is a Parnassus unto itself. If you have the means, the best thing is to put it on the third floor of a tower, following the model of Michel de Montaigne, whose ground floor was occupied by a chapel, and the second floor by 'a bedroom and dressing room', where the master of the house often slept 'in order to be alone'.[4] From his third-floor library, he commanded a view of the entire household, which was itself 'perched on a little hill, as its name indicates':[5] Montaigne, in other words, 'mountain'. A real Parnassus, even in the Bordeaux region.

As for an island, even one without water, the same author wrote:

> The shape of my library is round, the only flat side being the part needed by my table and chair; and curving round me it presents at a glance all my books, arranged in five rows of shelves on all sides. It offers rich and free views in three directions, and sixteen paces of free space in diameter.

As a perfect disk floating on the universe and an ideal viewpoint on reality and knowledge, with its three windows and five rows of shelves running along the walls, Montaigne's library seems like a utopia. Some 150 years later, Jonathan Swift would also imagine that scholars could live nowhere else but on a circular flying island: the traveller Gulliver's description of this island is very precise, but not devoid of irony directed at its inhabitants, who were more concerned with calculating a comet's trajectory than dealing with everyday business.[6] In this case, however, the target is the sciences rather than letters.

Despite appearances, Montaigne's library in a tower is barely less chimeric than the island of Laputa. 'In my library I spend most of the days of my life, and most of the hours of the day', Montaigne claimed, but it's hard to really believe him, knowing that his many domestic and political occupations clearly took up most of his time.[7] This self-portrait of the scholar able to devote his entire existence to study, without paying any attention to his other obligations, is a chimera, but a necessary one, inextricably linked with the scholar's status. The library presents itself as an ideal space, distinct from daily realities:

> There is my throne. I try to make my authority over it absolute, and to withdraw this one corner from all society, conjugal, filial, and civil. Everywhere else I have only a verbal authority, essentially divided.

Subject to all of life's vicissitudes, the scholar is in fact only an absolute master in his own kingdom. He has planted his flag on the island of books – whether surrounded by water, air, or walls – to exercise his sovereign freedom. This is the portrait of himself Montaigne wanted to leave for posterity, even if it doesn't exactly correspond with reality: that of a scholar up all day and night, always at the ready in the heart of his library.

This position also corresponds with his book's initial project, which consisted in commenting on other books: a book written in the midst of the other books he places at its centre.[8] Even the praise of perceptible and singular experience with which the *Essays* closes is never separable from the practice of citation, however erudite. To the non-scholar, this is a paradox, but to the scholar, it's evident: to him, the texts are not only a world in and of itself, liable to be explored, but the very things that have over time shaped his own way of understanding the real, so much so that the empirical world finishes by revealing itself to him through the obligatory intervention of books. Hence the figure of the island, tower, or mountain: both protected and with a 360-degree view, as blind as it is panoptic.

A real tower isn't even required: in Weimar, Goethe was content with putting his library in an isolated room of his house;[9]

books are adequate ramparts, as well as windows.

Inspired to imitate his library, the scholar chases the secret dream of composing a book that would be both an island and the world: an island because it focuses on a specific point of knowledge; a world through the infinite set of notes, allusions, and citations weaving a dense web that encompasses the totality of knowledge. All of culture would be refracted there.

Less than two decades after Montaigne's death, Shakespeare would use his final play to stage the scholar's omnipotence and ideal omniscience. Here the island was real (as much as a theatre will allow): after being expelled from Milan by his usurper of a brother, Prospero has landed on the island with his daughter Miranda twelve years before the action starts. Yet the island is equally metaphorical. Even when still in power, Prospero had left its implementation to his brother Antonio in order to fully devote himself to the 'liberal arts' and the 'secret studies'.[10] 'My library was dukedom enough',[11] he initially explains, before confessing a little later that he even prizes it above his own dukedom.[12] So long as the duke remains surrounded by his most precious texts, the difference between taking refuge among the books in his palace or being exiled to the land of Caliban is slim. Whether in Milan or in the middle of the sea, it's always an island.

Since the noble Gonzalo had allowed the deposed ruler to take a few of his most precious volumes into exile, Prospero's island proves to be a library, in the same way that Montaigne's library could be seen as an island; both men behave here like absolute rulers, and both find their power in books. Caliban is well aware of this. Plotting against his master, he recommends first and foremost to take possession of his books and burn them, 'for without them, he's but a sot.'[13] In fact, books are the reason Prospero is able to know everything that happens on land and in the sky. At the end of the play, it is also a book (of magic) that he promises to destroy as he abandons the island: he will drown it 'deeper than did ever plummet sound.'[14] The identity between island and library could not be more clearly expressed: you can't abandon one without the other.[15]

Now consider this borderline and desperate case: a single book can serve as an island – or a life preserver. In circumstances infinitely less fictional and otherwise more tragic than Shakespeare's play, another scholar, chased out of Germany by the Nazis, found himself forced to gradually give up the thousands of books that made up his library. In the end, the process of profligacy was so advanced that there remained only one volume, the memoirs of the Cardinal de Retz. 'Thus, alone in my room, I call on the "Grand Siècle"',[16] wrote Walter Benjamin in a letter of 19 July 1940, a testament to this last joy of reading, the final fragment of the lost island before the reef to which he clung also disappeared in the storm. Benjamin also managed to get his hands on *The Red and the Black* and the last volume of *Les Thibault*, which accompanied him in his flight.[17] But it was too late: when Benjamin took his own life a few weeks later, the island had sunk for all time, and Caliban had triumphed. Prosperos are more likely to survive on the stage.

XXIII

The Night

Night doesn't descend on everyone in the same way. The owl takes flight at dusk. Scholars are night people – and have always been considered as such, even before efficient, comfortable artificial lighting was invented, as if there were essential affinities between studying and nocturnal life.

One affinity has to do with solitude. In the first century AD, Quintilian was categorical: he advised orators to work at night rather than retire to the countryside or woods. Indeed, rustic landscapes exert an excessive power of seduction. As Quintilian put it: 'the charm of the woods, the gliding of the stream, the breeze that murmurs in the branches, the song of birds, and the very freedom with which our eyes may range, everything attracts us, and in my opinion the pleasure which they excite is more likely to relax than to concentrate our mind.'[1] On the contrary, Quintilian continued, you should follow Demosthenes's model and lock yourself up in a place where nothing can distract your attention:

> Therefore, let those of us who burn the midnight oil (*lucubrantes*) seclude ourselves in the silence of night, within closed doors, with nothing but a solitary lamp to shelter us.[2]

By putting all the senses to sleep, night allows thought to reach the necessary magnitude. Every space goes dark, with the exception of texts and books. This great adventure requires unfailing health, 'for we have fallen into the habit of devoting to relentless labour the hour which nature has appointed for rest and relaxation.'[3] You therefore should not undertake such an endeavour unless you have absolutely no other choice: to write, 'the hours of daylight are amply sufficient for one who has spare time; only the busy man is driven to encroach on the hours of darkness.'[4] Quintilian insists on this point by providing dietary advice: sobriety and frugality above all. A few years earlier, the doctor Celsus had offered scholars similar advice: 'if one must study by lamplight (*lucubrandum*), it should not be immediately after taking food, but after digestion.'[5] One cannot commit lightly to a nocturnal exploration: there is a dietetics of study.

Celsus and Quintilian use the same verb in their respective texts: *lucubrare*, translated in the Loeb Quintilian as 'burning the midnight oil' and in the Loeb Celsus, more precisely, as 'working by lamplight'. If one were to risk a neologism, one might even suggest 'lamping'. The noun *lucubration* is also used: when Quintilian declares that 'night work, so long as we come to it fresh and untired, provides by far the best form of privacy (*secreti*)',[6] you have to imagine the light of the lamp shining in the darkness behind the expression 'night work' (*lucubratio*). The scholar's night is defined first by this lamp, which manifestly carries a mythological dimension.

Gaston Bachelard devoted an entire book to the flame of a candle, an object of endless reverie for anyone who has ever worked by candlelight. 'The candle, companion of solitude, is above all the companion of solitary work', writes the philosopher:

> The candle doesn't illuminate an empty room, it illuminates a book.
>
> Alone at night, with a book illuminated by a candle – book and candle, double island of light against the double darkness of the night and of the mind.[7]

The flame of the candle delimits a space, an island lost in the night, a mountain described by the cone of the lamp, in which the scholar takes shelter: to inhabit the light that shines in the darkness is his vocation or, as Bachelard puts it, the 'primordial engraving'.[8]

But the flame is itself a mystery. Scientists long struggled with the problem of its existence:

> The system of the world was studied in large books, and now a simple flame – oh mockery of erudition! – insists upon its own enigma.[9]

What is a flame, after all? How is it born? What fuels it and how does it die? For many millennia, the mystery remained complete, obscurity in the very heart of darkness.

Perhaps this is the second affinity between study and night. Night leads us into another organisation of existence, where nothing is ever given in advance, where certainties are as unsteady as a flame, where shadows only retreat to settle further away, and where light itself is an enigma. In the night, another time takes hold, in which suddenly the ancient masters become the reader's contemporaries. There is some magic at work here: Between *grammar* and *grimoire*, the relationship is more than etymological. Every text is a grimoire for the scholar: it always demands tremendous effort to be mastered, because its meaning must be pieced together; it is always liable to contain a lost knowledge and create enchantment, just as it is always on the verge of remaining incomprehensible. The scholar isn't defined by the fact that he knows, but that he *wants* to know, and that if necessary he will achieve that knowledge by sacrificing what time he has to sleep. Quintilian literally said as much: the luminous night (*lucubratio*) is the scholar's secret (*secretum*).

XXIV

Death

On 25 February 1980, at approximately 3:45 p.m., a scholar was about to step onto the crosswalk facing 44, rue des Écoles, Paris. Having carefully looked to the left, then to the right, he set foot on the road, where a double-parked car was blocking the view. Suddenly a Sedaine laundry van emerged and knocked the scholar down. He was transported unconscious to the Salpêtrière hospital. He would remain there for a month.

At first, his state was not considered worrisome. His friends came to visit him. He chatted with them. Little by little, however, his old respiratory problems resurfaced (he had spent extended periods in sanatoria when he was young). He was intubated, then given a tracheotomy. Then he caught a nosocomial disease. It killed him on 26 March, at 1:40 p.m.[1] This was the end of Roland Barthes, holder of the Chair in Literary Semiology at the Collège de France.

Traffic accident, hospitalisation, surgical interventions: the death of the scholar bears little distinction from the ordinary mortal's. With rare exceptions (war or political turmoil), it features no fields of honour or executions. Nothing but banal, piddling, pitiful stuff. One can die a soldier's death, but one cannot die a scholar's death, other perhaps than by collapsing on one's desk, in the middle of a library, surrounded by open folio volumes.

If the scholar's life is essentially double, if it confers a biological level of presence to the immaterial signs of culture, how could his death not also be endowed with this double nature? How could this death not resonate with the studies that structured his life?

A passer of texts he brings back to life from the void, a conductor of souls – and first of his own – through the infinite cemeteries of culture, familiar with the dead more than the living, the scholar is the perfect infernal ferryman, or Hermes as psychopomp. He is a ferryman, however, who retraces Charon's steps in the opposite direction: not from memory to oblivion, as generously offered by the waters of the Lethe, but from oblivion to memory, from ignorance to knowledge, as it is drawn from texts.

The resuscitator's trade demands a particular awareness of death and its sadness: standing before Lazarus's tomb, Christ begins by crying.[2] Knowledge, the body, death: the three terms are more closely connected than one generally thinks. Barthes illustrated this triple dependence through a melancholy anecdote:

> as a student, the only teacher I loved and admired was the Hellenist Paul Mazon; when he died I never stopped regretting that so much knowledge of the Greek language would vanish with him, that another body should have to begin again the interminable trajectory of grammar, starting from the conjugation of *deiknumi*.

Barthes adds: 'Knowledge, like delight, dies with each body.'[3] Paradoxically, Barthes's observation seems akin to the famous statement by Amadou Hampâté Bâ at UNESCO: 'In Africa, when an old man dies, it is a library burning.'⁴ Here, Bâ was characterising the fragility of an essentially oral culture, as opposed to the written civilisations: the fragility of a world in which the individual is the custodian of a knowledge not contained in books.

The situation of the Western scholar is to all appearances completely different: Why lament his disappearance, as Barthes does, when his writings and library survive him? Bâ's old Sufi teacher Tierno Bokar answers the question in terms similar to those Plato might have used – which is no surprise, given that both thinkers belonged to a culture transitioning from the oral to the written: 'Writing is one thing and knowledge is another thing. Writing is a photograph of knowledge, but it is not knowledge itself. Knowledge is a light which is in man.'⁵

From this perspective, the distinction between oral and written civilisations recedes. However erudite it may be, even if it draws on an entire library, no knowledge exists outside of its actualisation in a human being; it is inseparable from a truly existential dimension. The scholar provides it with this embodiment at the price of constant labour against death and oblivion. This is what Paul Mazon's death revealed to Roland Barthes. Confucius said, 'Study as though you could never catch up, [and if you did,] you would still be fearful of losing it.'⁶

To ward off this vital threat, Barthes put his hopes in the seminar, conceived as a kind of insurance against the teacher's death. This regular gathering of students, colleagues, and friends allowed for the risks of loss to be pooled through a collectivisation of knowledge.⁷ One can say the undertaking was a success, given that more than thirty years after Barthes's death, his students continue to keep his thought alive and productive. The same approach was adopted by Confucius, whose disciples spread his teachings over the centuries and millennia.

Yet the moment of one's own death must necessarily arrive. Its approach becomes perceptible. The Chinese master had prophetic dreams: 'Mount Tai crumbles, the great beam breaks, the wise man withers away', he sang.[8] Barely less lyrical, Barthes also adopted the position of the wise man: more than ever, the knowledge he offered merged with his own existence. This was borne out in the last two years of his lecture courses at the Collège de France, which were deliberately anchored in a personal experience. The theme was 'The Preparation of the Novel'. As Barthes explained, it was not so much a question 'of collecting information on the techniques different novelists of the past used to prepare their novels',[9] but of personally experiencing the maturation and writing of a novel to share it with the course's audience. With this attempt to have the time of study coincide with that of life, the project takes on an eminently postmodern appearance. It blurs epistemological boundaries, by confirming the disappearance of metalanguage:[10] the critic and the writer are indissolubly combined.

But there is also something profoundly *premodern* about this undertaking. It recalls the early stages of written civilisations, when they were still hesitating between the written and the oral, and weren't clearly distinguishing between the moment of experience and that of knowledge, the lived and the thought. At the end of his life, Barthes rediscovered this constant of scholarly life since its beginnings: knowledge transforms man, and this transformation is the very condition for any real knowledge, no less than its test.

The end of the scholar, the end of his body, truly is the end of a knowledge. Hence the melancholy that comes over him in his final moments: Confucius complains that 'the world has long strayed from the true way';[11] Barthes notes the 'signs of desuetude' of a literature 'perhaps *in the process of dying*'.¹² He gradually lets himself be overcome by an acute sense of loss: Derrida was right to emphasise the omnipresence of death in his last texts.¹³

Something dies with the scholar, there is no denying it. But something also lives on: a teaching, disciples, texts, books. These immaterial excrescences of the scholar's body are all chances for immortality. 'It is beautiful, after death, to still live' (*È bello doppo il morire vivere anchora*).¹⁴ This was the motto of the Milanese humanist Bernardino Corio in the late fifteenth century. It could be any scholar's.

Take Barthes: in the final sessions of his last lecture course, he studied the concrete details of a writer's life, his home, illnesses, and schedule, thus resuscitating the embodied dimension of any enterprise in writing.¹⁵ In parallel, he was planning to write a piece on 'the art of living', in which he would combine reflections on 'the pleasures of studying and reading, of the relationship to food, to space, to travel, to friends'.¹⁶ 'Life as work',¹⁷ Barthes noted for his lecture: to his mind, this concerned the life of the novelist above all, but it is likely he hadn't given up on applying this description to himself – not mistakenly, for it is indeed an accurate definition of a scholar's life.

It could also be the title of this book, which looks at the material aspects of a scholarly existence, like his lecture course on 'the preparation of the novel' aimed to do for the writer. Perhaps the coincidence is not vain. A project pursued by Roland Barthes modestly inspires another one, a few decades later; a virtual work circulates from one generation to the next; a fragment of knowledge is reborn despite the passage of time: here is the proof, humble but tangible, that despite appearances, death is not the final chapter of a scholar's life.

A page is turned: the book is closed and put away; little by little, the library lights go out; darkness descends. Tomorrow, other readers will come.

Notes

1. Roland Barthes, *The Preparation of the Novel: Lecture courses and seminars at the Collège de France 1978–1979 and 1979–1980*, translated by Kate Briggs, text established, annotated, and introduced by Nathalie Léger (New York: Columbia University Press, 2011), 17. The translation has been slightly amended for the purposes of this epigraph.
2. Roland Barthes, *How to Live Together: Novelistic Simulations of Some Everyday Spaces. Notes for a lecture course and seminar at the Collège de France (1976–1977)*, translated by Kate Briggs, text established, annotated, and introduced by Claude Coste (New York: Columbia University Press, 2013), 4.

Preamble

1. Giacomo Leopardi, *Zibaldone*, revised version, edited by Michael Caesar and Franco D'Intino, translated by Kathleen Baldwin, Richard Dixon, David Gibbons, Ann Goldstein, Gerard Slowery, Martin Thom, and Pamela Williams. (New York: Farrar, Straus and Giroux, 2015), 1037. Pagination of the handwritten manuscript: 2453 (30 May 1822).

I. Birth

1. See Sima Qian, *Selections from Records of the Historian*, translated by Yang Hsien-yi and Gladys Yang (Peking: Foreign Language Press, 1979), 1.
2. Plutarch, *Cicero*, in *Lives*, vol. VII, English translation by Bernadette Perrin (Cambridge, MA: Loeb Classical Library, Harvard University Press, 1917), 84/85 (II, 1–861 c): 'anôdunôs kai aponôs.'
3. *The Analects of Confucius*, translated by Burton Watson (New York: Columbia University Press, 2007), 10 (2.4).
4. See Nehemiah, ch. 8, *The Bible: King James Version with Apocrypha* (New York:

Penguin, 2006), 606-607. Recounted in the Book of Ezra (ch. 7-10), Ezra's arrival in Jerusalem took place in the seventh year of Artaxerxes's reign, that is to say in 458 BC, if the chronicler who wrote books I and II of the Chronicles and the books of Ezra and Nehemiah is referring to Artaxerxes I. The text is ambiguous: if it is Artaxerxes II who is referred to, then Ezra's arrival took place in 398 BC. In a Jewish tradition subsequent to the canonical texts, the scribe Ezra becomes a prophet subject to apocalyptic visions who under divine inspiration is able to reconstruct the burned text of the Scriptures by dictating it to five secretaries over forty days (see the Second Book of Ezra in *The Bible: King James Version with Apocrypha*, 1281-1314). Christian tradition would bring back the figure of the prophet Esdras/Ezra in several apocryphal texts; see *Vision of Ezra*, introduced and translated by J. R. Mueller and G. A. Robbins in *The Old Testament Pseudepigrapha*, vol. 1, ed. James H. Charlesworth (Garden City, NY: Doubleday & Company, 1985), 581-590.

5. Literally, 'leisure with dignity'. See Cicero, *Pro Sestio* (Cambridge, MA: Loeb Classical Library, Harvard University Press, 1984), 168 (XLV-98); *The Letters to his Friends*, vol. I, translated by W. Glynn Williams (Cambridge, MA: Loeb Classical Library, Harvard University Press, 1958), 80/81 (*Ad familiar*, I, 9, 21).

6. See, for example, *The Analects*, 23 and 28 (2.23 and 3.14).

7. Sima Qian, *Selections from Records of the Historian*, 1.

8. Cicero, *Laws* in *The Republic and The Laws*, translated by Niall Rudd (Oxford: Oxford University Press, 1998), 98 (1. I, 1-5).

II. The Body

1. Ernst H. Kantorowicz, *The King's Two Bodies: A Study in Medieval Political Theology* (Princeton, NJ: Princeton University Press, 1997), 7-9.

2. *Selections from Records of the Historian*, 2. Translator's note: The height given in the English translation is 'well over six feet'. The height has been altered here to match the French translation cited by the author.

3. The entrance halls at the foot of the towers have 88-foot ceilings, the reading rooms 39-foot ceilings. See the plans by Dominique Perrault, *Bibliothèque nationale de France, 1989-1995* (Basel: Birkhäuser, 1995), 130-143.

4. Celsus, *De medicina*, English translation by W. G. Spencer (Cambridge, MA: Loeb Classical Library, Harvard University Press, 1971), 44/45 (1. I, 2, 1).

5. Giacomo Leopardi, letter to Pietro Giordani, 2 March 1818, in *Lettere* (Milan: Mondadori, 2006), 128: '[...] io mi sono rovinato con sette anni di studio matto e disperatissimo in quel tempo che mi s'andava formando e mi si doveva assodare la complessione. E mi sono rovinato infelicemente e senza rimedio per tutta la vita, e rendutomi l'aspetto miserabile, e dispregevolissima tutta

quella gran parte dell'uomo, che è la sola a cui guardino i più [...].' English translation in Giacomo Leopardi, *Essays, Dialogues and Thoughts*, translated by James V. Thomson (London: George Routledge & Sons, 1905), 11–12.

6. Giacomo Leopardi, *Zibaldone*, vol. I (Milan: Mondadori, 1997), 2453. Pagination of the handwritten manuscript (30 May 1822): 'Ed è cosa già osservata che il vigor del corpo nuoce alle facoltà intellettuali, e favorisce le immaginative, e per lo contrario l'imbecillità del corpo è favorevolissima al riflettere [...].' English translation from *Zibaldone*, 101–102.

7. Ibid., 1597–1598 (31 August – 1 September 1821): '[...] la debolezza corporale giova, e il vigore nuoce all'esercizio e allo sviluppo delle facoltà mentali massime appartenenti alla ragione. E viceversa l'esercizio e lo sviluppo di queste facoltà nuoce estremamente al vigore e al ben essere del corpo. Onde Celso fa derivare l'indebolimento degli uomini e le malattie dagli studi, e ciascun pensatore o studioso ne fa l'esperienza in se, quanto al deterioramento individuale del suo sorpo.' English translation from *Zibaldone*, revised edition, 738.

8. Ibid., vol. II, 2702 (20 May 1823). 'Lo studio è cosa faticosissima.' English translation from *Zibaldone*, 1124.

9. Ibid., vol. I, 1610 (2 September 1821). '[...] i gobbi hanno molto spirito.' English translation from *Zibaldone*, 743.

10. Ibid., 207–208 (11 August 1820); 233 (8 September 1820); 1599–1602 (31 August – 1 September 1821). English translation from *Zibaldone*, revised edition, 152–153; 165; 739–740.

11. See Jorge Luis Borges, 'An Autobiographical Essay', in *The Aleph and Other Stories 1933–1969*, edited and translated by Norman Thomas di Giovanni in collaboration with the author (New York: E.P. Dutton, 1978), 250.

12. J. L. Borges, 'Poema de los dones' (1959) in *El hacedor*, collected in *Obras completas, vol. II: 1952–1972* (Barcelona: Emecé, 1989), 187: 'De hambre y de sed (narra une historia griega) / Muere un rey entre fuentes y jardines ; / Yo fatigo sin rumbo los confines / De esa alta y honda biblioteca ciega.' English translation by Alastair Reid as 'Poem of the Gifts' in Borges, *Selected Poems* (New York: Viking, 1999), 95.

III. Gender

1. Virginia Woolf, *A Room of One's Own* (1929) (Oxford: Oxford University Press, 1992), 60–62.

2. Ibid., 9.

3. Émilie du Châtelet, *Les Lettres de la marquise du Châtelet*, vol. II (Geneva: Institut et Musée Voltaire, 1958), 294 (letter to Jean-François de Saint-Lambert,

around 15 June 1749); cited by Robert Mauzi in his edition of *Discours sur le bonheur* (Paris: Les Belles lettres, 1961), 54-55.

4. See Cicero, *Pro Archia Poeta* (The Speech on Behalf of Archias the Poet) in *The Speeches of Cicero*, English translation by N. H. Watts (Cambridge, MA: Loeb Classical Library, Harvard University Press, 1965), 19-25 (§ 12-16), as well as *Tusculan Disputations*, English translation by J.E. King (Cambridge, MA: Loeb Classical Library, Harvard University Press, 1966), 2-5 (1.I, § 1-8) and 494-501 (1.V, § 68-72).

5. The quotes from Madame du Châtelet are taken from her *Discours sur le bonheur* (Paris: Payot & Rivages, 1997), 52-55.

6. Sei Shōnagon describes this event at the end of her *Pillow Book*; see *The Pillow Book*, translated by Meredith McKinney (London: Penguin Books, 2006), 256.

IV. Schedule

1. This is the traditional Latin translation of Hippocrates's first aphorism [*Works*] vol. IV (Cambridge, MA: Loeb Classical Library, Harvard University Press, 1992) (*Aphorismoi* [Aphorisms]), I, 1): 'Ho bios brakhus, hê de tekhnê makrê [...].'

2. Jules Barthélémy-Saint-Hilaire, *M. Victor Cousin, sa vie et sa correspondance* (Paris: Hachette, 1895), vol. II, 510-513.

3. See Ehrgott Andreas Christoph Wasianski, *Immanuel Kant in seinen letzen Lebensjahren. Ein Beitrag zur Kenntnis seines Charakters und häuslichen Lebens aus dem täglichen Umgange mit ihm* in Ludwig Ernest Borowski et al., *Wer war Kant?* (n.l.: Neske, 1974), 225: 'kann ein Mensch gesunder sein, als ich?'

4. See Theodor Gottlieb von Hippel, *Der Mann nach der Uhr, oder der ordentliche Mann. Ein Lustspiel in einem Auzuge* (1766) in *Sämmtliche Werke*, vol. 10: *Kleinere Schriften* (Berlin: Reimer, 1828), 371-416. French translation, *L'Homme à la minute, comédie en un acte* in Adrien Chrétien Friedel, ed., *Nouveau théâtre allemand*, vol. IV (Paris, 1782), 255-328.

5. François Rabelais, *Gargantua* (1535), ch. XXIII in *Œuvres complètes* (Paris: Gallimard, 1994), 65. English translation by M. A. Screech in *Gargantua and Pantagruel* (London: Penguin Books, 2006), 279.

6. Pierre de Ronsard, *Discours des misères de ce temps* in *Œuvres complètes*, vol. II (Paris: Gallimard, 1994), 1055-1057. ('Response de Pierre de Ronsard aux injures et calomnies de je ne sçay quels predicantereaux et ministreaux de Genève', 1563, v. 477-552). See Yvonne Bellanger, *Le Jour dans la poésie française au temps de la Renaissance* (Tübingen: Gunter Narr, 1978), 77-78.

V. Education

1. See Nicola Spinosa, *Ribera* (Naples: Electa Napoli, 2003), 244.
2. In the catalogue used by Spinosa, the *Diogenes* is numbered A177 (a fine reproduction can be found in Alfonso E. Pérez Sánchez and N. Spinosa, *Jusepe de Ribera 1591–1652* {New York: Metropolitan Museum of Art, 1992}, 122), the *Astronomer* A209 (reproduction in Fernando Benito Doménech, *Ribera 1591–1652* {Valencia: Bancaja, 1991}, 129), *Isaac and Jacob* A170 (reproduced on 126–127). In a far more hypothetical manner, one could recognise the same model, but without a beard, in the *Philosopher* (1631) in the collections of the University of Arizona Museum of Art in Tucson (A72; reproduced in F. B. Doménech, 70) and, with white hair, in the *Saint Philip* (A85) at the Prado and the *Beggar* (A236) in the collection of the Count of Derby at Knowsley Hall, dated 1640. Additionally, independently of the question of the model, the lighting of the Tucson *Philosopher* is similar to that of the canvas in Bordeaux: only the head and hands are illuminated. There is also a copy of a lost Ribera painting representing a *Philosopher with a Mirror* (B15).
3. I noticed this plate when I visited the museum in April 2007.
4. René Descartes, *Discours de la méthode* (1637), I, in *Œuvres et Lettres* (Paris: Gallimard, Bibliothèque de la Pléiade, 1953), 131. English translation by F. E. Sutcliffe in *Discourse on Method and the Meditations* (London: Penguin Books, 1968), 33.
5. Ibid., 134 (*Discours II*). English translation, *Discourse on Method*, 37 (*Discourse 2*).
6. Jean Baudoin, *Iconologie* (Paris: Mathieu Guillemot, 1644), II, 194 (s. v. 'Desir d'apprendre').
7. See Guy de Tervarent, *Attributs et Symboles dans l'art profane* (Geneva: Droz, 1997), 298; *ill.* 26.
8. Cesare Ripa, *Iconologia* (1593) (Rome: 1603), 444–445 (s. v. 'Scienza').
9. Ibid., 499 (s. v. 'Verità'): 'Il libro aperto, accenna, che ne i libri si suona la verità delle cose, & per ciò è lo studio delle scienze.'
10. Ibid., 501 (s. v. 'Verità'): 'Et lo specchio insegna, che la verità allora, è in sua perfettione, quando, come si è detto, l'intelletto si conferma con le cose intelligibili, come lo specchio è buono quando rende la vera forma della cosa, che vi risplende [...].' The passage's context (there is a reference above to 'the conformity [*conformità*] of the intellect with intelligible things') forces one to read *si conferma* as *si conforma*.
11. Ibid., 18 (s. v. 'Ammaestramento'): 'Huomo d'aspetto magnifico, & venerabile, con habito longo, e ripieno di magnanima grauità, con vno specchio in

mano, intorno al quale sarà vna cartella con queste parole. INSPICE, CAVTVS ERIS.'

12. Ibid., 18 (s. v. 'Ammaestramento'): 'lo specchio ci da intendere, che ogni nostra attione deue esser calcolata, & compassata con l'attioni de gl'altri.'

13. Jean Baudoin, *Iconologie*, II, 129 (s.v. 'Instruction').

14. C. Ripa, *Iconologia*, 445 (s. v. 'Scienza'): 'senza libri solo con la voce del Maestro difficilmente si può capire, & ritenere gran copia di cose, che partoriscono la cognitione, & la scienza in noi stessi.'

VI. The Examination

1. Robert Borgen, *Sugawara no Michizane and the Early Heian Court* (Cambridge: Harvard University Press, 1986), 107.

2. Ibid., 111.

VII. The Study

1. For a photograph and a description of this object, see Eric Gubel, ed., *Le Sphinx de Vienne* (Brussels: Ludion, 1993), 168-169.

2. See *Le Jardin du lettré* (Boulogne-Billancourt: Musée Albert-Kahn, 2004), 264-271.

3. See ibid., 226-229; David Holzman, 'Les Sept sages de la forêt des bambous et la société de leur temps', *T'oung Pao*, vol. XLIV, 1956, 328-346; Audrey Spiro, *Contemplating the Ancients* (Berkeley: University of California Press, 1990), 44-64 and passim.

4. Cicero, *Tusculanes*, v, 105: 'scholarly leisure'.

5. Edmund Engelman, *Berggasse 19: Sigmund Freud's Home and Offices, Vienna 1938* (New York: Basic Books, 1976), plates 24, 27, 28, 35 and passim.

6. Sigmund Freud, *Briefe an Wilhelm Fliess, 1887-1904* (Frankfurt: Fischer, 1986), 399 (letter dated 1 August 1899): 'Meine von Dir so wenig anerkannten alten und dreckigen Götter beteiligen sich als Manuskriptbeschwerer an der Arbeit.' Quoted by Lydia Marinelli in L. Marinelli, ed., *'Meine... alten und dreckigen Götter'* (Frankfurt: Stroemfeld, 1998), 11.

7. S. Freud, letter to Stefan Zweig dated 17 February 1931, in S. Zweig, *Briefwechsel mit Hermann Bahr, Sigmund Freud, Rainer Maria Rilke und Arthur Schnitzler* (Frankfurt: Fischer, 1987), 192: '[...] daß ich bei aller gerühmten Anspruchslosigkeit viel Opfer für meine Sammlung griechischer, römischer und egyptischer Antiquitäten gebracht und eigentlich mehr Archeologie als Psychologie gelesen habe [...].'

8. On the history and composition of this collection, see the studies by Peter

Gay, Wendy Botting and J. Keith Davies, notably in Lynn Gamwell & Richard Wells, eds., *Sigmund Freud and Art* (London: Thames and Hudson, 1989), 15-16, 184-185 and passim, as well as Joachim Sliwa, *Egyptian Scarabs and Seal Amulets from the Collection of Sigmund Freud* (Krakow: Polska Akademia Umiejetnosci, 1999).

9. Edmund Engelman, *Berggasse 19*, 138.

10. Ibid.

11. Aside from the works cited earlier, on this subject see Stephen Barker, ed., *Excavations and Their Objects* (Albany: State University of New York Press, 1996); Janine Burke, *The Sphinx on the Table* (New York: Walker, 2006).

12. In particular, one thinks of Antonello da Messina's *Saint Jerome*, on view at the National Gallery in London, and of the Saint Augustine painted by Vittorio Carpaccio in the Venetian Scuola di San Giorgio degli Schiavoni (on this fresco, see the chapter below, 'The Animal'). Petrarch was the first scholar to be represented in his study. See Wolfgang Liebenwein, *Studiolo* (Modena: Panini, 1988), 39-40; Dora Thornton, *The Scholar in His Study* (New Haven: Yale University Press, 1997); Jean Clair, 'La mélancolie du savoir', in J. Clair, *La Mélancolie* (Paris: Gallimard, 2005), 204.

13. Gilles Corrozet, 'Le blason de l'estude', in *Les blasons domestiques*, Paris, 1539, f. 33-35 v°; cited by D. Thornton, *The Scholar in His Study*, 178-179.

14. S. Freud, *Gesammelte Werke*, vol. X, (Frankfurt: Fischer, 1973), 430-431 ('Trauer und Melancholie [Mourning and Melancholia]', 1915): 'einen dem Bewußtsein entzogenen Objektverlust [...], zum Unterschied von der Trauer, bei welcher nichts an dem Verluste unbewußt ist.' Translated under the general editorship of James Strachey in collaboration with Anna Freud, in *The Standard Edition of the Complete Psychological Works*, vol. XIV (London: The Hogarth Press and The Institute of Psycho-Analysis, 1957), 245. On the ambiguous place of reflection on melancholia in Freud, see Alexandra Triandafillidis, *La Dépression et son inquiétante familiarité* (Paris: Éditions universitaires, 1991).

15. This distress is not without positive qualities, as emphasised by Anne Larue, *L'Autre Mélancolie* (Paris: Hermann, 2001), 114-121.

VIII. Economy

1. Juvenal, *The Sixteen Satires*, 3rd edition, translated by Peter Green (London: Penguin Books, 1998), 110 (VII, 65-71): 'Magnæ mentis opus nec de lodice paranda / attonitæ, currus et equos faciesque deorum / aspicere et qualis Rutulum confudat Erinys. / Nam si Vergilio puer et tolerabile deesset / hospitium, caderent omnes a crinibus hydri, / surda nihil gemeret grave bucina.' See also Virgil, *The Aeneid*, translated by Robert Fagles (New York: Penguin Books, 2006), 227

(VII, 445-447); 230 (511-522).

2. For the contemporary period, see Bernard Lahire's masterful sociological study, *La Condition littéraire* (Paris: La Découverte, 2006).

3. Aristotle, *The Nicomachean Ethics* (Cambridge, MA: Loeb Classical Library, Harvard University Press, 1990), 612 (X, VII, 1, 1177 a 18).

4. Aristotle, *The Metaphysics*, vol. I, English translation by Hugh Tredennik (Cambridge, MA: Loeb Classical Library, Harvard University Press, 1989), 8 (I, I, 981 b 23): 'prôton en toutois tois topois houper eskholasan.'

5. Aristotle, *The Nicomachean Ethics*, 612 (X, VII, 4, 1177 a 28).

6. See the history of this curse in the modern era in Pascal Brissette, *La Malédiction littéraire* (Montreal: Presses de l'Université de Montréal, 2005).

7. Julien Benda, *La Trahison des clercs* (1927) (Paris: Grasset, 1995), 131 *sqq*. English translation by Richard Aldington, *The Treason of the Intellectuals* (New York: W. W. Norton & Company, 1969), 43 *sqq*.

8. See the instructive notes and documents provided by Ch. Urbain and E. Levesque in their edition of Jacques Bénigne Bossuet, *Correspondance* (Paris: Hachette, 1909), vol. I, 253-254, as well as Georges Minois, *Bossuet* (Paris: Perrin, 2003), 212-214.

9. J. B. Bossuet, letter to Maréchal de Bellefonds, 9 September 1672, in *Correspondance*, vol. I, 253.

10. Ibid.

11. Ibid., 254-255.

12. See Ch. Urbain & E. Levesque (eds.), Bossuet, *Correspondance*, 493-494.

13. See G. Minois, *Bossuet*, 230 *sqq*.

IX. The Home

1. The details of the events of 15 June 1889 are drawn from the next day's *Journal officiel de la République française* and the following days' *Journal des débats*.

2. Ernest Renan, *Œuvres complètes* (Paris: Calmann-Lévy, 1948), vol. II, 1010-1011 ('Peut-on travailler en province?', in *Feuilles détachées*).

3. *Grand Dictionnaire universel du XIX*^{e} *siècle* (Paris: Larousse, 1866-1879), vol. XIII, 1385 (art. 'Rose').

4. Maurice Barrès, *Huit jours chez M. Renan* (1886) (Paris: Émile-Paul, 1913).

5. See *Le Livre d'or de Renan* (Paris: Joanin, 1903), 43; Léon Dubreuil, *Rosmapamon* (Paris: Ariane, 1945), 74; Anne-Marie de Brem, *Tréguier et la maison d'Ernest Renan* (Paris: Monum – Éditions du patrimoine, 2004), 39.

6. Martin Heidegger, *Holzwege* (Frankfurt: Klostermann, 1977), 28 ('Der Ursprung des Kunstwerkes', 1936): 'Im Aufgehenden west die Erde als das Bergende.' Translation by Julian Young and Kenneth Haynes, 'The Origin of the Work of Art' in *Off the Beaten Track* (Cambridge and New York: Cambridge University Press, 2002), 21.

X. The Garden

1. See Mark Morford, 'The Stoic Garden', *Journal of Garden History*, vol. VII, no. 2, April-June 1987, 154-155.

2. See Pierre Grimal, *Les Jardins romains* (Paris: Fayard, 1984), 361-362.

3. Cicero, *On the Orator*, English translation by E. W. Sutton (Cambridge, MA: Loeb Classical Library, Harvard University Press, 1967), vol. I, 23 (I, VII-29).

4. Ibid., vol. I, 213 (II, V-21).

5. Ibid., (II, V-22): 'eosque incredibiliter repuerescere esse solitos, quom rus ex urbe tamquam e uinclis euolauissent.'

6. Petrarch, *The Life of Solitude* (*De vita solitaria*, 1346-1366), translated by Jacob Zeitlin (Champaign, IL: University of Illinois Press, 1924), 109-121 (l. I, sect. 2).

7. Ibid., 268-291 (l. II, sect. 7-9).

8. Leon Battista Alberti, *I libri della famiglia* (approx. 1433) (Turin: Giulio Einaudi, 1994), 244 (III): 'La villa sola sopra tutti si truova conoscente, graziosa, fidata, veridica. Se tu la governi con diligenza e con amore, mai a lei parerà averti satisfatto ; sempre agiugne premio a' premii. Alla primavera la villa ti dona infiniti sollazzi, verzure, fiori, odori, canti ; sforzasi in piú modi farti lieto, tutta ti ride e ti promette grandissima ricolta, émpieti di buona speranza e di piaceri assai.' English translation by Renée Neu Watkins, *The Family in Renaissance Florence* (Long Grove, IL: Waveland Press, 1994), vol. III, 61.

9. Desiderius Erasmus, *Opera omnia*, vol. I, 3: *Colloquia* (Amsterdam: North-Holland Publishing Company, 1972), 235 (*Convivium religiosum*): 'Abstine, inquit, sus, non tibi spiro.'

10. Lucretius, *On the Nature of Things* (*De rerum natura*), English translation by W. H. D. Rouse, revised by Martin F. Smith, (Cambridge, MA: Loeb Classical Library, Harvard University Press, 1992), 567 (VI, 973-975); Aulus Gellius, *Attic Nights* (*Noctes Atticae*), English translation by John Rolfe (Cambridge, MA: Loeb Classical Library, Harvard University Press, 1927), vol. I, preface, XXXV.

11. Justus Lipsius, *Opera omnia* (Wesel: André van Hoogenhuysen, 1675), vol. II, 507-508 (*Epistolarum selectarum centuria quinta miscellanea postuma*, 77, to Gaspar van Diemen, 12 November 1605): 'Post libros, duæ sunt avocationes, vel solatia: Hortus, & Canes.' Cited by Jan Papy, 'Lipsius and His Dogs: Humanist

Tradition, Iconography and Rubens's Four Philosophers', *Journal of the Warburg and Courtauld Institutes*, LXII, 1999, 167.

12. See Justus Lipsius, *Opera omnia*, 776-788 (*Epistolarum selectarum centuria prima ad Belgas*, 44).

13. See Justus Lipsius, *Opera omnia*, 112 (*Epistolarum selectarum centuria prima miscellanea*, *91*, *to Charles de l'Écluse*): 'Cariores mihi bulbi illi Tuliparum selectarum, quos ad me mittis, quam si globulos totidem ex auro vel argento. Vulgus non credat? ego de meo animo & ex animo loquor. Grandes tibi gratias habeo: & cùm habeo, debeo: ac debebo semper.' Partially quoted by Mark Morford, 'The Stoic Garden', 167-168.

14. See J. Papy, 'Lipsius and His Dogs: Humanist Tradition, Iconography and Rubens's Four Philosophers', 190-197.

15. Justus Lipsius, *De constantia* (Antwerp: Plantin, 1599), 43 (II, II): 'O gaudii & liquidæ voluptatis vere fons! ô Venerum & Gratiarum sedes! mihi in vestris umbraculis quies & vita sit: mihi fas remoto extra civicos tumultus, inter has herbas, inter hos noti ignotique orbis flores, hilari & hiante oculo oberrare: & modò ad hunc occidentem, modò ad illum exorientem manum vultumque circumferre: & cum vagâ quadam allucinatione, curarum hîc omnium falli & laborum.' Translation from the Tours edition, 1592.

16. Ibid., 45-46 (II, III): 'Itaque vides veteres illos Sapientes? in hortis habitarunt. Eruditas hodie doctasque animas? hortis delectantur, & in iis divina illa pleraque scripta procusa, quæ miramur, & quæ nulla temporum series aut senectus abolebit. Viridi illi Lycæo tot dissertiones de naturâ debemus: umbriferæ Academiæ, & moribus, & ex hortorum spatiis diffusi uberes illi Sapientiæ rivi quos bibimus, & qui fæcundâ diluvie orbem terræ inundarunt. Scilicet attollit se magis erigitque ad alta iste animus, cùm liber & solutus videt suum cælum, quàm cum ædium aut urbium carceribus tenetur inclusus. Hîc mihi vos poëtæ duraturum aliquod carmen pangite, hîc vos litterati meditamini & scribite, hic vos Philosophi de tranquillitate, de constantiâ, de vitâ & morte disputate. En Lipsi, quæ vera hortorum usio & finis, otium inquam, secessio, meditatio, lectio, scriptio: & ea tamen omnia velut per remissionem & per lusum. Ut pictores, longâ intentione hebetatos oculos, ad specula quædam & virores colligunt: sic nos hîc animum defessum, aut aberrantem. Et cur celem te meum institutum? Pergulam illam topiario opere vides? Hæc musarum mihi domus est, hæc sapientiæ meæ gymnasium & palæstra.' Translation from the Tours edition, 1592.

17. Justus Lipsius, *Opera omnia*, vol. II, 143 (*Ep. sel. cent. II misc.*, 15, to Dominique Lampson, 19 June 1587: 'Lipsiani horti lex'): 'K. III. SERMONES etiam ne exléges. / JOCARI licet. / NARRARE licet: / ROGARE licet: / Sed nihil SERIUM. / GRATIARUM hic locus est. / K. IV. Siquid AMOENIUS tamen in STUDIIS; / Inter AMBULANDUM / Dissere, doce, disce. / Et MUSARUM hic locus est.'

Cited by Nathalie Dauvois-Lavialle, 'Juste Lipse et l'esthétique du jardin', in C. Mouchel, ed., *Juste Lipse (1547-1606) en son temps* (Paris: Champion, 1996), 229-230. See Mark Morford, 'The Stoic Garden', 151-154.

XI. The Animal

1. Montaigne, *Essais* (Paris: Presses universitaires de France, 1992), 661 (II, XVII). English translation by Donald M. Frame, *The Complete Essays of Montaigne* (Stanford, CA: Stanford University Press, 1958), 502.

2. The poet was Louis Le Jars. See Michèle Fogel, *Marie de Gournay* (Paris: Fayard, 2004), 27.

3. Gédéon Tallemant des Réaux, *Historiettes* (Paris: Gallimard, 1960), vol. I, 380.

4. Justus Lipsius, letter dated 5 May 1597, in Marie de Gournay, *Œuvres complètes* (Paris: Champion, 2002), vol. II, 1941.

5. The same reservations as above apply to the source of this remark.

6. See Jean-Marc Chatelain, *La Bibliothèque de l'honnête homme* (Paris: Bibliothèque nationale de France, 2003), 13-18.

7. Marie de Gournay, *Œuvres complètes*, vol. I, 565-567.

8. Ibid., vol. I, 1811-1812.

9. Gédéon Tallemant des Réaux, *Historiettes*, vol. I, 380.

10. Maurice Cauchie, 'Nicole Jamin, la suivante de Mlle de Gournay, est-elle fille d'Amadis Jamin?', *Revue des bibliothèques*, 32nd year, no. 10-12, October-December 1922, 289-292.

11. Michel de Marolles, *Suite des Mémoires de Michel de Marolles, abbé de Villeloin* (Paris: Sommaville, 1657), 99.

12. The first scholar to correctly identify the subject of this image was Helen I. Roberts, 'St. Augustine in *St. Jerome's Study*: Carpaccio's Painting and Its Legendary Source', *The Art Bulletin*, vol. XLI, no. 4, December 1959, 283-297. Claudia Cieri Via offers an interesting analysis of this fresco in her preface to Wolfgang Liebenwein, *Studiolo* (Modena: Panini, 1988), XV-XVI.

13. *Hieronymus: vita et transitus*, Venice, 1485, fol. 22. Quoted by Helen I. Roberts, 'St. Augustine in *St. Jerome's Study*', 297.

14. Other examples of scholars' dogs: the engraving that serves as the frontispiece of Bernardino Corio's book, *Patria historia*, Milan, 1503; Lorenzo Lotto's watercolour representing a member of the church in his study, c. 1530, in the collection of the British Museum, London; the portrait of a gentleman attributed to Girolamo da Carpi, c. 1526, in the collection of the Palazzo Barberini, Rome. See the corresponding illustrations in Dora Thornton, *The*

Scholar in His Study (New Haven: Yale University Press, 1997), 7 (*fig.* 7), 38 (*fig.* 24), 141 (*fig.* 87). Regarding the presence of dogs in representations of scholars' studies, see Patrick Reuterswärd, 'The Dog in the Humanist's Study', *Konsthistorisk tidskrift*, vol. L, no. 2, 1981, 53-69.

15. Translator's note: The original French reads 'des grands sphinx allongés au fond des solitudes'. The English translation is by Richard Howard in *Les Fleurs du Mal: The Complete Text of The Flowers of Evil* (Boston: David R. Godine, 1982), 69.

16. See Tommaso Landolfi, 'La petite chatte de Pétrarque' ('La gattina del Petrarca'), in *Sinon la réalité* (*Se non la realtà*, 1960) (Paris: Christian Bourgois, 2006), 53-62.

XII. Sexuality

1. 'Comme un cadavre' [Like a cadaver] (Jesuit motto).

2. François Rabelais, *Gargantua*, ch. LIII, in *Œuvres complètes*, (Paris: Gallimard, 1994), 140. English translation by Burton Raffel, *Gargantua and Pantagruel* (New York: W.W. Norton & Company, 1990), 118.

3. See *Report of the Royal Commission on the Universities of Oxford and Cambridge*, 1874.

4. William Empson, *Seven Types of Ambiguity* (1930) (New York: New Directions, 1966).

5. *College Orders and Memoranda 1907-1946*, 210. Quoted by John Haffenden, *William Empson* (Oxford: Oxford University Press, 2005), vol. I, 242. My account of this episode is entirely based on Haffenden's exceptional biography of Empson, particularly vol. I, 230-273.

6. William Empson, letter to I. A. Richards, quoted by John Haffendfenden, *William Empson*, 250.

7. See Thomas Walter Laqueur, *Solitary Sex* (New York: Zone Books, 2004).

8. John Haffenden, *William Empson*, vol. I, 232-239; vol. II, 376-431.

9. William Empson, 'Letter I', in *Collected Poems* (San Diego: Harcourt Brace Jovanovich, 1956), 19.

XIII. Food

1. *Select Letters of St. Jerome*, English translation by F. A. Wright (Cambridge, MA: Loeb Classical Library, Harvard University Press, 1933), 247 (letter LIV to Furia in 395, 10).

2. Or at least that's what is claimed in the fiction *The Conferences of John Cassian*, translated by Boniface Ramsey (New York: Newman Press, 1997), 291

(VIII, I); cited by René Draguet in *Les Pères du désert* (Paris: Plon, 1949), XLVI. See Roland Barthes, *Comment vivre ensemble* (Paris: Seuil / IMEC, 2002, 144–147). English translation by Kate Briggs, *How to Live Together* (New York: Columbia University Press, 2013), 102–104.

3. See Armand Jean de Rancé, *Réponse au Traité des études monastiques* (Paris: François Muguet, 1692), 54–65 (I, ch. VII: 'Réponse à ce que l'on dit, *que les Études ont esté établies par saint Benoist même dans ses Monasteres ; & à ce que l'on prétend, qu'elles ont esté en usage dans les plus anciens Monasteres, c'est-à-dire dans ceux de l'Orient.*' [Reply to what is said, *that Studies were established by Saint Benoist himself in his Monasteries; & the claim that they were in use in the most ancient Monasteries, that is to say in those of the Orient*']; Alfred de Vigny, *Daphné* (c. 1837) (Paris: Garnier, 1970), 304–305 (1st letter); Anatole France, *Thaïs* (1890), in *Œuvres*, vol. I (Paris: Gallimard, 1984), 721 *sqq*.

4. Georg Wilhelm Friedrich Hegel, *Briefe von und an Hegel*, vol. III: *1823–1831* (Hamburg: Felix Meiner, 1969), 185. Letter 559, 3 September 1827: 'wir haben uns nicht lange beim déjeuner verweilt (d. h. um 11 Uhr Koteletts gegessen und eine Bouteille Wein getrunken).' English translation adapted from *Hegel: The Letters*, translated by Clark Butler and Christiane Seile (Bloomington: Indiana University Press, 1984), 650.

5. Ibid., 188 (letter 560, 9 September). English translation in *Hegel: The Letters*, 654.

6. Ibid., 188–189 (letter 561, 13 September): 'Lavements, Fomentationen und Tisanen ganz auf französische Weise.' English translation in *Hegel: The Letters*, 655.

7. Ibid., 193–194 (letter 563, 26 September), 197. Letter 564, 30 September. English translation in *Hegel: The Letters*, 658, 659.

8. Ehrgott Andreas Christoph Wasianski, *Immanuel Kant in seinen letzten Lebensjahren*, in Ludwig Ernest Borowski *et al.*, *Wer war Kant?*, (no location given, Neske: 1974), 220 and 228.

9. L. E. Borowski, *Darstellung des Lebens und Charakters Immanuel Kants. Von Kant selbst genau revidiert und berichtigt*, in *Wer war Kant?*, 193: 'Sein Tisch bestand aus drei Schüsseln, nebst einem Beisatz von Butter und Käse und im Sommer noch von Gartenfrüchten. Die erste Schüssel enthielt jederzeit eine Fleisch-, größtenteils Kalbssuppe mit Reis, Graupen oder Haarnudeln. Er hatte die Gewohnheit, auf seinen Teller noch Semmel zur Suppe zu schneiden, um sie dadurch desto bündiger zu machen. In der zweiten Schüssel wechselten trocknes Obst mit verschiedenen Beisätzen, durchgeschlagene Hülsenfrüchte und Fische miteinander ab. In der dritten folgte ein Braten; ich erinnere mich aber nicht, jemals Wildbret bei ihm gegessen zu haben. Des Senfs bediente er sich fast zu jeder Speise, auch liebte er sehr die dicke Butter zu Gemüsen und Fleischspeisen und sann selbst darüber nach, wie die dicke Butter am besten

durch fixe Luft zubereitet werden könnte. Butter und Käse machten für ihn noch einen wesentlichen Nachtisch aus. Und da er selbst so sehr den Käse liebte, so sahe er es auch gern, wenn seine Gäste Freunde vom Käse waren. Daher scherzte er oft mit meinem Bruder, daß dieser über zwei wichtige Gegenstände der Unterhaltung, nämlich über Käse und Tobakrauchen, nicht mitsprechen könnte. Er aß ein feines, zweimal gebackenes Roggenbrot, das sehr wohlschmeckend war. Der Käse wurde öfters fein gerieben auf den Tisch gesetzt. Unter allen Käsesorten war ihm der englische am liebsten, aber nicht der rötliche, der ihm mit Moorrübensaft gefärbt zu sein und deshalb so leicht seinen Geschmack zu verändern schien, sondern der seltnere weiße. Bei großen Gesellschaften kam noch eine Schüssel und ein Beisatz von Kuchen hinzu. Die Lieblingsspeise Kants war Kabeljau. Er versicherte mich eines Tages, als er schon völlig gesättigt war, daß er noch mit vielem Appetit einen tiefen Teller mit Kabeljau zu sich nehmen könnte.'

10. Ibid., 194: 'einen leichten roten Wein, gewöhnlich Medoc.'

11. Giacomo Leopardi, *Zibaldone* (Milan: Arnoldo Mondadori, 1997), vol. III, 4184 (pagination of the handwritten manuscript): 'molti si trovano, che dando allo studio o al ritiro p. qualunque causa tutto il resto del giorno, non conversano che a tavola, e sarebbero *bien fachés* [sic] di trovarsi soli e di tacere in quell'ora.' English translation from *Zibaldone*, revised edition, 1829.

12. Matthew, XV, 11.

13. One thinks, for example, of the famous Good Friday dinner Sainte-Beuve hosted at his home on rue du Montparnasse, on 10 April 1868 (see Wolf Lepenies, *Sainte-Beuve* {Paris: Gallimard, 2002}, 84).

14. Plutarch, *Dinner of the Seven Wise Men* (*Tôn hepta sophôn symposion*), 156 D, in *Moralia*, vol. II, translated by Frank Cole Babbitt (Cambridge, MA: Loeb Classical Library, Harvard University Press, 1928), 405. 'Hotan de toioutoi sunelosin andres, hoious ho Periandros humas parakeklêken, ouden ergon estin oimai kulikos oud' oinokhoês, all' hai Mousai kathaper kratêra nêphalion en mesôi prothemenai ton logon hôi pleiston hêdonês hama kai paidias kai spoudês enestin, egeirousi toutôi kai katardousi kai diakheousi tên philophrosunên, eôsai ta polla tên oinokhoên atrema keisthai kratêros huperthen [...].' English translation here adapted from Babbitt. Quoted by Florence Dupont, *Le Plaisir et la Loi* (Paris: La Découverte, 2013), 68. The oenochoe is the small jug with which wine is drawn from the krater and poured in the cup.

15. All these questions are borrowed from Plutarch's *Table-Talk* (*Sumposiaka*) in *Moralia*, vol. VIII-IX, English translation by Paul A. Clement, Herbert B. Hoffleit, Edwin L. Minar Jr., F. H. Sandbach, and W. C. Helmbold (Cambridge, MA: Loeb Classical Library, Harvard University Press, 1961-1969).

16. See Christian Jacob, 'Athenaeus the Librarian', in D. Braund and J. Wilkins, eds., *Athenaeus and His World* (Exeter: University of Exeter Press, 2000), 103.

17. Two potential Greek equivalents for the French 'lettré'.

18. Plutarch, *Advice about Keeping Well* (*Hugieina paraggelmata*), XX, 133 A, in *Moralia*, vol. II, 271. English translation adapted from the Loeb translation by Frank Cole Babbitt.

XIV. Melancholy

1. Aristotle, *Problems*, English translation by W. S. Hett (Cambridge, MA: Loeb Classical Library, Harvard University Press, 1957), vol. II, 164–165 (XXX, 1, 954 b 16-18): 'pollakis gar houtôs ekhomen hôste lupeisthai, eph' hotôi de, ouk an ekhoimen eipein; hote de euthumôs, eph' hôi de, ou dêlon.' Several writers attribute this *Problem* not to the master, but to his school, and in particular to Theophrastus. On melancholy, the essential reference is Raymond Klibansky, Erwin Panofsky and Fritz Saxl, *Saturn and Melancholy* (1964) (Montreal: McGill-Queen's University Press, 2019).

2. Ibid., vol. II, 154-155 (953 a 10-14): 'Dia ti pantes hosoi perittoi gegonasin andres ê kata philosophian ê politikên ê poiêsin ê tekhnas phainontai melagkholikoi ontes, kai hoi men houtôs hôste kai lambanesthai tois apo melainês kholês arrôstêmasin, hoionlegetai tôn te hêrôïkôn ta peri ton Hêraklea?'

3. Ibid., 156-157 (953 a 25-29): 'Kai alloi de polloi tôn hêrôôn homoiopatheis phainontai toutois. Tôn de husteron Empedoklês kai Platôn kai Sôkratês kai heteroi sukhnoi tôn gnôrimôn.'

4. Ibid., 162-163 (954 a 39-40). English translation adapted from that by W. S. Hett.

5. Cicero, *Tusculan Disputations* (Cambridge, MA: Loeb Classical Library, Harvard University Press, 1966), 94-95 (I, XXXIII-80): 'Aristoteles quidem ait omnis ingeniosos melancholicos esse, ut ego me tardiorem esse non moleste feram.' One could also translate 'ingeniosos' by *men of genius*. Cited by Pierre Louis in the French edition of Aristotle, *Problèmes* (Paris: Les Belles Lettres, 1994), vol. III, 25. English translation adapted from that by J. E. King.

6. Yves Hersant, 'L'acédie et ses enfants', in Jean Clair ed., *Mélancolie* (Paris: Gallimard, 2005), 54.

7. Marsilio Ficino, *Three Books on Life* (*De vita*, 1489), critical edition and translation by Carol V. Kaske and John R. Clarke (Binghamton, NY: Center for Medieval and Early Renaissance Studies, 1989), 113-121 (I, III-VI): 'Litterati pituitæ et atræ bili obnoxii sunt'; 'Quot sint causæ quibus litterati melancholici sint vel fiant'; 'Cur melancholici ingeniosi sint et quales melancholici sint eiusmodi, quales contra'; 'Quo pacto atra bilis conducat ingenio.'

8. E. Panofsky, *The Life and Art of Albrecht Dürer* (Princeton, NJ: Princeton University Press, 1955), 166. See also Peter-Klaus Schuster, '*Melencolia I*: Dürer

et sa postérité' in J. Clair ed., *Mélancolie*, 90–103; and see, in this book, the chapter on 'The Study'.

9. Meury Riflant, *Le Miroir des melancholicques* [Rouen] (Petit, 1543), frontispiece. Compare with the more literal version on the second to last page: 'Every animal becomes melancholic / After the act of copulation.' See Aristotle, *Problems*, vol. II, 168–169 (XXX, 1, 955 a 23).

10. Aristotle, *Problems*, vol. II, 162–163 (XXX, 1, 954 b 1–4).

11. Marsilio Ficino, *Three Books on Life*, 112–115 (I, IV).

12. Timothy Bright, *A Treatise of Melancholy* (1586) (London: Stansby, 1613), 296 (XXXVII): 'aboue all, abandon working of your braine by any studie, or conceit.' All quotes from Timothy Bright adapted to modern English in the body of the text by the translator.

13. Ibid., 295: 'Of the labours of the minde, studies haue great force to procure Melancholy if they be vehement and of difficult matters and high mysteries: and therefore chiefly they are to bee avoided.'

14. Ibid., 296: 'such matter of study is to be made choise of, as requireth no great contention, but with a certaine mediocritie, may vnbend that stresse of the minde, through that ouervehement action, and withall carie a contentedness thereto, and ioy to the affection.'

15. Leon Battista Alberti, *Avantages et inconvénients des lettres* (*De commodis litterarum atque incommodis*, c. 1430) (Grenoble: Millon, 2004). A literal English translation of the title would be *Advantages and Inconveniences of Literary Studies*; the book does not appear to have been translated into English.

16. Robert Burton, *The Anatomy of Melancholy* (1621) (Oxford: Clarendon Press, 1989–2000), vol. I, 307 (part. 1, sect. 2, memb. 3, subd. 15): 'wee can make *Maiors* and officers every yeare, but not Schollers: Kings can invest Knights and Barons, as *Sigismond* the Emperour confessed; Universities can give degrees; and *Tu quod es, è populo quilibet esse potest*; but he nor they, nor all the world can give learning, make Philosophers, Artists, Orators, Poets.' Italics by the author. Adapted to modern English in the body of the text by the translator.

17. See Wolf Lepenies, *Melancholie und Gesellschaft* (Frankfurt: Suhrkamp, 1969), 22–37; Pascal Brissette, *La Malédiction littéraire* (Montreal: Presses de l'Université de Montréal, 2005); J. Clair, 'Une mélancolie faustienne', in J. Clair, ed., *Mélancolie* (Paris: Gallimard, 2005), 452–461.

18. Aristotle, *Problems*, vol. II, 168–169 (XXX, 1, 955 a 36–39).

XV. The Soul

1. Thomas à Kempis, *The Imitation of Christ*, translated by Ronald Knox and

Michael Oakley (New York, Sheed & Ward Inc., 1959), 20-21 (l. I, chap. II): 'Quiesce a nimio sciendi desiderio, quia magna ibi invenitur distractio et deceptio. / Scientes libenter volunt videri et sapientes dici. / Multa sunt, quæ scire parum vel nihil animæ prosunt. / Et valde insipiens est qui aliquibus aliis intendit, quam his quæ saluti suæ deserviunt. / Multa verba non satiant animam, sed bona vita refrigerat mentem, et pura conscientia magnam ad Deum præstat confidentiam.'

2. See Petrarch, letter to Boccaccio, 28 May 1362, in *Letters of Old Age*, vol. I, translated by Aldo S. Bernardo and Saul Levin (New York: Italic Press, 2005), 15-26 (I, 5); French translation cited by Ugo Dotti, *Pétrarque* (Paris: Fayard, 1991), 294-295.

3. For my account of this controversy, I owe a great deal to Blandine Kriegel, *L'Histoire à l'âge classique* (1988) (Paris: Presses universitaires de France, 1996), particularly vol. I: *Jean Mabillon*, 103-160; vol. II: *Les Académies de l'histoire*, 19-167.

4. See *Questions proposées à tous les Religieux Bénédictins de la Congrégation de Saint Maur, par le Bureau de Littérature, établi à l'Abbaye de Saint Germain des Prés* [Questions suggested to all the Benedictine monks of the Congregation of Saint-Maur, by the Bureau of Literature, based at the Abbey of Saint Germain des Prés] (Paris: Valleyre l'aîné, rue de la vieille Bouclerie, à l'Arbre de Jessé, 1767). These *Questions* were published as an appendix to Mabillon's treatise *De monasticorum studiorum ratione*, which is on pages 1-12. The examples of research topics are drawn from pages 13-17. Mabillon had himself established a long 'Liste des Principales Difficultez qui se rencontrent dans la lecture des Conciles, des Peres, & de l'histoire ecclesiastique par ordre des siècles' ['List of the principal difficulties encountered in reading the councils, the Fathers & church history, arranged according to century'] at the end of his *Traité des Etudes monastiques*, 2nd ed. (Paris: Charles Robustel, 1692), vol. II, 198-254. The English translation of Mabillon's treatise is *Treatise on Monastic Studies*, translated by John Paul McDonald (Lanham, MD: University Press of America, 2004). The list of difficulties is on pages 255-283.

5. At this stage, the French controversy over 'pagan miracles' was over a century old. See Marc Fumaroli, 'Les dieux païens dans *Phèdre*', in *Exercices de lecture* (Paris: Gallimard, 2006), 228-231.

6. According to the rules applicable to their congregation, Maurists could change monasteries.

7. Armand Jean de Rancé, *De la sainteté et des devoirs de la vie monastique. Seconde Édition, reveuë & augmentée* (Paris: François Muguet, 1683), vol. I, 262-263 (ch. IX, question V). English translation by 'a religious of the Abbey of Melleray, La Trappe', *A Treatise on the Sanctity and on the Duties of the Monastic State* (Dublin: Richard Grace, 1830), 143.

8. These were the nuns of Clairêts. See Jean Mabillon, *Réflexions sur la réponse de M. l'Abbé de La Trappe. Au Traité des Études monastiques*, 2ⁿᵈ ed., vol. I (Paris: Charles Robustel, 1693), ch. XVII, 225.

9. A. J. de Rancé, letter to Abbé Nicaise, 4 June 1693, quoted by François René de Chateaubriand, *Vie de Rancé* (1844) (Paris: Marcel Didier, 1955), vol. II, 265.

10. A. J. de Rancé, *Réponse au Traité des Études monastiques. Par M. l'Abbé de la Trappe* (Paris: François Muguet, 1692), 150 (ch. XIV).

11. J. Mabillon, *De monasticorum studiorum ratione ad juniores studiososque congregationis sancti Mauri monachos* (Paris: Valleyre l'aîné, 1767), 4: 'Cibus animæ lectio est, quam si non subinde ipsi suppedites, jejuna & languens ad omnia erit. Non experientia quævis, non labor qui corpore exercetur, non ipsa divina officia sapient, si animus piarum lectionum usu non fuerit recreatus. Inde cor siccum & aridum erit, pigra erunt rerum spiritalium desideria, quæ flammæ instar, sublatolectionis oleo & alimento, restinguentur.'

12. J. Mabillon, *Reflexions sur la réponse de M. l'Abbé de La Trappe*, vol. I, 227 (ch. xvii); cited by B. Kriegel, *L'Histoire à l'âge classique*, vol. I, 153. Mabillon is referring to the Gospel According to Saint John, v, 39.

13. J. Mabillon, *Traité des Études monastiques*, vol. I, 20-22 (part I, ch. II).

14. J. Mabillon, *Reflexions sur la réponse de M. l'Abbé de La Trappe*, vol. I, 203-204 (ch. XV).

15. J. Mabillon, *Traité des Études monastiques*, vol. II, 195 (part III, ch. V): 'Quotidie morimur, quotidie commutamur: & tamen æternos nos esse credimus. Hoc ipsum quod dicto, quod relego, quod emendo, de vita mea tollitur. Quot puncta notarii, tot meorum damna sunt temporum. Scribimus atque rescribimus: transeunt maria epistolæ, & scindente sulcum carina, per singulos fluctus ætatis nostræ momenta minuuntur. Hoc solum habemus lucri, quod Christi nobis amore sociamur.'

XVI. Religion

1. The episode is reported in several Talmudic sources, including *The Fathers According to Rabbi Nathan* (Atlanta: Scholars Press, 1986), 42-44 (*Abot de rabbi Natan*, ch. iv); *Hebrew-English Edition of the Babylonian Talmud*, vol. XIV (London: Soncino, 1990), 255-259 (*Gittin* 56 b). See Jacob Neusner, *A Life of Yohanan ben Zakkai* (Leiden: Brill, 1970), 157-166; Solomon Schechter and Wilhelm Bacher, 'Johanan b. Zakkai', in Isidore Singer, ed., *The Jewish Encyclopedia* (New York: Funk and Wagnalls, 1901-1906), vol. VII, 214-217.

2. Gustave Flaubert, *Correspondance* (Paris: Gallimard, 1991), vol. III, 191 (letter to Edma Roger des Genettes, 1861); cited by Marguerite Yourcenar, *Œuvres romanesques* (Paris: Gallimard, 1982), 519 (*Carnets de notes de « Mémoires d'Hadrien »*). Flaubert's italics. English translation by Francis Steegmuller in

The Letters of Gustave Flaubert 1857–1880 (Cambridge, MA: The Belknap Press of Harvard University Press, 1982), 20.

3. François Rabelais, *Quart Livre*, ch. XXVIII; after Plutarch, *The Obsolescence of Oracles* (*Peri tôn ekleloipotôn krhêstêriôn*), 419 b–d, in *Moralia*, vol. V (Cambridge, MA: Harvard University Press, 2003), 400–402. See Jean-Christophe Bailly's beautiful commentary, *Adieu: essai sur la mort des dieux* (La Tour d'Aigues: Éditions de l'Aube, 1993). English translation of Rabelais by Burton Raffel, *Gargantua and Pantagruel*, 445–446.

4. Lactantius, *The Divine Institutes*, IV, 28.

5. Michel de Montaigne, *Essais* (Paris: Presses universitaires de France, 1992), 601–603 (II, XII); after Plutarch, *The E at Delphi* (*Peri tou ei tou en Delphois*), 392 e – 393 b (19–20), in *Moralia*, vol. V, 242–244. English translation by Donald M. Frame, *The Complete Essays of Montaigne*, 455–457.

6. Plutarch, *The E at Delphi*, 394 c (21), 252: 'Alla ge tôi ei to "gnôthi sauton" eoike pôs antikeisthai kai tropon tina palin sunadein; to men gar ekplêxei kai sebasmôi pros ton theon hôs onta dia pantos anapephônêtai, to d' hupomnêsis esti tôi thnêtôi tês peri auton phuseôs kai astheneias.' English translation by Donald M. Frame, *The Complete Essays of Montaigne*, 456–457.

7. Heraclitus, Diels-Kranz 93; cited by Plutarch, *The Oracles at Delphi no longer given in verse* (*Peri tou mê khran emmetra nun tên Puthian*), 404 d (21), in *Moralia*, vol. V, 314: 'ho anax, hou to manteion esti to en Delphois, oute legei oute kruptei alla sêmainei.'

8. Charles Baudelaire, *Les Fleurs du mal* ('Élévation'). English translation by Richard Howard, 'Elevation', *Les Fleurs du Mal, The Complete Text of The Flowers of Evil*, 14.

9. Plutarch, *The E at Delphi*, 393 c – 394 a (21), 246–250.

XVII. Quarrel

1. For example, see Letter CV to Augustine, written in 403, in St. Jerome, *Letters and Select Works*, translated by the Hon. W. H. Freemantle (New York: A Select Library of Nicene and Post-Nicene Fathers of the Christian Church, 1893), 189.

2. *Select Letters of St. Jerome*, translated by F. A. Wright, 166–167 (letter XL, to Marcella, written in 384).

3. Literally, Jerome compares them to 'geldings worthy of eunuch priests' (*Gallicis canteriis*) (St. Jerome, *Letters and Select Works*, 44: letter XXVII, to Marcella, written in 384). English translation adapted by the translator.

4. St. Jerome, *Letters and Select Works*, 44.

5. See, for example, *The Analects of Confucius*, translated by Burton Watson, 30

(III, 26).

6. Theodor Wiesengrund Adorno, *Prisms* (*Prismen*, 1955), translated by Samuel and Shierry Weber (Cambridge, MA: The MIT Press, 1983), 17-34 ('Cultural Criticism and Society', 1951).

7. See Jean-Michel Rey, *L'Enjeu des signes* (Paris: Seuil, 1971); Viktor Pöschl, 'Nietzsche und die klassische Philologie', in Hellmut Flashar, Karlfried Gründer and Axel Horstmann, eds., *Philologie und Hermeneutik im 19. Jahrhundert* (Göttingen: Vandenhoeck & Ruprecht, 1979), 141-155; Éric Blondel, *Nietzsche, le corps et la culture* (Paris: Presses universitaires de France, 1986), 133-189.

8. Friedrich Nietzsche, *Kritische Studienausgabe*, 8 (Munich: Deutsche Taschenbuch Verlag, 1988), 38 (3 [76]): 'Die griechische Cultur vollständig begreifend sehen wir also ein, dass es vorbei ist. So ist der Philologe der grosse Skeptiker in unseren Zuständen der Bildung und Erziehung : das ist seine Mission. – Glücklich, wenn er, wie Wagner und Schopenhauer, die verheissungsvollen Kräfte ahnt, in denen eine neue Cultur sich regt.' Translation by William Arrowsmith, 'Notes for "We Philologists"' in *Arion: A Journal of Humanities and the Classics*, New Series, vol. 1, no. 2 (1973/1974), 303.

9. This was the title of the original 1872 edition (*Die Geburt der Tragödie aus dem Geiste der Musik*). The new edition of 1886 would replace it by *The Birth of Tragedy, or: Hellenism and Pessimism* (*Die Geburt der Tragödie. Oder: Griechenthum und Pessimismus*).

10. F. Nietzsche, *The Birth of Tragedy*, translated by Douglas Smith (Oxford: Oxford University Press, 2000), 5-6 ('Attempt at a Self-Criticism' ['Versuch einer Selbstkritik', 1886], 3).

11. See Charles Andler, *Nietzsche*, vol. I (Paris: Gallimard, 1979 [1st ed.: 1958]), 438-441; William Musgrave Calder III, 'The Wilamowitz-Nietzsche Struggle: New Documents and a Reappraisal', *Nietzsche-Studien*, vol. 12, 1983, 214-254; Michèle Cohen-Halimi, 'Une philologie excentrique', in *Querelle autour de "La Naissance de la tragédie"* (Paris: Vrin, 1995), 11-24.

12. Friedrich Ritschl, letter to F. Nietzsche, 14 February 1872, in *Querelle autour de "La Naissance de la tragédie"*, 35.

13. F. Nietzsche, letter to Erwin Rohde, 30 April 1872, in ibid., 73.

14. Ulrich von Wilamowitz-Möllendorff, *Zukunftsphilologie! Eine erwidrung auf Friedrich Nietzsches, ord. professors der classischen philologie zu Basel, "geburt der tragödie"*, in *Der Streit um Nietzsches "Geburt der Tragödie"* (1969) (Hildesheim: Olms, 1989), 27. Contrary to traditional German usage, Wilamowitz's original text does not capitalise the first letters of nouns. An English translation by G. Postl, B. Babich, and H. Schmid was published as *Future Philology!* in *New Nietzsche Studies*, vol. 4: nos. 1 & 2, Summer/Fall 2000, 1-33.

15. Ibid., 31: 'jede geschichtlich gewordene erscheinung allein aus den voraussetzungen der zeit, in der sie sich entwickelt, zu begreifen.' English translation, *Future Philology!* in *New Nietzsche Studies*, 5. The expression 'philology of the future' also echoes the Wagnerian formula the 'artwork of the future' (*Kunstwerk der Zukunft*, 1850) and its parody by Ludwig Bischoff, 'music of the future' (*Zukunftsmusik*, 1859) (see M. Cohen-Halimi, 'Une philologie excentrique', 18). For his part, Nietzsche would refer to a 'philosophy of the future' (*Philosophie der Zukunft*) in the subtitle to *Beyond Good and Evil* (*Jenseits von Gut und Böse*, 1886).

16. Ibid., 55: 'ergreife er den thyrsos, ziehe er von Indien nach Griechenland, aber steige er herab vom katheder, auf welchem er wissenschaft lehren soll; sammle er tiger und panther zu seinen knieen, aber nicht Deutschlands philologische jugend.' English translation, *Future Philology!* in *New Nietzsche Studies*, 24.

17. In private, Rohde's remarks were more revolting: 'That is really a scandal in all its repugnant Jewish opulence', he wrote to Nietzsche just after the appearance of Wilamowitz's pamphlet ('Da wäre ja der Skandal, in widerwärtigster Judenüppigkeit!', letter of 5 June 1872, in *Nietzsche Briefwechsel*, vol. II, vol. 4 {Berlin: De Gruyter, 1978}, 11; translation after Max Marcuzzi, in *Querelle autour de "La Naissance de la tragédie"*, 128).

18. *Zukunftsphilologie!*, 27. English translation, *Future Philology!* in *New Nietzsche Studies*, 1.

19. See C. Andler, *Nietzsche*, vol. I, 439.

20. Heraclitus, Diels-Kranz 53: 'polemos pantôn men patêr esti.'

21. See Caroline Noirot, 'Présentation', in U. v. Wilamowitz, *Qu'est-ce qu'une tragédie attique?* (Paris: Les Belles Lettres, 2001), XVI.

XVIII. The Academy

1. Giovanni Pico della Mirandola, *Conclusiones nongentae* (Florence: Olschki, 1995), 6: 'De adscriptis Numero Noningentis Dialecticis, Moralibus, Physicis, Mathematicis, Meta-Physicis, Theologicis, Magicis, Cabalisticis, cum suis tum sapientium Chaldaeorum, Arabum, Hebraeorum, Graecorum, Aegyptiorum, Latinorumque placitis, disputabit publice Johannes Picus Mirandulanus Concordiae Comes.' English translation by S. A. Farmer in *Syncretism in the West: Pico's 900 Theses (1486)* (Tempe, AZ: Medieval & Renaissance Texts & Studies, 1998), 211.

2. Ibid., XII. English translation, *Syncretism in the West*, 553.

3. See Olivier Boulnois, 'Humanisme et dignité de l'homme selon Pic de la Mirandole', in Pico della Mirandola, *Œuvres philosophiques* (Paris: Presses universitaires de France, 1993), 328–332.

4. *Syncretism in the West*, conclusion 268 (23.7), 312 (Latin)/313 (English translation): 'Nulla est vis coelestium astrorum quantum est in se malefica'; no. 161 (7.6), 252/253: 'Possibile est hominem ex putrefactione generari'; no. 350 (27.5), 340/341: 'Nihil est in mundo expers vitæ'; no. 784 (9>13), 498/499: 'Magicam operari non est aliud quam maritare mundum'; no. 585 (4>15), 428/429: 'Si non peccasset Adam, Deus fuisset incarnatus, sed non crucifixus'; no. 884 (11>56), 542/543: 'Qui sciuerit explicare quaternarium in denarium, habebit modum, si sit peritus Cabalæ, deducendi ex nomine ineffabili nomen LXXII literarum'; no. 882 (11>54), 542/543: 'Quod dicunt Cabalistæ, beatificandos nos in speculo lucente reposito sanctis in futuro seculo, idem est præcise sequendo fundamenta eorum, cum eo, quod nos dicimus, beatificandos sanctos in filio.'

5. See Giuseppe Tognon, preface, in Pico, *Œuvres philosophiques*, XXXIV-XXXV.

6. See the first preface, or epistle to the reader, *Syncretism in the West*, 210/212: 'In quibus recitandis, non Romanæ linguæ nitorem, sed celebratissimorum Parisiensium disputatorum dicendi genus est imitatus, propterea quod eo nostri temporis philosophi plerique omnes utuntur.' Translation: 'In reciting these opinions, he has not imitated the splendor of the Roman language, but the style of speaking of the most celebrated Parisian disputers, since this is used by almost all philosophers of our time.'

7. See Giovanni Pico della Mirandola, *On the Dignity of Man* (*De hominis dignitate*), translated by Charles Glenn Wallis (Indianapolis, IN: The Bobbs Merrill Company, 1965), 19.

8. Aristotle, *The Nicomachean Ethics*, English translation by H. Rackham (Cambridge: Harvard University Press, 1990), 614/615 (X, 1177 a): 'ho de sophos kai kath' hauton ôn dunatai theôrein, kai hosôi an sophôteros êi mallon; beltion d' isôs sunergous ekhôn, all' homôs autarkestatos.'

9. See Blandine Kriegel, *L'Histoire à l'âge classique*, vol. III: *Les Académies de l'histoire* (Paris: Presses universitaires de France, 1996), 171-220. The Académie des Inscriptions' area of expertise is clearly defined in article XXI of its regulations, *Règlement Pour l'Académie royale des Inscriptions & Belles-Lettres. Du 22 Décembre 1786* (Paris: Imprimerie royale, 1787), 5-6.

10. Art. XIV-XVII of *Règlement ordonné par le Roy pour l'Academie Royale des Inscriptions & Medailles* (16 July 1701), in *Lettres patentes du Roy, Qui confirment l'établissement des Academies Royales des Inscriptions & des Sciences* (Paris: Muguet, 1713), 5.

11. Ibid., 6, art. XXI.

12. Ibid, art. XXIV.

13. Ibid, art. XXVI.

14. *Règlement Pour l'Académie royale des Inscriptions & Belles-Lettres. Du 22 Décembre 1786*, 6-7, art. XXII.

XIX. Politics

1. Aristotle, *The Nicomachean Ethics*, 614-616 (X, VII, 1177 b 12-15).
2. Ibid., 614 (X, VII, 1177 b 1): 'Doxai t' an autê monê di' hautên agapasthai; ouden gar ap' autês ginetai para to theôrêsai, apo de tôn praktikôn ê pleion ê elatton peripoioumetha para tên praxin.'
3. See the commentary by René Antoine Gauthier and Jean Yves Jolif, in Aristotle, *L'Éthique à Nicomaque* (Louvain-la-Neuve: Peeters, 2002), book II, vol. 2, 855-860.
4. Aristotle, *The Nicomachean Ethics*, 612 (X, VII, 1177 a 28).
5. Philostratus, *The Life of Apollonius of Tyana*, English translation by F. C. Conybeare (London: Loeb Classical Library, William Heinemann, 1912), vol. 1, 431-487 (IV, 35-V, 11); vol. 2, 147-395 (VII, 1-VIII, 27).
6. In his state, Plato reserves the highest office to the magistrate responsible for education. See *Laws*, English translation by R.G. Bury (Cambridge, MA: Loeb Classical Library, Harvard University Press, 1967), vol. 1, 438/439 (VI, 765 e).
7. Aristotle, *Politics*, English translation by H. Rackham (Cambridge, MA: Loeb Classical Library, Harvard University Press, 1986), 540/541 (VII, II, 1324 a 16).
8. Ibid., 548, 550/549, 551 (VII, III, 1325 a 16 - 1325 b 32).
9. Julien Benda, *La Trahison des clercs* (1927) (Paris: Grasset, 1995), 132. English translation by Richard Aldington, *The Treason of the Intellectuals*, 45.
10. Ibid., 131-132. English translation, *The Treason of the Intellectuals*, 43.
11. Julien Benda, *La Fin de l'éternel* (1928) (Paris: Gallimard, 1977), 53.
12. *The Analects of Confucius*, translated by Burton Watson (XI, 26).
13. See Anne Cheng, *Histoire de la pensée chinoise* (Paris: Seuil, 1997), 277.
14. Nobusada Nishitakatsuji, *Dazaifu Tenman-gu* (Fukuoka: Dazaifu Tenman-gu, 1982), 50-57.
15. Cicero, *The Republic* and *The Laws*, translated by Niall Rudd, 7 (VI-10): '[...] in qua quid facere potuissem, nisi tum consul fuissem? Consul autem esse qui potui, nisi eum uitae cursum tenuissem a pueritia per quem, equestri loco natus, peruenirem ad honorem amplissimum?'
16. Plutarch, *Cicero* in *Lives*, vol. VII, 206 (48, 2 - 885 d): 'en grammasin eleutheriois kai mathêmasin.' English translation adapted from the French translation by Robert Flacelière and Émile Chambry.
17. Ibid., 208/209 (49, 3 - 886 a): 'tas sarkas apotemnonta tas hautou kata mikron optan, eit' esthiein ênagkasen.'
18. Ibid., 208/209 (49, 5 - 886 b).

XX. War

1. *Description de l'Égypte ou recueil des observations et des recherches qui ont été faites en Égypte pendant l'expédition de l'armée française* (Paris: Imprimerie impériale, then Imprimerie royale, 1809-1828), 22 vol. See Robert Solé, *Les Savants de Bonaparte* (Paris: Seuil, 2001), 207-212.

2. Paul-Louis Courier, letter of 6 March 1808, in *Correspondance générale* (Paris: Klincksieck, 1978), vol. II, 13.

3. Horace, *Epistles*, in *Satires, Epistles, Ars Poetica*, English translation by H. Rushton Fairclough (Cambridge, MA: Loeb Classical Library, Harvard University Press, 1942), 406/407 (II, I, 116). Translator's note: Fairclough's translation is 'carpenters handle carpenters' tools'. The translation given here is closer to the French translation cited by the author.

4. Albert Thibaudet, *La Campagne avec Thucydide* (1922), in Thucydide, *Histoire de la guerre du Péloponnèse* (Paris: Laffont, 1990), 7. In the slang of the *poilus*, Azor referred to a backpack.

5. Auguste Dupouy, *Écrivains morts pour la patrie*, in Charles Le Goffic, *La Littérature française aux XIXe et XXe siècles*, vol. II (Paris: Larousse, 1919 [or rather 1923]), 286-289. The first four volumes of *Anthologie des écrivains morts à la guerre* [Anthology of Writers Who Died in the War] (ed. Thierry Sandre {Amiens: Malfère, 1924-1926}) also lists 450 names, to which the fifth volume adds about one hundred additional names of writers who didn't die directly in combat.

6. Albert Thibaudet, *La Campagne avec Thucydide*.

7. See Ray Monk, *Ludwig Wittgenstein* (London: Cape, 1990), 137-166.

8. Alain, *Souvenirs de guerre* (1937), in *Les Passions et la Sagesse* (Paris: Gallimard, 1972), 503.

9. Ibid., 537.

10. Ibid., 544.

11. Albert Thibaudet, *La Campagne avec Thucydide*, 3.

12. René Descartes, *Discours de la méthode* (1637), II, in *Œuvres et Lettres*, 132. English translation by F.E. Sutcliffe in *Discourse on Method and the Meditations*, 25.

13. Adrien Baillet, *La Vie de Monsieur Descartes* (Paris: Horthemels, 1691), vol. I, 91 (II, II).

14. Ibid., 41 (I, IX).

15. Ibid., 82-83, 86 (II, I).

16. Ibid., 84. This is probably the gist of the unfinished *Olympiques* of 1619-1620, of which there remains only indirect accounts, in particular in the notes

taken by Leibniz (see R. Descartes, *Œuvres philosophiques*, vol. I: 1618-1637 {Paris: Garnier, 1992}), 61-62.

XXI. The Coronation

1. Petrarch, *Rerum familiarum libri* [Letters on Familiar Matters] (Albany, NY: State University of New York Press, 1975), 188-189 (l. IV, 4). See also letters 5 to 9, in ibid., 190-197. On Petrarch's coronation, above all see Ernest Hatch Wilkins, 'The Coronation of Petrarch' (1943) in *The Making of the 'Canzoniere' and Other Petrarchan Studies* (Rome: Storia e Letteratura, 1951), 9-69, and *Vita del Petrarca* (Milan: Feltrinelli, 1990), 43-48, as well as Ugo Dotti, *Pétrarque* (Paris: Fayard, 1991), 62-77. For a study of the coronation of the poet in general, see Marc Fumaroli, *L'École du silence* (Paris: Flammarion, 1994), 129-134.

2. Petrarch believed as much (*Collatio laureationis*, VI, 1, 1264). English translation by Ernest H. Wilkins, *Petrarch's Coronation Oration* in PMLA, vol. 68, no. 5 (Dec. 1953), 1245.

3. *Collatio laureationis*, VI, 2, 1264-1266. English translation, *Petrarch's Coronation Oration*, 1245.

4. Petrarch, *Lettera ai posteri*, 31, 56: 'a meridie ad vesperam'; cited by E. H. Wilkins, 'The Coronation of Petrarch', 47.

5. Petrarch, *Epistolæ metricæ*, II, 1, v. 38-53, quoted by E. H. Wilkins in 'The Coronation of Petrarch', 63-64: 'subitumque vocati / Romulei proceres coeunt; capitolia læto / Murmure complentur; muros tectumque vetustum / Congaudere putes; cecinerunt classica; vulgus / Agmina certatim glomerat, cupidumque videndi / Obstrepit. Ipse etiam lachrymas, ni fallor, amicis / Compressis pietate animis, in pectore vidi. / Ascendo; siluere tubæ, murmurque resedit. / Vna quidem nostri vox primum oblata Maronis / Principium dedit oranti, nec multa profatus; / Nam neque mos vatum patitur, nec iura sacrarum / Pyeridum violasse leve est; de vertice Cyrræ / Avulsas paulum mediis habitare coegi / Vrbibus ac populis. Post facundissimus Vrsus / Subsequitur fando. Tandem mihi Delphica serta / Imposuit, populo circumplaudente Quiritum.'

6. Petrarch, *Rerum familiarum libri* [Letters on Familiar Matters], IV, 8, 196.

7. See Jean-François Chevalier, 'Albertino Mussato', in Albertino Mussato, *Écérinide* (Paris: Les Belles Lettres, 2000), XI-XVIII; Manlio Dazzi, *Il Mussato preumanista* (Vicence: Neri Pozza, 1964), 67-68; E. H. Wilkins, 'The Coronation of Petrarch', 21-23.

8. Virgil, *Georgics*, III, v. 291-292, cited by Petrarch, *Collatio laureationis*, in *Opere latine di Francesco Petrarca*, vol. II (1975) (Turin: Unione tipografico-editrice torinese, 1987), 1256: 'Sed me Parnasi deserta per ardua dulcis / raptat amor.'

9. Petrarch, *Collatio laureationis*, VIII, 2, 1268: 'me in tam laborioso et michi quidem periculoso calle ducem prebere non expavi, multos posthac, ut arbitror, secuturos.'

10. Ibid., XI, 25, 1282: 'laurea tam cesarea quam poetica.'

11. For a detailed discussion of the legitimacy of the coronation, see E. H. Wilkins, 'The Coronation of Petrarch', 29-35.

12. Petrarch, *Canzoniere*, translated by Mark Musa (Bloomington, IN: Indiana University Press, 1996), 8 (7: *La gola e 'l somno...*, v. 9) and 26 (23: *Nel dolce tempo...*, v. 43-44).

13. Petrarch, *Le "Senili" secondo l'edizione Basilea 1581 (Epistolæ seniles)* (Savigliano: L'Artistica Editrice, 2006), 295 (XVI or XVII, 2, letter dated 28 April 1373); cited by Wilkins, 'The Coronation of Petrarch', 69.

XXII. The Island

1. Virgil, *Georgics*, III, v. 291-292, cited by Petrarch, *Collatio laureationis*, 1256: 'Sed me Parnasi deserta per ardua dulcis / raptat amor.'

2. See Marc Fumaroli, 'Académie, Arcadie, Parnasse: trois lieux allégoriques du loisir lettré', in *L'École du silence* (Paris: Flammarion, 1994), 22-23.

3. See Michele Feo, 'La biblioteca', in M. Feo (ed.), *Petrarca nel tempo* (no location: Comitato nazionale per le celebrazioni del VII centenario della nascita di Francesco Petrarca, 2003), 458.

4. Montaigne, *Essais*, 869 (III, III). English translation by Donald M. Frame, *The Complete Essays of Montaigne*, 629.

5. Ibid., 870. English translation by Donald M. Frame, *The Complete Essays of Montaigne*, 629. Same references for the following quotes from Montaigne.

6. Jonathan Swift, *Gulliver's Travels* (1726) (London: Penguin Books, 2001), 155-162.

7. See Alain Legros, *Essais sur poutres* (Paris: Klincksieck, 2000), 223.

8. On the importance and ambiguity of citation in Montaigne, see Antoine Compagnon, *La Seconde Main* (Paris: Seuil, 1979), notably 278-306.

9. See Gisela Maul & Margarete Oppel, *Goethes Wohnhaus in Weimar* (Weimar: Stiftung Weimarer Klassik, 2002), 90-91.

10. William Shakespeare, *The Tempest* (1611) (Oxford: Oxford University Press, 1998), 105 (I, 2, v. 73 and 77).

11. Ibid., 107 (v. 109-110).

12. Ibid., 110 (v. 168-169): 'volumes that / I prize above my dukedom.'

13. Ibid., 160 (III, 2, v. 83-84).

14. Ibid., 190 (V, 1, v. 56–57).

15. In Peter Greenaway's spectacular film adaptation of *The Tempest*, the choice to give Prospero's books the leading role is most perceptive (*Prospero's Books*, 1991).

16. Walter Benjamin, letter to Gretel Adorno (19 July 1940), in *Gesammelte Briefe*, vol. VI: *1938–1940* (Frankfurt: Suhrkamp, 2000), 470 (Benjamin uses the French expression 'Grand Siècle'). See also the letter to Hannah Arendt (8 July 1940), on page 468 of the same volume. An English translation of the letter to Arendt is in *The Correspondence of Walter Benjamin 1910–1940*, translated by Manfred R. Jacobson and Evelyn M. Jacobson (Chicago: The University of Chicago Press, 1994), 637.

17. See Walter Benjamin, letters to Alfred Cohn (20 July 1940) and Hannah Arendt (9 August 1940), *Gesammelte Briefe*, vol. VI: 1938–1940, 471 and 479.

XXIII. The Night

1. Quintilian, *Institutio Oratoria*, English translation by H. E. Butler (Cambridge, MA: Loeb Classical Library, Harvard University Press, 1920), vol. IV, 104/105 (X, III, 24): 'siluarum amoenitas et praeterlabentia flumina et inspirantes ramis arborum aurae uolucrumque cantus, et ipsa late circumspiciendi libertas ad se trahunt, ut mihi remittere potius uoluptas ista uideatur cogitationem quam intendere.' English translation adapted from Butler's rendition.

2. Ibid., 121–122 (X, III, 25): 'Ideoque lucubrantes silentium noctis et clausum cubiculum et lumen unum uelut tectos maxime teneat.' Translation adapted from Butler's translation. Cited by Petrarch, *The Life of Solitude* (*De vita solitaria*, 1346–1366), 156 (I, VII, 7).

3. Ibid., 104/105 (X, III, 26): 'cum tempora ab ipsa rerum natura ad quietem refectionemque nobis data, in acerrimum laborem conuertimus.'

4. Ibid., (X, III, 27): 'abunde si uacet lucis spatia sufficiunt: occupatos in noctem necessitas agit.' English translation adapted from Butler's rendition.

5. Celsus, *On Medicine* (*De medicina*) vol. I: Books 1–4, English translation by W. G. Spencer (Cambridge, MA: Loeb Classical Library, Harvard University Press, 1935), 46/47 (I, II, 5): 'sin lucubrandum est, non post cibum id facere, sed post concoctionem.'

6. Quintilian, *Institutio Oratoria*, 104/105 (X, III, 27): 'Est tamen lucubratio, quotiens ad eam integri ac refecti uenimus, optimum secreti genus.'

7. Gaston Bachelard, *La Flamme d'une chandelle* (1961) (Paris: Presses universitaires de France, 1984), 54–55. English translation by Joni Caldwell, *The Flame of a Candle* (Dallas, TX: The Dallas Institute of Humanities and Culture, 1988), 37.

8. Ibid., 108. English translation, *The Flame of a Candle*, 76.

9. Ibid., 20. English translation, *The Flame of a Candle*, 13.

XXIV. Death

1. The details of this account are borrowed from the 28 March 1980 issue of the newspaper *Le Monde*, 27, and from Louis-Jean Calvet, *Roland Barthes* (Paris: Flammarion, 1990), 292–302; Éric Marty, *Roland Barthes, le métier d'écrire* (Paris: Seuil, 2006), 102–105; Hervé Algalarrondo, *Les Derniers Jours de Roland B.* (Paris: Stock, 2006), 266–267.

2. Gospel of John, XI, 35.

3. Roland Barthes, 'Au séminaire' (1974), in *Œuvres complètes*, vol. IV: *1972–1976* (Paris: Seuil, 2002), 508. Entitled 'Le savoir, la mort', the fragment is cited and commented on by Philippe Roger in *Roland Barthes, roman* (Paris: Grasset, 1986), 341–342. Fragment entitled 'Knowledge, death' in the English translation by Richard Howard, 'To the Seminar' in *The Rustle of Language* (Berkeley, CA: University of California Press, 1989), 338–339.

4. These words were spoken in 1960 or 1962. See Amadou Hampâté Bâ, *Aspects de la civilisation africaine* (Paris: Présence africaine, 1972), 21 ('Remarques sur la culture. La sagesse et la question linguistique en Afrique noire'). English translation by Susan B. Hunt, 'Remarks on Culture: Wisdom and the Linguistic Question in Black Africa', *Aspects of African Civilization*, https://www.academia.edu/49073084/Aspects_of_African_Civilization_Amadou_Hampate_Ba, 8.

5. Tierno Bokar, quoted in *Aspects de la civilisation africaine*, 22. English translation, https://www.academia.edu/49073084/Aspects_of_African_Civilization_Amadou_Hampate_Ba, 9.

6. *The Analects of Confucius*, translated by Burton Watson, 56 (VIII, 17).

7. See Roland Barthes, 'Au séminaire', 502–511. English translation, 'To the Seminar', 332–342.

8. Sima Qian, *Selections from Records of the Historian*, 25.

9. Roland Barthes, *La Préparation du roman* (Paris: Seuil / IMEC, 2003), 459 (summary of the lecture course for the Collège de France catalogue, 1979). English translation by Kate Briggs, *The Preparation of the Novel*, 377.

10. See Éric Marty, *Roland Barthes, le métier d'écrire*, 227–234, as well as the discussions at the 1977 Colloque de Cerisy, in Antoine Compagnon, ed., *Prétexte: Roland Barthes* (Paris: Christian Bourgois, 2003), 242–243.

11. Sima Qian, *Selections from Records of the Historian*, 25.

12. Roland Barthes, *La Préparation du roman*, 353 (session of 16 February 1980; Barthes' italics). English translation, *The Preparation of the Novel*, 277.

13. Jacques Derrida, 'Les morts de Roland Barthes', *Poétique*, no. 47, September 1981, 269-292. English translation by Pascale-Anne Brault and Michael Naas, 'The Deaths of Roland Barthes', in Jacques Derrida, *The Work of Mourning* (Chicago: University of Chicago Press, 2001), 34-67. See also Dominique Carlat, *Témoins de l'inactuel* (Paris: Corti, 2007), 91-123.

14. A motto visible in an engraving of the edition of Bernardino Corio, *Patria historia* (Milan, 1503); reproduced in Dora Thornton, *The Scholar in His Study*, 7, *fig. 7*.

15. Roland Barthes, *La Préparation du roman*, 275-349 (sessions of 19 January to 9 February 1980). English translation, *The Preparation of the Novel*, 207-274.

16. Louis-Jean Calvet, *Roland Barthes*, 299.

17. Roland Barthes, *La Préparation du roman*, 275. English translation, *The Preparation of the Novel*, 207.

Bibliography

Adorno, Theodor Wiesengrund. *Prismes: critique de la culture et société*. Trans. Geneviève and Rainer Rochlitz. Paris: Payot, 2003.

Adorno, Theodor Wiesengrund. *Prisms*. Trans. Samuel and Shierry Weber. Cambridge, MA: The MIT Press, 1983.

Alain. *Les Passions et la Sagesse*. Paris: Bibliothèque de la Pléiade, Gallimard, 1972.

Alberti, Leon Battista. *Avantages et inconvénients des lettres*. Trans. Christophe Carraud and Rebecca Lenoir. Grenoble: Jérôme Millon, 2004.

Alberti, Leon Battista. *I libri della famiglia*. Ed. Ruggiero Romano, Alberto Tenenti and Francesco Furlan. Turin: Giulio Einaudi, 1994.

Alberti, Leon Battista. *The Family in Renaissance Florence*. Trans. Renée Neu Watkins. Long Grove, IL: Waveland Press, 1994.

Algalarrondo, Hervé. *Les Derniers Jours de Roland B.*. Paris: Stock, 2006.

Andler, Charles. *Nietzsche: sa vie et sa pensée. Les précurseurs de Nietzsche. La jeunesse de Nietzsche*. Paris: Bibliothèque des idées, Gallimard, 1979.

Aristotle. *L'Éthique à Nicomaque*. Ed. René Antoine Gauthier and Jean Yves Jolif. Louvain-la-Neuve: Peeters, 2002.

Aristotle. *Politique*. III, l. VII. Ed. Jean Aubonnet. Paris: Collection des universités de France, Les Belles Lettres, 1986.

Aristotle. *Problèmes*. III. Ed. Pierre Louis. Paris: Collection des universités de France, Les Belles Lettres, 1994.

Aristotle. *The Metaphysics*. I. Ed. Hugh Tredennick. Cambridge, MA: Loeb Classical Library, Harvard University Press, 1989.

Aristotle. *The Nicomachean Ethics*. Trans. H. Rackham. Cambridge, MA: Harvard University Press, 1990.

Aristotle. *Politics*. Trans. H. Rackham. Cambridge, MA: Loeb Classical Library, Harvard University Press, 1986.

Aristotle. *Problems*. Trans. W. S. Hett. Cambridge, MA: Loeb Classical Library, Harvard University Press, 1957.

Arrowsmith, William. 'Notes for "We Philologists"' in *Arion: A Journal of Humanities and the Classics*, New Series, vol. 1, no. 2 (1973/1974), 279–380.

Athenaeus. *The Deipnosophists*. Trans. Charles Burton Gulick. London: Loeb Classical Library, Heinemann, 1969–1971.

Aulus Gellius. *Les Nuits attiques*. Books I-IV. Trans. René Marache. Paris: Collection des universités de France, Les Belles Lettres, 1967.

Aulus Gellius. *Attic Nights*. Trans. John Rolfe. Cambridge, MA: Loeb Classical Library, Harvard University Press, 1927.

Bâ, Amadou Hampâté. *Aspects de la civilisation africaine*. Paris: Présence africaine, 1972.

Bachelard, Gaston. *La Flamme d'une chandelle*. Paris: Quadrige, Presses universitaires de France, 1984.

Bachelard, Gaston. *The Flame of a Candle*. Trans. Joni Caldwell. Dallas, TX: The Dallas Institute of Humanities and Culture, 1988.

Baillet, Adrien. *La Vie de Monsieur Descartes*. Paris: Daniel Horthemels, 1691; Hildesheim: Georg Olms, 1972.

Bailly, Jean-Christophe. *Adieu: essai sur la mort des dieux*. La Tour d'Aigues: Éditions de l'Aube, 1993.

Barker, Stephen (ed.). *Excavations and Their Objects: Freud's Collection of Antiquity*. Albany: State University of New York Press, 1996.

Barrès Maurice. *Huit jours chez M. Renan*. Paris: Émile-Paul, 1913.

Barthelemy-Saint-Hilaire Jules. *M. Victor Cousin, sa vie et sa correspondance*. II. Paris: Hachette, 1895.

Barthes, Roland. *Le Bruissement de la langue: Essais critiques IV*. Paris: Éditions du Seuil, 1984.

Barthes, Roland. *Comment vivre ensemble: simulations romanesques de quelques espaces quotidiens. Notes de cours et de séminaires au Collège de France, 1976-1977*. Ed. Claude Coste, under the direction of Éric Marty. Paris: Seuil / IMEC, 2002.

Barthes, Roland. *Œuvres complètes*. IV: *1972-1976*. Ed. Éric Marty. Paris: Seuil, 2002.

Barthes, Roland. *La Préparation du roman. I et II. Notes de cours et de séminaires au Collège de France, 1978-1979 et 1979-1980*. Ed. Nathalie Léger, under the direction of Éric Marty. Paris: Seuil / IMEC, 2003.

Barthes, Roland. *How to Live Together: Novelistic Simulations of Some Everyday Spaces. Notes for a lecture course and seminar at the Collège de France (1976-1977)*. Trans. Kate Briggs. Ed. Claude Coste. New York: Columbia University Press,

2013.

Barthes, Roland. *The Preparation of the Novel: Lecture courses and seminars at the Collège de France 1978-1979 and 1979-1980*. Trans. Kate Briggs. Ed. Nathalie Léger. New York: Columbia University Press, 2011.

Barthes, Roland. *The Rustle of Language*. Trans. Richard Howard. Berkeley, CA: University of California Press, 1989.

Baudelaire, Charles. *Les Fleurs du Mal: The Complete Text of The Flowers of Evil*. Trans. Richard Howard. Boston: David R. Godine, 1982.

Baudoin, Jean. *Iconologie, ou, explication nouvelle de plusieurs images, emblemes, et autres figures Hyerogliphiques des Vertus, des Vices, des Arts, des Sciences, des Causes naturelles, des Humeurs differentes, & des Passions humaines*. Paris: Mathieu Guillemot, 1644.

Benda, Julien. *La Fin de l'éternel*. Paris: Gallimard, 1977.

Benda, Julien. *La Trahison des clercs*. Paris: Les Cahiers rouges, Grasset, 1995.

Benda, Julien. *The Treason of the Intellectuals*. Trans. Richard Aldington. New York: W. W. Norton & Company, 1969.

Benjamin, Walter. *Gesammelte Briefe*. VI: *1938-1940*. Ed. Christoph Gödde and Henri Lonitz. Frankfurt: Suhrkamp, 2000.

Benjamin, Walter. *Je déballe ma bibliothèque: une pratique de la collection*. Trans. Philippe Ivernel. Paris: Rivages, 2000.

Benjamin, Walter. *The Correspondence of Walter Benjamin 1910-1940*. Trans. Manfred R. Jacobson and Evelyn M. Jacobson. Chicago: The University of Chicago Press, 1994.

La Bible de Jérusalem, édition de référence avec notes et augmentée de clefs de lectures. Paris: Fleurus / Cerf, 2001.

La Bible: écrits intertestamentaires. Ed. André Dupont-Sommer and Marc Philonenko. Paris: Bibliothèque de la Pléiade, Gallimard, 1987.

The Bible: King James Version with Apocrypha. New York: Penguin, 2006.

Blondel, Éric. *Nietzsche, le corps et la culture: la philosophie comme généalogie philologique*. Paris: Philosophie d'aujourd'hui, Presses universitaires de France, 1986.

Bonnefis, Philippe and Lyotard, Dolorès (eds.). *Pascal Quignard, figures d'un lettré*. Paris: Galilée, 2005.

Borgen, Robert. *Sugawara no Michizane and the Early Heian Court*. Cambridge, MA: Harvard University Press, 1986.

Borges, Jorge Luis. *Livre de préfaces*, suivi de *Essai d'autobiographie*. Trans. Françoise-Marie Rosset and Michel Seymour Tripier. Paris: Du monde entier, Gallimard, 1980.

Borges, Jorge Luis. *Obras completas*. II: *1952-1972*. Ed. Carlos V. Frías. Barcelona: Emecé, 1989.

Borges, Jorge Luis. *Œuvres complètes*. Ed. Jean-Pierre Bernès. Paris: Bibliothèque de la Pléiade, Gallimard, 1993-1999.

Borges, Jorge Luis. *The Aleph and Other Stories 1933-1969*. Trans. Norman Thomas di Giovanni. New York: E.P. Dutton, 1978.

Borges, Jorge Luis. *Selected Poems*. Ed. Alexander Coleman. New York: Viking, 1999.

Borowski, L. E., Jachmann, R. B., and Wasiansi, E. A. C.. *Immanuel Kant. Ein Lebensbild nach Darstellungen der Zeitgenossen: Jachmann, Borowski, Wasianski*. Ed. Alfons Hoffmann. Halle, Hugo Peter, 1902.

Borowski, L. E., Jachmann, R. B., and Wasiansi, E. A. C.. *Kant intime*. Trans. Jean Mistler. Paris: Grasset, 1985.

Borowski, L. E., Jachmann, R. B., and Wasiansi, E. A. C.. *Wer war Kant? Drei zeitgenössiche Biographien von Ludwig Ernst Borowski, Reinhold Bernhard Jachmann und E. A. Ch. Wasianski*. Ed. Siegried Drescher: s. l., Neske, 1974.

Bossuet, Jacques Bénigne. *Correspondance*. I: *1651-1676*. Ed. Ch. Urbain and E. Levesque. Paris: Les Grands Écrivains de la France, Hachette, 1909.

Brem, Anne-Marie de. *Tréguier et la maison d'Ernest Renan*. Paris: Monum – Éditions du patrimoine, 2004.

Bright, Timothy. *A Treatise of Melancholy. Containing the Causes Thereof, And Reasons of the strange effects it worketh in our minds and bodies: with the Physicke Cure, and spirituall consolation for such as haue thereto adioyned afflicted Conscience. The Difference betwixt it, and Melancholy, With diuers Philosophicall discourses touching actions, and affections of Soule, Spirit, and Body: the particulars whereof are to be seene before the Booke. By T. Bright Doctor of Physicke. Newly Corrected and amended*. London: William Stansby, 1613.

Bright, Timothy. *Hygieina, id est, de sanitate tuenda, medicinae pars prima, auctore Timotheo Brighto, Cantabrigiensi, medicinae doctore, cui accesserunt de studiosorum sanitate libri III Marsilii Ficini*. Mayence: Nicolaus Heyll, 1647.

Bright, Timothy. *Traité de la mélancolie*. Trans. Éliane Cuvelier. Grenoble: Jérôme Millon, 1996.

Brissette, Pascal. *La Malédiction littéraire: du poète crotté au génie malheureux*. Montréal: Presses de l'Université de Montréal, 2005.

Burke, Janine. *The Sphinx on the Table: Sigmund Freud's Art Collection and the Development of Psychoanalysis*. New York: Walker, 2006.

Burton, Robert. *The Anatomy of Melancholy*. Ed. Thomas C. Faulkner, Nicolas K. Kiessling and Rhonda L. Blair. Oxford: Clarendon Press, 1989-2000.

Calder III, William Musgrave. 'The Wilamowitz-Nietzsche Struggle: New Documents and a Reappraisal' in *Nietzsche-Studien*. Berlin: Walter de Gruyter, vol. 12, 1983, 214-254.

Calvet, Louis-Jean. *Roland Barthes*. Paris: Flammarion, 1990.

Carlat, Dominique. *Témoins de l'inactuel: quatre écrivains contemporains face au deuil*. Paris: Les Essais, José Corti, 2007.

Saint Cassian, John. *Conférences*. II: VIII-XVII. Trans. Dom Eugène Pichery. Paris: Sources chrétiennes, Éditions du Cerf, 1958.

Saint Cassian, John. *The Conferences of John Cassian*. Trans. Boniface Ramsey. New York: Newman Press, 1997.

Cauchie, Maurice. 'Nicole Jamin, la suivante de Mlle de Gournay, est-elle fille d'Amadis Jamin ?' in *Revue des bibliothèques*, 32e année, n° 10-12, October-December 1922, 289-292.

Celsus. *De medicina*. Trans. W. G. Spencer. London: Loeb Classical Library, William Heinemann, 1971.

Celsus. *On Medicine*. I, Books 1-4. Trans. W. G. Spencer. Cambridge, MA: Loeb Classical Library, Harvard University Press, 1935.

Chateaubriand, François René de. *Vie de Rancé*. Ed. Fernand Letessier. Paris: Société des textes français modernes, Marcel Didier, 1955.

Chatelain, Jean-Marc. *La Bibliothèque de l'honnête homme: livres, lectures et collections en France à l'âge classique*. Paris: Bibliothèque nationale de France, 2003.

Châtelet, Émilie du. *Discours sur le bonheur*. Ed. Robert Mauzi. Paris: Bibliothèque de la faculté des lettres de Lyon, Les Belles Lettres, 1961.

Châtelet, Émilie du. *Discours sur le bonheur*. Preface by Élisabeth Badinter. Paris: Payot & Rivages, 1997.

Châtelet, Émilie du. *Les Lettres de la marquise du Châtelet*. Ed. Theodore Besterman. Genève: Institut et Musée Voltaire, 1958.

Cheng, Anne. *Histoire de la pensée chinoise*. Paris: Seuil, 1997.

Chevalier, Jean-Frédéric. 'Albertino Mussato ou la renaissance de l'Humanisme à Padoue' in Albertino Mussato, *Écérinide, Épîtres métriques sur la poésie, Songe*. Ed. J.-F. Chevalier. Paris, Les Belles Lettres, 2000, XI-XLII.

Cicero. *Correspondance*. III. Ed. & trans. L.-A. Constans. Paris: Collection des universités de France, Les Belles Lettres, 1971.

Cicero. *Discours*. XII: *Pour le poète Archias, Pour L. Flaccus*. Ed. & trans. Félix Gaffiot and André Boulanger. Revised by Philippe Moreau. Paris: Collection des universités de France, Les Belles Lettres, 1989.

Cicero. *De l'orateur*. Ed. & trans. Henri Bornecque and Edmond Courbaud. Paris: Collection des universités de France, Les Belles Lettres, 1966-1985.

Cicero. *La République*. Book I. Ed. & trans. Esther Bréguet. Paris, Collection des universités de France, Les Belles Lettres, 1989.

Cicero. *Traité des lois*. Ed. & trans. Georges de Plinval. Paris, Collection des universités de France, Les Belles Lettres, 1968.

Cicero. *Tusculanes*. Ed. & trans. Georges Fohlen and Jules Humbert. Paris: Collection des universités de France, Les Belles Lettres, 1968-1970.

Cicero. *The Letters to his Friends*. I. Trans. W. Glynn Williams. Cambridge, MA: Loeb Classical Library, Harvard University Press, 1958.

Cicero. *On the Orator*. Trans. E. W. Sutton. Cambridge, MA: Loeb Classical Library, Harvard University Press, 1967.

Cicero. *The Republic* and *The Laws*. Trans. Niall Rudd. Oxford: Oxford University Press, 1998.

Cicero. *The Speeches of Cicero*. Trans. N. H. Watts. Cambridge, MA: Loeb Classical Library, Harvard University Press, 1965.

Cicero. *Tusculan Disputations*. Trans. J. E. King. Cambridge, MA: Loeb Classical Library, Harvard University Press, 1966.

Cicero. *Works*. XII: *Pro Sestio, In Vatinium*. Ed. & trans. Robert Gardner. Cambridge, MA: Loeb Classical Library, Harvard University Press, 1984.

Cieri Via, Claudia. 'Il luogo della mente e della memoria' in Wolfgang Liebenwein, *Studiolo: storia e tipologia di uno spazio culturale*. Modène: Panini, 1988. VII-XXX.

Clair, Jean (ed.). *Mélancolie: génie et folie en Occident*. Paris: Gallimard, 2005.

Compagnon, Antoine (ed.). *Prétexte: Roland Barthes. Colloque de Cerisy*. Paris: Christian Bourgois, 2003.

Compagnon, Antoine (ed.). *La Seconde Main ou le travail de la citation*. Paris: Seuil, 1979.

Confucius: à l'aube de l'humanisme chinois. Paris: Réunion des musées nationaux, 2003.

Confucius. *Analects, with selections from traditional commentaries*. Trans. Edward Slingerland. Indianapolis: Hackett, 2003.

Confucius. *Entretiens avec ses disciples*. Trans. André Lévy. Paris: Flammarion, 1994.

Confucius. *Les Entretiens de Confucius*. Trans. Anne Cheng. Paris: Points Sagesses, Seuil, 1981.

Confucius. *Les Entretiens de Confucius*. Trans. Pierre Ryckmans. Preface by Étiemble. Paris: Connaissance de l'Orient, Gallimard, 1989.

Confucius. *Les Quatre Livres, avec un commentaire abrégé en chinois, une double traduction en français et en latin et un vocabulaire des lettres et des noms propres*. Ed. Séraphin Couvreur. Taipei, 1972.

The Analects of Confucius. Trans. Burton Watson. New York: Columbia University Press, 2007.

Corrozet, Gilles. *Les blasons domestiques contenantz la decoration d'une maison honneste, & du mesnage estant en icelle: Inuention ioyeuse, & moderne*. Paris: Gilles Corrozet, 1539.

Courier, Paul-Louis. *Correspondance générale*. Ed. Geneviève Viollet-le-Duc. Paris: Bibliothèque du XIXe siècle, Klincksieck, 1976-1985.

Courier, Paul-Louis. *Œuvres complètes*. Ed. Maurice Allem. Paris: Bibliothèque de la Pléiade, Gallimard, 1964.

Damiani, Rolando. *All'apparir del vero. Vita di Giacomo Leopardi*. Milan: Arnoldo Mondadori, 1998.

Dauvois-Lavialle, Nathalie. 'Juste Lipse et l'esthétique du jardin' in Christian Mouchel (ed.), *Juste Lipse (1547-1606) en son temps. Actes du colloque de Strasbourg, 1994*. Paris: Honoré Champion, 1996, 215-232.

Davies, J. Keith and Botting, Wendy. 'La bibliothèque de Freud' in Eric Gubel (ed.), *Le Sphinx de Vienne: Sigmund Freud, l'art et l'archéologie*. Bruxelles: Ludion, 1993, 198-201.

Dazzi, Manlio. *Il Mussato preumanista (1261-1329): l'ambiente e l'opera*. Vicence: Neri Pozza, 1964.

Derrida, Jacques. *Chaque fois unique, la fin du monde*. Paris: Éditions Galillé, 2003.

Derrida, Jacques. 'Les morts de Roland Barthes' in *Poétique*, n° 47, September 1981, 269-292.

Derrida, Jacques. *The Work of Mourning*. Trans. Pascale-Anne Brault and Michael Naas. Chicago: University of Chicago Press, 2001.

Descartes, René. *Œuvres et Lettres*. Ed. André Bridoux. Paris: Bibliothèque de la Pléiade, Gallimard, 1953.

Descartes, René. *Œuvres philosophiques*. I: *1618-1637*. Ed. Ferdinand Alquié. Paris: Classiques, Garnier, 1992.

Descartes, René. *Discourse on Method and the Meditations*. Trans. F. E. Sutcliffe. London: Penguin Books, 1968.

Description de l'Égypte ou recueil des observations et des recherches qui ont été faites en Égypte pendant l'expédition de l'armée française. Paris: Imprimerie impériale, puis royale, 1809-1828.

Doménech, Fernando Benito. *Ribera 1591-1652*. Valence: Bancaja, 1991.

Dotti, Ugo. *Pétrarque*. Trans. Jérôme Nicolas. Paris: Fayard, 1991.

Dubreuil, Léon. *Rosmapamon: la vieillesse bretonne de Renan*. Paris: Ariane, 1945.

Dupont, Florence. *Le Plaisir et la Loi. Du « Banquet » de Platon au « Satiricon »*. Paris: [Re]découverte, La Découverte, 2002.

Écrits apocryphes chrétiens, Ed. François Bovon and Pierre Geoltrain. Paris: Bibliothèque de la Pléiade, Gallimard, 1997.

Empson, William. *Collected Poems*. San Diego: Harcourt Brace Jovanovich, 1956.

Empson, William. *Seven Types of Ambiguity*. New York: New Directions, 1966.

Engelman, Edmund. *La Maison de Freud, Berggasse 19, Vienne*. Paris: Seuil, 1979.

Erasmus. *Éloge de la folie, Adages, Colloques, Réflexions sur l'art, l'éducation, la religion, la guerre, la philosophie, Correspondance*. Trans. Claude Blum, André Godin, Jean-Claude Margolin and Daniel Ménager. Paris: Bouquins, Robert Laffont, 1992.

Erasmus. *Œuvres choisies*. Trans. Jacques Chomarat. Paris: Le Livre de poche, Librairie générale française, 1991.

Erasmus. *Opera omnia*. I, 3: *Colloquia*. Ed. L.-E. Halkin, F. Bierlaire and R. Hoven. Amsterdam: North-Holland Publishing Company, 1972.

Étiemble, René. *Confucius*. Paris: Folio essais, Gallimard, 1986.

Feo, Michele (ed.). *Petrarca nel tempo: tradizione lettori e immagini delle opere*. Comitato nazionale per le celebrazioni del VII centenario della nascita di Francesco Petrarca. Pontedera: Bandecchi & Vivaldi, 2003.

Flaubert, Gustave. *The Letters of Gustave Flaubert 1857-1880*. Trans. Francis Steegmuller. Cambridge, MA: The Belknap Press of Harvard University Press, 1982.

Ficin, Marsile. *Three Books on Life*. Trans. Carol V. Kaske and John R. Clark. Binghamton (New York): Center for Medieval and Early Renaissance Studies, 1989.

Fogel, Michèle. *Marie de Gournay: itinéraires d'une femme savante*. Paris: Fayard, 2004.

France, Anatole. *Œuvres*. I. Ed. Marie-Claire Bancquart. Paris: Bibliothèque de la Pléiade, Gallimard, 1984.

Freud, Sigmund. *Briefe an Wilhelm Fliess, 1887-1904*. Frankfurt, Fischer, 1986.

Freud, Sigmund. *Gesammelte Werke. X: Werke aus den Jahren 1913-1917*. Frankfurt, Fischer, 1973.

Freud, Sigmund. *Œuvres complètes*. XIII: *1914-1915*. Ed. André Bourguignon, Pierre Cotet and Jean Laplanche. Paris: Presses universitaires de France, 1994.

Freud, Sigmund. *The Standard Edition of the Complete Psychological Works*. XIV. Trans. James Strachey. London: The Hogarth Press and The Institute of Psychoanalysis, 1957.

Friedel, Adrien Chrétien (ed.). *Nouveau Théâtre allemand*. IV. Paris, 1782.

Fumaroli, Marc. *Exercices de lecture: de Rabelais à Paul Valéry*. Paris: Bibliothèque des idées, Gallimard, 2006.

Fumaroli, Marc. *L'École du silence. Le sentiment des images au XVIIe siècle*. Paris: Idées et Recherches, Flammarion, 1994.

Furetiere, Antoine. *Dictionnaire universel, contenant généralement tous les mots françois, tant vieux que modernes, & les termes des sciences et des arts*. La Haye, 1727; Hildesheim: Georg Olms, 1972.

Gamwell, Lynn. 'Les origines de la collection de Freud' in Eric Gubel (ed.), *Le Sphinx de Vienne: Sigmund Freud, l'art et l'archéologie*. Bruxelles: Ludion, 1993, 179-188.

Gamwell, Lynn and Wells, Richard (eds.). *Sigmund Freud and Art: His Personal Collection of Antiquities*. London: Thames and Hudson, 1989.

Gournay, Marie de. *Œuvres complètes*. Ed. Jean-Claude Arnould. Paris: Champion, 2002.

Grand Dictionnaire universel du XIXe siècle. Paris: Larousse, 1866-1879.

Grimal, Pierre. *Cicéron*. Paris: Fayard, 1986.

Grimal, Pierre. *Les Jardins romains*. Paris: Fayard, 1984.

Gubel, Eric (ed.). *Le Sphinx de Vienne: Sigmund Freud, l'art et l'archéologie*. Bruxelles: Ludion, 1993.

Haffenden, John. *William Empson*. Oxford: Oxford University Press, 2005-2006.

Hegel, Georg Wilhelm Friedrich. *Briefe von und an Hegel*. III: *1823-1831*. Ed. Johannes Hoffmeister. Hamburg: Felix Meiner, 1969.

Hegel, Georg Wilhelm Friedrich. *Correspondance*. III: *1823-1831*. Ed. Johannes Hoffmeister. Trans. Jean Carrère. Paris: Gallimard, 1990.

Hegel, Georg Wilhelm Friedrich. *Hegel: The Letters*. Trans. Clark Butler and Christiane Seile. Bloomington: Indiana University Press, 1984.

Heidegger, Martin. *Holzwege*. Frankfurt: Klostermann, 1977.

Heidegger, Martin. *Off the Beaten Track*. Ed. & Trans. Julian Young and Kenneth Haynes. Cambridge and New York: Cambridge University Press, 2002.

Heraclitus. *Fragments*. Ed. Marcel Conche. Paris: Épiméthée, Presses universitaires de France, 1986.

Hersant, Yves. 'L'acédie et ses enfants' in Jean Clair (ed.), *Mélancolie: génie et folie en Occident*. Paris: Gallimard, 2005, 54-59.

Hersant, Yves. *Mélancolies: de l'Antiquité au XXe siècle*. Paris: Bouquins, Robert Laffont, 2005.

Hippel, Theodor Gottlieb von. *Sämmtliche Werke*. X: *Kleinere Schriften*. Berlin: G. Reimer, 1828.

Hippocrates. [*Œuvres*]. IV. Trans. W. H. S. Jones. Cambridge, MA: Loeb Classical Library, Harvard University Press, 1992.

Hippocrates. [*Works*]. IV. Trans. W. H. S. Jones. Cambridge, MA: Loeb Classical Library, Harvard University Press, 1992.

Holzman, David. 'Les sept sages de la forêt des bambous et la société de leur temps' in *T'oung Pao*, vol. XLIV, 1956, 317-346.

Horace. *Satires, Epistles, Ars Poetica*. Trans. H. Rushton Fairclough. Cambridge, MA: Loeb Classical Library, Harvard University Press, 1942.

Hummel, Pascale. *Moeurs érudites: étude sur la micrologie littéraire* (Allemagne, XVIe-XVIIIe siècles). Genève: Froz, 2002.

Hummel, Pascale. *Philologus auctor: le philologue et son œuvre*. Berne: Peter Lang, 2003.

L'Imitation de Jésus-Christ. Trans. Félicité Robert de Lamennais. Paris: Bibliothèque spirituelle du chrétien lettré, Plon, 1950.

Jacob, Christian. 'Athenaeus the Librarian' in David Braund and John Wilkins (eds.), *Athenaeus and His World: Reading Greek Culture in the Roman Empire*. Exeter: University of Exeter Press, 2000, 85-110.

Jacob, Christian (ed.). *Des Alexandries II: les métamorphoses du lecteur*. Paris: Bibliothèque nationale de France, 2003.

Jacob, Christian (ed.). *Lieux de savoir*. I: *Espaces et communautés*. Paris: Albin Michel, 2007.

Le Jardin du lettré: synthèse des arts en Chine. Boulogne-Billancourt: Musée Albert-Kahn, 2004.

St. Jerome. *Lettres*. Trans. Jérôme Labourt. Paris: Collection des universités de France, Les Belles Lettres, 1949.

St. Jerome. *Select Letters of St. Jerome*. Trans. F. A. Wright. Cambridge, MA: Loeb Classical Library, Harvard University Press, 1933.

St. Jerome. *Letters and Select Works*. Trans. Hon. W. H. Freemantle. New York: A Select Library of Nicene and Post-Nicene Fathers of the Christian Church, 1893.

Journal officiel de la République française, 21e année, n° 160, 16 June 1889, 2783-2786 ('Assemblée générale du congrès annuel des sociétés savantes et des sociétés de beaux-arts de Paris et des départements, le 15 juin 1889, dans le grand amphithéâtre de la Sorbonne, sous la présidence de M. Fallières, ministre de l'instruction publique et des beaux-arts').

Juvenal. *Satires*. Ed. P. de Labriolle, F. Villeneuve and J. Gérard. Paris: Collection des universités de France, Les Belles Lettres, 1983.

Juvenal. *The Sixteen Satires*. Trans. Peter Green. London: Penguin Books, 1998.

Kantorowicz, Ernst Hartwig. *Œuvres: L'Empereur Frédéric II, Les Deux Corps du Roi*. Postscript by Alain Boureau. Paris: Quarto, Gallimard, 2000.

Klibansky, R., Panofsky, E., and Saxl, F.. *Saturne et la mélancolie. Études historiques et philosophiques: nature, religion, médecine et art*. Trans. Fabienne Durand-Bogaert and Louis Évrard. Paris: Gallimard, 1989.

Kriegel, Blandine. *L'Histoire à l'âge classique (Les Historiens et la Monarchie*, 1988). Paris: Quadrige, Presses universitaires de France, 1996.

Kuspit, Donald. 'A Mighty Metaphor: The Analogy of Archaeology and Psychoanalysis' in Lynn Gamwell and Richard Wells (eds.), *Sigmund Freud and Art: His Personal Collection of Antiquities*. London: Thames and Hudson, 1989, 133–151.

Lahire, Bernard. *La Condition littéraire: la double vie des écrivains*. Paris: La Découverte, 2006.

Landolfi, Tommaso. *Sinon la réalité*. Trans. Monique Baccelli. Paris: Christian Bourgois, 2006.

Laqueur, Thomas Walter. *Solitary Sex: A Cultural History of Masturbation*. New York: Zone Books, 2003.

Larue, Anne. *L'Autre Mélancolie:* Acedia, *ou les chambres de l'esprit*. Paris: Hermann, 2001.

Le Goffic, Charles. *La Littérature française aux XIXe et XXe siècles: tableau général accompagné de pages types*. II, with an appendix on *les Écrivains morts pour la patrie* by Auguste Dupouy. Paris: Larousse, 1919 [rather 1923].

Legros, Alain. *Essais sur poutres: peintures et inscriptions chez Montaigne*. Preface by Michael A. Screech. Paris: Klincksieck, 2000.

Leopardi, Giacomo. *Lettere*. Ed. Rolando Damiani. Milan: I Meridiani, Arnoldo Mondadori, 2006.

Leopardi, Giacomo. *Zibaldone*. Ed. Rolando Damiani. Milan: I Meridiani, Arnoldo Mondadori, 1997.

Leopardi, Giacomo. *Essays, Dialogues and Thoughts*. Trans. James V. Thomson. London: George Routledge & Sons, 1905.

Leopardi, Giacomo. *Zibaldone*. Trans. Kathleen Baldwin, Richard Dixon, David Gibbons, Ann Goldstein, Gerard Slowery, Martin Thom, and Pamela Williams. Ed. Michael Caesar and Franco D'Intino. New York: Farrar, Straus and Giroux, 2015.

Lepenies, Wolf. *Melancholie und Gesellschaft*. Frankfurt: Suhrkamp, 1969.

Lepenies, Wolf. *Sainte-Beuve. Au seuil de la modernité*. Trans. Jeanne Étoré and Bernard Lortholary. Paris: Bibliothèque des idées, Gallimard, 2002.

Lettres patentes du Roy, Qui confirment l'établissement des Academies Royales des Inscriptions & des Sciences. Avec les Reglemens pour lesdites deux Academies. Données à Marly au mois de Fevrier 1713. Registrées en Parlement le 3. May 1713. Paris: Chez la Veuve François Muguet & Hubert Muguet, 1713.

Li Chu-Tsing and Watt, J. C. Y. (eds.). *The Chinese Scholar's Studio: Artistic Life in the Late Ming period.* New York: Thames and Hudson, 1987.

Liebenwein, Wolfgang. *Studiolo: storia e tipologia di uno spazio culturale (Studiolo: die Entstehung eines Raumtyps und seine Entwicklung bis um 1600).* Ed. Claudia Cieri Via. Modène: Panini, 1988.

Lipsius, Justus. *Les Deux Livres de la Constance, Esquels en forme de devis familier est discouru des afflictions, et principalement des publiques, et comme il se faut résoudre à les supporter.* Trans. anonymous. Paris: Noxia, 2000.

Lipsius, Justus. *Iusti Lipsi de constantia libri duo, Qui alloquium præcipuè continent in Publicis malis. Vltima editio, castigata.* Anvers: Plantin, 1599.

Lipsius, Justus. *Justi Lipsi V. C. opera omnia, postremum ab ipso aucta et recensita: nunc primum copioso rerum indice illustrata.* Wesel: André van Hoogenhuysen, 1675.

Le Livre d'or de Renan. Paris: Joanin, 1903.

Lucian. *Œuvres.* II: *Opuscules 11–20.* Ed. & trans. Jacques Bompaire. Paris: Collection des universités de France, Les Belles Lettres, 2003.

Lucretius. *De la nature.* II: Books IV–VI. Ed. & trans. Alfred Ernout. Paris: Collection des universités de France, Les Belles Lettres, 1985.

Lucretius. *On the Nature of Things.* Trans. W. H. D. Rouse. Cambridge, MA: Loeb Classical Library, Harvard University Press, 1992.

Mabillon, Jean. *De monasticorum studiorum ratione ad juniores studiososque congregationis sancti Mauri monachos D. J. Mabillonius. Suivi de Questions proposées à tous les Religieux Bénédictins de la Congrégation de Saint Maur, par le Bureau de Littérature, établi à l'Abbaye de Saint Germain des Prés.* Paris: Valleyre l'aîné, 1767.

Mabillon, Jean. *Reflexions sur la réponse de M. l'Abbé de la Trappe, Au Traité des Etudes monastiques. Divisées en deux parties; Par Dom Jean Mabillon, Religieux Benedictin de la Congregation de S. Maur. Seconde édition revûë & corrigée.* Paris: Charles Robustel, 1693.

Mabillon, Jean. *Traité des Etudes monastiques, divisé en trois parties; avec une liste des principales Difficultes, qui se rencontrent en chaque siécle dans la lecture des Originaux; & un Catalogue de livres choisis pour composer une Biblioteque ecclesiastique. Par Dom Jean Mabillon, Religieux Benedictin de la Congregation de S. Maur. Seconde édition revûë & corigée (sic).* Paris: Charles Robustel, 1692.

Mabillon, Jean. *Treatise on Monastic Studies.* Trans. John Paul McDonald. Lanham, MD: University Press of America, 2004.

Macrobius. [*Les Saturnales*] *I saturnali (Saturnaliorum convivia).* Ed. & trans. Nino Marinone. Turin: Unione tipografico-editrice torinese, 1997.

Marcel, Antoine. *Le Jardin du lettré.* Paris: Alternatives, 2004.

Marinelli, Lydia (ed.). *'Meine... alten und dreckigen Götter': aus Sigmund Freuds Sammlung*. Frankfurt: Stroemfeld, 1998.

Marolles, Michel de. *Suitte des Mémoires de Michel de Marolles, abbé de Villeloin. Contenant douze traitez sur divers Sujets Curieux, dont les noms sont imprimez dans la page suivante*. Paris: Antoine de Sommaville, 1657.

Marty, Éric. *Roland Barthes, le métier d'écrire*, Paris: Fiction & Cie, Seuil, 2006.

Maul, G. and Oppel, M.. *Goethes Wohnhaus in Weimar*. Weimar: Stiftung Weimarer Klassik, 2002.

Michel, Alain. 'De Virgile à Juste Lipse: sagesse et rêverie dans le jardin' in Jackie Pigeaud and Jean-Paul Barbe (eds.), *Histoires de jardins: lieux et imaginaire*. Paris: Perspectives littéraires, Presses universitaires de France, 2001, 85–95.

Minois, Georges. *Bossuet: entre Dieu et le Soleil*. Paris: Perrin, 2003.

Le Monde, 28 March 1980, 26–27 ('La mort de Roland Barthes').

Monk, Ray. *Ludwig Wittgenstein: The Duty of Genius*. London: Jonathan Cape, 1990.

Montaigne, Michel de. *Essais*. Ed. Pierre Villey. Paris: Presses universitaires de France, 1992.

Montaigne, Michel de. *Les Essais*. Ed. Jean Balsamo, Michel Magnien and Catherine Magnien-Simonin. Paris: Bibliothèque de la Pléiade, Gallimard, 2007.

Montaigne, Michel de. *The Complete Essays of Montaigne*. Trans. Donald M. Frame. Stanford, CA: Stanford University Press, 1958.

Morford, Mark. 'The Stoic Garden' in *Journal of Garden History*, vol. VII, nº 2, April-June 1987, 151-175.

Neusner, Jacob. *A Life of Yohanan ben Zakkai (Ca. 1–80 C. E.)*. Leiden: Studia post-biblica, Brill, 1970.

Nietzsche, Friedrich. *Die Geburt der Tragödie*. Stuttgart: Universal-Bibliothek, Reclam, 2002.

Nietzsche, Friedrich. *Kritische Studienausgabe. 8: Nachgelassene Fragmente 1875–1879*. Ed. Giorgio Colli and Mazzino Montinari. Munich: Deutsche Taschenbuch Verlag, 1988.

Nietzsche, Friedrich. *Nietzsche Briefwechsel: kritische Gesamtausgabe*. II, vol. 4: *Briefe an Friedrich Nietzsche: Mai 1872 – Dezember 1874*. Ed. Giorgio Colli and Mazzino Montinari. Berlin: Walter de Gruyter, 1978.

Nietzsche, Friedrich. *Introduction aux leçons sur l'Œdipe-Roi de Sophocle. Introduction aux études de philologie classique*. Trans. Françoise Dastur and Michel Haar. La Versanne: Encre marine, 1994.

Nietzsche, Friedrich. *La Naissance de la tragédie*. Trans. Philippe Lacoue-

Labarthe. Paris: Folio essais, Gallimard, 2002.

Nietzsche, Friedrich. *Œuvres philosophiques complètes. Considérations inactuelles, III et IV: Schopenhauer éducateur, Richard Wagner à Bayreuth. Fragments posthumes (début 1874 – printemps 1876)*. Ed. Giorgio Colli and Mazzino Montinari. Trans. Henri-Alexis Baatsch et al.. Paris: Gallimard, 1988.

Nietzsche, Friedrich. *Querelle autour de « La Naissance de la tragédie »: écrits et lettres de Friedrich Nietzsche, Friedrich Ritschl, Erwin Rohde, Ulrich von Wilamowitz-Möllendorff, Richard et Cosima Wagner*. Trans. M. Cohen-Halimi, Hélène Poitevin and Max Marcuzzi. Paris: Tradition de la pensée classique, Vrin, 1995.

Nietzsche, Friedrich. *The Birth of Tragedy*. Trans. Douglas Smith. Oxford: Oxford University Press, 2000.

Nishitakatsuji, Nobusada. *Dazaifu Tenman-gu*. Trans. Chase Frank Richard Fukuoka: Dazaifu Tenman-gu, 1982.

Panofsky, Erwin. *La Vie et l'Art d'Albrecht Dürer*. Trans. Dominique Le Bourg. Paris: Hazan, 1987.

Papy, Jan. 'Lipsius and His Dogs: Humanist Tradition, Iconography and Rubens's Four Philosophers' in *Journal of the Warburg and Courtauld Institutes*, LXII, 1999, 167-198.

Les Pères du désert. Ed. René Draguet. Paris: Bibliothèque spirituelle du chrétien lettré, Plon, 1949.

Perez Sanchez, A. E. and Spinosa N.. *Jusepe de Ribera 1591-1652*. New York: Metropolitan Museum of Art, 1992.

Perrault, Dominique. *Bibliothèque nationale de France, 1989-1995*. Basel: Birkhäuser, 1995.

Petrarch. *Canzoniere / Le Chansonnier*. Ed & trans. Pierre Blanc. Paris: Classiques Garnier, Bordas, 1989.

Petrarch. *Collatio laureationis*, in *Opere latine di Francesco Petrarca*, edited by Antonietta Bufano et al., vol. II (1975). Turin: Unione tipografico-editrice torinese, 1987, 1257-1283.

Petrarch. *Lettera ai posteri*. Ed. Gianni Villani. Rome: Salerno, 1990.

Petrarch. *Lettres de la vieillesse*. I: Livres I-III. Ed. Elvira Nota et al.. Paris: Les Belles Lettres, 2002.

Petrarch. *Lettres familières*. Ed. Ugo Dotti. Trans. André Longpré. Paris: Les Belles Lettres, 2002.

Petrarch. *Le « Senili » secondo l'edizione Basilea 1581*. Ed. Marziano Guglielminetti. Savigliano: L'Artistica Editrice, 2006.

Petrarch. *La Vie solitaire*. Ed. & trans. Christophe Carraud. Grenoble: Jérôme Millon, 1999.

Petrarch. *Letters on Familiar Matters*. Trans. Aldo S. Bernardo. Albany, NY: State University of New York Press, 1975.

Petrarch. *The Life of Solitude*. Trans. Jacob Zeitlin. Champaign, IL: University of Illinois Press, 1924.

Petrarch. *Letters of Old Age*. I. Trans. Aldo S. Bernardo and Saul Levin. New York: Italic Press, 2005.

Philostratus. *The Life of Apollonius of Tyana*. Trans. F.C. Conybeare. London: Loeb Classical Library, William Heinemann, 1912.

Pico della Mirandola, Giovanni. *Conclusiones nongentae: le novecento tesi dell'anno 1486*. Ed. Albano Biondi. Florence: Leo S. Olschki, 1995.

Pico della Mirandola, Giovanni. *De la dignité de l'homme*. Ed. Yves Hersant. Paris: Éditions de l'Éclat, 2005.

Pico della Mirandola, Giovanni. *900 conclusions philosophiques, cabalistiques et théologiques*. Ed. Bertrand Schefer. Paris: Allia, 1999.

Pico della Mirandola, Giovanni. *Œuvres philosophiques*. Ed. Olivier Boulnois and Giuseppe Tognon. Paris: Presses universitaires de France, 1993.

Pico della Mirandola, Giovanni. *On the Dignity of Man*. Trans. Charles Glenn Wallis. Indianapolis, IN: The Bobbs Merrill Company, 1965.

Plato. *Les Lois: livres III-VI*. Ed. & trans. Édouard des Places. Paris: Collection des universités de France, Les Belles Lettres, 1975.

Plato. *Laws*. Trans. R. G. Bury. Cambridge, MA: Loeb Classical Library, Harvard University Press, 1967.

Plutarch. *Dialogues pythiques*. Ed. & trans. Robert Flacelière. Paris: Collection des universités de France, Les Belles Lettres, 1974.

Plutarch. *Dialogues pythiques*. Trans. Frédérique Ildefonse. Paris: Flammarion, 2006.

Plutarch. *Moralia*. V. Ed. & trans. Frank Cole Babbitt. Cambridge, MA: Loeb Classical Library, Harvard University Press, 2003.

Plutarch. *Œuvres morales*. II: *Consolation à Apollonios, Préceptes de santé, Préceptes de mariage, Le Banquet des sept sages, De la superstition*. Ed. & trans. Jean Defradas, Jean Hani and Robert Klaerr. Paris: Collection des universités de France, Les Belles Lettres, 1985.

Plutarch. *Propos de table*, dans *Œuvres morales*. IX. Ed. & trans. François Fuhrmann, Françoise Frazier and Jean Sirinelli. Paris: Collection des universités de France, Les Belles Lettres, 1972-1996.

Plutarch. *Vies.* XII: *Démosthène - Cicéron*. Ed. & trans. Robert Flacelière and Émile Chambry. Paris: Collection des universités de France, Les Belles Lettres, 1976.

Plutarch. *Lives.* VII. Trans. Bernadette Perrin. Cambridge, MA: Loeb Classical Library, Harvard University Press, 1917.

Plutarch. *Moralia.* II. Trans. Frank Cole Babbitt. Cambridge, MA: Loeb Classical Library, Harvard University Press, 1928.

Plutarch. *Moralia.* VIII-IX. Trans. Paul A. Clement, Herbert B. Hoffleit, Edwin L. Minar Jr., F. H. Sandbach, and W. C. Helmbold. Cambridge, MA: Loeb Classical Library, Harvard University Press, 1961-1969.

Pommier, Édouard. 'Notes sur le jardin dans la littérature artistique de la Renaissance italienne', in Jackie Pigeaud and Jean-Paul Barbe (eds.), *Histoires de jardins: lieux et imaginaire*. Paris: Perspectives littéraires, Presses universitaires de France, 2001, 127-140.

Pöschl, Viktor. 'Nietzsche und die klassische Philologie', in Hellmut Flashar, Karlfried Gründer and Axel Horstmann (eds.), *Philologie und Hermeneutik im 19. Jahrhundert*, Göttingen: Vandenhoeck & Ruprecht, 1979, 141-155.

Quintilian, *Institution oratoire*. VI: *Livres X et XI*. Ed. & trans. Jean Cousin. Paris: Collection des universités de France, Les Belles Lettres, 1979.

Quintilian. *Institutio Oratoria*. Trans. H. E. Butler. Cambridge, MA: Loeb Classical Library, Harvard University Press, 1920.

Rabelais, François. *Œuvres complètes*. Ed. Mireille Huchon. Paris: Bibliothèque de la Pléiade, Gallimard, 1994.

Rabelais, François. *Gargantua and Pantagruel*. Trans. M. A. Screech. London: Penguin Books, 2006.

Rabelais, François. *Gargantua and Pantagruel*. Trans. Burton Raffel. New York: W. W. Norton & Company, 1990.

Rancé, Armand Jean le Bouthillier de. *Réponse au Traité des études monastiques. Par M. l'Abbé de la Trappe*. Paris: François Muguet, 1692.

Rancé, Armand Jean le Bouthillier de. *De la sainteté et des devoirs de la vie monastique. Seconde Edition, reveuë & augmentée*. Paris: François Muguet, 1683.

Rancé, Armand Jean le Bouthillier de. *A Treatise on the Sanctity and on the Duties of the Monastic State*. Trans. A religious of the Abbey of Melleray, La Trappe. Dublin: Richard Grace, 1830.

Règlement Pour l'Académie royale des Inscriptions & Belles-Lettres. Du 22 Décembre 1786. Paris: Imprimerie royale, 1787.

Renan, Ernest. 'Peut-on travailler en province ?' (1889) in *Feuilles détachées*, in *Œuvres complètes*, Henriette Psichari (ed.). Paris: Calmann-Lévy, 1948, II, 1005-1018.

Reuterswärd, Patrick. 'The Dog in the Humanist's Study' in *Konsthistorisk tidskrift*, vol. L, n° 2, 1981, 53–69.

Rey, Jean-Michel. *L'Enjeu des signes: lecture de Nietzsche*. Paris: L'Ordre philosophique, Seuil, 1971.

Riflant, Meury. *Le Miroir des melancholicques, décrit en la XXXe section des « Problèmes » d'Aristote, concernant ce qui appartient à prudence, entendement et sapience, traduit de grec en français, par Meury Riflant*. [Rouen], Jehan Petit (imprimeur), Nicolas de Burges (libraire), 1543.

Ripa, Cesare. *Iconologia overo Descrittione di diverse Imagini cauate dall'antichità, & di propria inuentione*. Rome: Lepido Faeii, 1603.

Roberts, Helen I.. 'St. Augustine in *St. Jerome's Study*: Carpaccio's Painting and Its Legendary Source', *The Art Bulletin*, vol. XLI, n° 4, December 1959, 283-297.

Rodriguez Monegal, Emir. *Jorge Luis Borges: biographie littéraire*. Trans. Alain Delahaye. Paris: Gallimard, 1983.

Roger, Philippe. *Roland Barthes, roman*. Paris: Grasset, 1986.

Rohde, Erwin. *Der Streit um Nietzsches « Geburt der Tragödie » : die Schriften von E. Rohde, R. Wagner, U. v. Wilamowitz-Möllendorff*. Ed. Karlfried Gründer. Hildesheim: Georg Olms, 1989.

Romans grecs et latins. Trans. Pierre Grimal. Paris: Bibliothèque de la Pléiade, Gallimard, 1976.

Ronsard, Pierre de. *Œuvres complètes*. II. Ed. Jean Céard, Daniel Ménager and Michel Simonin. Paris: Bibliothèque de la Pléiade, Gallimard, 1994.

Sandre, Thierry (ed.). *Anthologie des écrivains morts à la guerre (1914-1918)*. Amiens: Bibliothèque du Hérisson, Edgar Malfère, 1924-1926.

Schechter, S. and Bacher, W. 'Johanan b. Zakkai' in Isidore Singer (ed.), *The Jewish Encyclopedia*. New York: Funk and Wagnalls, 1901-1906, VII, 214-217.

Schlanger, Judith. *La Mémoire des œuvres*. Paris: Le texte à l'œuvre, Nathan, 1992.

Schuster, Peter-Klaus. '*Melencolia I*: Dürer et sa postérité', trans. Jeanne Étoré-Lortholary, in Jean Clair (ed.), *Mélancolie: génie et folie en Occident*. Paris: Gallimard, 2005, 90-103.

Sei Shōnagon. *Notes de chevet*. Trans. André Beaujard. Paris: Connaissance de l'Orient, Gallimard / UNESCO, 1985.

Sei Shōnagon. *The Pillow Book*. Trans. Meredith McKinney. London: Penguin Books, 2006.

Shakespeare, William. *Œuvres complètes: Tragicomédies II, Poésies*. Ed. Michel Grivelet and Gilles Monsarrat. Paris: Bouquins, Robert Laffont, 2002.

Sima Qian. *Selections from Records of the Historian*. Trans. Yang Hsien-yi and

Gladys Yang. Peking: Foreign Language Press, 1979.

Sliwa, Joachim. *Egyptian Scarabs and Seal Amulets from the Collection of Sigmund Freud*. Cracovie: Polska Akademia Umiejetnosci, 1999.

Sole, Robert. *Les Savants de Bonaparte*. Paris: Points, Seuil, 2001.

Spinosa, Nicola. *Ribera: l'opera completa*. Naples: Electa Napoli, 2003.

Spiro, Audrey. *Contemplating the Ancients: Aesthetic and Social Issues in Early Chinese Portraiture*. Berkeley: University of California Press, 1990.

Stockreiter, Karl. 'Am Rand der Aufklärungsmetapher: Korrespondenzen zwischen Archäologie und Psychoanalyse', in Lydia Marinelli (ed.), « Meine... alten und dreckigen Götter »: *aus Sigmund Freuds Sammlung*, Frankfurt, Stroemfeld, 1998, 81-93.

Swift, Jonathan. *Œuvres*. Ed. Émile Pons, Paris: Bibliothèque de la Pléiade, Gallimard, 1988.

Swift, Jonathan. *Major Works*. Ed. Andus Ross and David Woolley. Oxford: Oxford University Press, 2003.

Syncretism in the West: Pico's 900 Theses (1486). Ed. S. A. Farmer. Tempe, AZ: Medieval & Renaissance Texts & Studies, 1998.

Tallemant des Réaux, Gédéon. *Historiettes*. I. Ed. Antoine Adam. Paris: Bibliothèque de la Pléiade, Gallimard, 1960.

[Talmud. Abot de rabbi Natan] *The Fathers According to Rabbi Nathan. An Analytical Translation and Explanation*. Ed. Jacob Neusner. Atlanta: Brown Judaic Studies, Scholars Press, 1986.

[Talmud. Michna. Seder Nashim. Gittin] *Hebrew-English Edition of the Babylonian Talmud*. XIV. Ed. Isidore Epstein. Trans. Maurice Simon. London: Soncino, 1990.

Tervarent, Guy de. *Attributs et Symboles dans l'art profane: dictionnaire d'un langage perdu (1450-1600)*. Genève: Droz, 1997.

Thibaudet, Albert. *La Campagne avec Thucydide in Thucydide, Histoire de la guerre du Péloponnèse*. Paris: Bouquins, Robert Laffont, 1990, 1-140.

Thornton, Dora. *The Scholar in His Study: Ownership and Experience in Renaissance Italy*. New Haven: Yale University Press, 1997.

Triandafillidis, Alexandra. *La Dépression et son inquiétante familiarité: esquisse d'une théorie de la dépression dans le négatif de l'œuvre freudienne*. Paris: Éditions universitaires, 1991.

Vigny, Alfred de. *Stello, Daphné*. Ed. François Germain. Paris: Classiques, Garnier, 1970.

Virgil. *Énéide, livres V-VIII*. Ed. Jacques Perret. Paris: Collection des universités de France, Les Belles Lettres, 1989.

Virgil. *The Aeneid*. Trans. Robert Fagles. New York: Penguin Books, 2006.

Vision of Ezra. Trans. J. R. Mueller and G. A. Robbins in *The Old Testament Pseudepigrapha*. vol. 1. Ed. James H. Charlesworth. Garden City, NY: Doubleday & Company, 1985.

Wilamowitz-Möllendorff, Ulrich von. *Qu'est-ce qu'une tragédie attique ? Introduction à la tragédie grecque*. Trans. Alexandre Hasnaoui. Paris: Les Belles Lettres, 2001.

Wilamowitz-Möllendorff, Ulrich von. *Future Philology!* Trans. G. Postl, B. Babich, and H. Schmid, in *New Nietzsche Studies*, vol. 4: nos. 1 & 2, Summer/Fall 2000, 1–33.

Wilkins, Ernest Hatch. *The Making of the « Canzoniere » and Other Petrarchan Studies*. Rome: Storia e Letteratura, 1951.

Wilkins, Ernest Hatch. *Vita del Petrarca*. Trans. Remo Cesarani. Milan: Feltrinelli, 1990.

Wilkins, Ernest Hatch. *Petrarch's Coronation Oration* in PMLA, vol. 68, no. 5 (Dec. 1953), 1241–1250.

Woolf, Virginia. *Une chambre à soi*. Trans. Clara Malraux. Paris: 10–18, 1996.

Woolf, Virginia. *A Room of One's Own* (1929), *Three Guineas* (1938). Ed. Morag Shiach. Oxford: The World's Classics, Oxford University Press, 1992.

Zilsel, Edgar. *Le Génie: histoire d'une notion de l'Antiquité à la Renaissance*. Trans. Michel Thévenaz. Paris: Minuit, 1993.

Zweig, Stefan. *Briefwechsel mit Hermann Bahr, Sigmund Freud, Rainer Maria Rilke und Arthur Schnitzler*. Ed. Jeffrey B. Berlin, Hans-Ulrich Lindken and Donald A. Prater. Frankfurt: Fischer, 1987.

Index

Adorno, Gretel 227
Adorno, Theodor Wiesengrund 145
Aemilian 135–37
Alain 175
Alberti, Leon Battista 84, 117
Algalarrondo, Hervé 228
Andler, Charles 220, 221
Anguillara, Orso dell' 181
Antisthenes 82
Antonello da Messina 64
Antony, Mark 169
Apollonius of Tyana 162
Arendt, Hannah 227
Aristophanes 151
Aristotle 41, 69–70, 82, 111–19, 156 161–64, 167
Artaxerxes 21, 202
Asinius Pollio 170
Athenaeus 109

Saint Augustine 64, 66, 95–96, 121, 132, 144
Augustus 68–69, 170
Aulus Gellius 84
Avicenna 154

Bâ, Amadou Hampâté 195–96
Bachelard, Gaston 191–92
Bacher, Wilhelm 218
Baillet, Adrien 176
Bailly, Jean-Christophe 219
Bardi, Roberto de 179
Barker, Stephen 207
Barrès, Maurice 79
Barthelemy-Saint-Hilaire, Jules 186
Barthes, Roland 9, 194–98, 213
Baudelaire, Charles 96, 219
Baudoin, Jean 48–49

Beatrice 130
Bellanger, Yvonne 204
Bellefonds, Bernardin de 72–73
Benda, Julien 71, 164–65
Saint Benedict of Nursia 123
Benjamin, Walter 118, 189
Saint Bernard of Clairvaux 78
Bischoff, Ludwig 221
Blondel, Éric 220
Boccaccio 121, 183
Boisrobert, François de 91–93
Bokar, Tierno 196
Bonaparte, Marie 63
Bonaparte, Napoléon 171
Borgen, Robert 206
Borges, Jorge Luis 29
Borowski, Ludwig Ernest 106–7, 204, 213
Bossuet, Jacques Bénigne 71–75
Botting, Wendy 207
Boulnois, Olivier 221–22
Brem, Anne-Marie de 208
Bright, Timothy 116–17
Brissette, Pascal 208, 216
Buddha 53
Burckhardt, Jakob
Burke, Janine 207
Burton, Robert 115, 117–18

Caesar 69, 168, 172
Calder III, William Musgrave 220
Calvet, Louis-Jean 228
Carlat, Dominique 229
Carnot, Sadi 76
Carpaccio, Victor 64, 94–95

Catiline 168
Cato the Elder 22
Cauchie, Maurice 211
Celsus 27–28, 191
Charlemagne 123
Charles V 170
Chateaubriand, François René de 121, 218
Chatelain, Jean-Marc 211
Châtelet, Émilie du 32–34, 36
Cheng, Anne 223
Chevalier, Jean-François 225
Christine de Pisan 35
Chuang-tzu 53
Cicero 19, 21–23, 28, 33, 41, 61, 69, 82–84, 113–14, 135, 168–70
Cieri Via, Claudia 211
Clair, Jean 207, 215, 216,
Cohen-Halimi, Michèle 220, 221
Cohn, Alfred 227
Cola di Rienzo 181
Colonna, Giovanni 178, 183
Colonna, Stefano 180, 183
Compagnon, Antoine 226
Confucius 19–23, 26, 53, 59, 144, 165–67, 196–97
Convenevole de Prato 181, 183
Corio, Bernardino 198, 211
Corrozet, Gilles 64
Courier, Paul-Louis 172
Cousin, Victor 38–39, 105
Crassus 82
Croesus 133

Emperor Daigo 167
Dante 131, 181, 183

Dauvois-Lavialle, Nathalie   211
Davies, J. Keith   207
Dazzi, Manlio   225
Demetrius   162
Demosthenes   190
Derrida, Jacques   198
Descartes, René   46–47, 90, 175–76
Do, Giovanni (Juan)   44, 51
Domenech, Fernando Benito   205
Domitian   134, 162, 179
Dotti, Ugo   217, 225
Draguet, René   213
Dubreuil, Léon   208
Dupont, Florence   214
Dupouy, Auguste   224
Dürer, Albrecht   66–67, 74–75, 115

Empedocles   112
Empson, William   99–103
Engelman, Edmund   62, 64
Epicurus   82, 108
Epitherses   135–37
Erasmus   84, 118, 165
Estienne, Henri   90
Eusebius of Caesarea   137
Ezra   21, 23, 202

Fallières, Armand   77
Feo, Michele   226
Ficino, Marsilio   114–16, 118, 157
Flaubert, Gustave   108, 134
Fliess, Wilhelm   63
Fogel, Michèle   211
Foucault, Michel   112
France, Anatole   17, 105

Freud, Sigmund   62–66
Friedel, Adrien Chrétien   204
Fujiwara no Sadako   35
Fumaroli, Marc   217
Furia   104

Gaetano, Marini   172
Gamwell, Lynn   207
Gaulle, Charles de   172
Gauthier, René Antoine   223
Gay, Peter   206–7
Gemistos Plethon, Georgios   157
Saint George   96
Giordani, Pietro   202
Girolamo Da Carpi   211
Goethe, Johann Wolfgang von   187
Gournay, Marie de   35, 89–93, 96
Greenaway, Peter   227
Grimal, Pierre   209
Groussac, Paul   29
Gubel, Eric   206

Haffenden, John   212
Hegel, Georg Wilhelm Friedrich   105–6, 137
Heidegger, Martin   60, 80
Heraclitus   141, 152
Hermes Trismegistus   154
Herodotus   23
Hersant, Yves   215
Hippel, Theodor Gottlieb von   204
Hippocrates   37
Holzman, David   206
Homer   109, 132
Horace   83–84, 170, 172,
Hypatia of Alexandria   35

Iamblichus 154
Pope Innocent VIII 155

Jacob, Christian 214
Jamin, Amadis 91–92
Jamin, Nicole 91–92
Saint Cassian, John 104
Saint Jerome 64, 66, 74–75, 94–96, 104–5, 121, 128–29, 144
Jesus 129, 137, 165, 180
Ji Kang 61
Jolif, Jean Yves 223
Juvenal 68

Kant, Emmanuel 38–39, 106–7, 165
Kantorowicz, Ernst H. 24
Kiyohara, Motosuke 36
Kleist, Heinrich von 172
Klibansky, Raymond 215
Kriegel, Blandine 217, 218, 222

Lactantius 138
Laelius 83
Lahire, Bernard 208
Lampson, Dominique 210
Landolfi, Tommaso 212
Langius, Charles 86–87
Lao Tzu 59
Laqueur, Thomas Walter 212
Larue, Anne 207
Laura 183
l'Écluse, Charles de 210
Le Jars, Louis 211
Legros, Alain 226
Leibniz, Gottfried Wilhelm 32, 225
Leonardo da Vinci 175
Leopardi, Giacomo 13, 27–29, 107, 118

Lepenies, Wolf 214, 216
Leto, Giulio Pomponio 157
Levesque, E. 208
Liebenwein, Wolfgang 207, 211
Lipsius, Justus 85–88
Livy 69
Longus 172
Lotto, Lorenzo 211
Louis, Pierre 215
Louis XVI 159
Lucian of Samosata 69, 108
Lucretius 84

Mabillon, Jean 121–22, 125–28, 217
Macrobius 108
Malherbe, François de 90
Manutius, Aldus 157
Marcella 219
Marcus Aurelius 135
Marinelli, Lydia 206
Marmol, José 29
Marolles, Michel de 93
Martin du Gard, Roger 189
Marty, Éric 228
Maul, Gisela 226
Mauzi, Robert 204
Mazarin, Jules 90
Mazon, Paul 195–96
Maecenas 68
Michelangelo 175
Minois, Georges 208
Moses 21, 64, 123
Molière 31, 93, 121
Monk, Ray 224
Monluc, Blaise de 172
Montaigne, Michel de 89–90, 93, 139, 141, 173–74, 186–88

Montbazon, Marie de   121
Morford, Mark   209-11
Musonius Rufus   162
Mussato, Albertino   181, 183

Nehemiah   201
Nero   133, 162
Neusner, Jacob   218
Newton, Isaac   32, 36
Nicaise, Claude   218
Nietzsche, Friedrich   118, 137-38, 145-51
Nishitakatsuji, Nobusada   223
Noirot, Caroline   221

Oppel, Margarete   226

Panofsky, Erwin   215
Panormita, Antonio   157
Papy, Jan   209
Pascal, Blaise   93
Pepin the Short   123
Perez Sánchez, Alfonso E.   205
Perrault, Dominique   80, 202
Petrarch   83, 85, 96, 121, 178-85, 207, 226-27
Phaedrus   82
Philologos   170
Philostratus   162
Pico della Mirandola, Giovanni   221-22
Pietroni, Pietro   121
Pilate, Ponce   165
Plato   28, 41, 82, 108-10, 112, 116, 118, 156, 163, 196
Pliny the Elder   69
Plutarch   19, 69, 108, 110, 133-42, 170

Pontano, Giovanni   157
Pöschl, Viktor   220
Proust, Marcel   17

Quintilian   190-91, 193

Rabelais, François   26, 40, 98, 135-37
Rancé, Armand Jean de   72-74, 105, 121-22, 125-28
Raphael   175
Renan, Ernest   76-79, 108, 165
Cardinal de Retz   189
Reuterswärd, Patrick   212
Rey, Jean-Michel   220
Ribera, Jusepe de   44, 47, 51
Richards, Ivor Armstrong   99-101
Richelieu, Armand Jean de   90-93
Riflant, Meury   216
Rigaud, Hyacinthe   75
Ripa, Cesare   48-49
Ritschl, Friedrich   148
Robert of Anjou   179-81
Roberts, Helen I.   211
Roger, Philippe   228
Roger des Genettes, Edma   218
Rohde, Erwin   148-51
Ronsard, Pierre de   40, 89-92
Rousseau, Jean-Jacques   29
Rubens, Pierre Paul   85
Rufinus of Aquileia   144

Sainte-Beuve, Charles Augustin   108
Saint-Lambert, Jean François de   32
Sandre, Thierry   224
Saxl, Fritz   215
Schechter, Solomon   218

Schopenhauer, Arthur 146, 150
Schuster, Peter-Klaus 215
Scipio 22, 83
Sei Shōnagon 35–36
Seneca 83
Abbot Serenus 104
Shakespeare, William 31, 102, 115, 188–89
Silber, Eucharius 153
Sima Qian 26, 201–2, 228–29
Simon, Richard 125
Sliwa, Joachim 207
Socrates 54, 82, 90, 108, 112
Solé, Robert 224
Spinosa, Nicola 205
Spinoza, Baruch 125
Spiro, Audrey 206
Stendhal 172, 189
Sugawara no Michizane 53, 167
Swift, Jonathan 186

Taine, Hippolyte 108
Tallemant des Réaux, Gédéon 91, 211
Tarquin the Proud 173
Tervarent, Guy de 205
Theophrastus 215
Thibaudet, Albert 173–76
Thornton, Dora 207, 211, 229
Thucydides 173–74
Tiberius 136–38, 170
Tissot, Samuel Auguste 102
Tognon, Giuseppe 222
Trajan 170
Triandafillidis, Alexandra 207

Urbain, Ch. 208

Valéry, Paul 118
Van Diemen, Gaspar 209
Varro 69
Vespasian 131, 170
Vigny, Alfred de 105, 172
Virgil 68, 75, 84, 132, 170, 173–74, 180–82, 185
Voltaire 32–33, 36

Wagner, Cosima 148
Wagner, Richard 146–50
Wang Wei 59
Wasianski, Ehrgott Andreas Chistoph 204, 213
Wells, Richard 238
Wilamowitz-Möllendorff, Ulrich von 149–52
Wilkins, Ernest Hatch 149–52
Wittgenstein, Ludwig 174
Woolf, Virginia 31–32, 34–35

Xenophon 84, 108, 172

Yohanan Ben Zakkai 131, 134
Yourcenar, Marguerite 135

Zeng, Dian (Xi) 166
Zidane, Zinedine 112
Zweig, Stefan 63